Other books published by Broadway Press:

Backstage Forms, by Paul Carter

Backstage Handbook:
An Illustrated Almanac of Technical Information, third edition, by Paul Carter

Lighting the Stage: Art and Practice, third edition, by Willard F. Bellman

Photometrics Handbook, second edition, by Robert C. Mumm

Also by Bill Raoul

Sound Designer's Companion
A resource of classical and popular music to help sound designers sift through humdreds of composers, styles of music, and songs. The author's often whimsical descriptions of essential musical knowledge includes classical composers from before the Renaissance to the end of the 20th century, as well as virtually every popular song from 1900 through the Big Band era.

Stock Scenery Construction Handbook Companion Videos
Four short videos on a DVD written and directed by Bill Raoul which illustrate the techniques found in his book for building a flat.

The Magic of Scene Painting Video
Professional scenic artists from Cobalt Studios in New York demonstrate how to paint a complete set consisting of a floorcloth, a backdrop, a cut border, and a three-dimensional fence with a stone gate and an arbor. Video is written and produced by Bill Raoul.

For more information, call toll-free, 800-869-6372,
or visit our Web site, www.broadwaypress.com

STOCK SCENERY
CONSTRUCTION
HANDBOOK

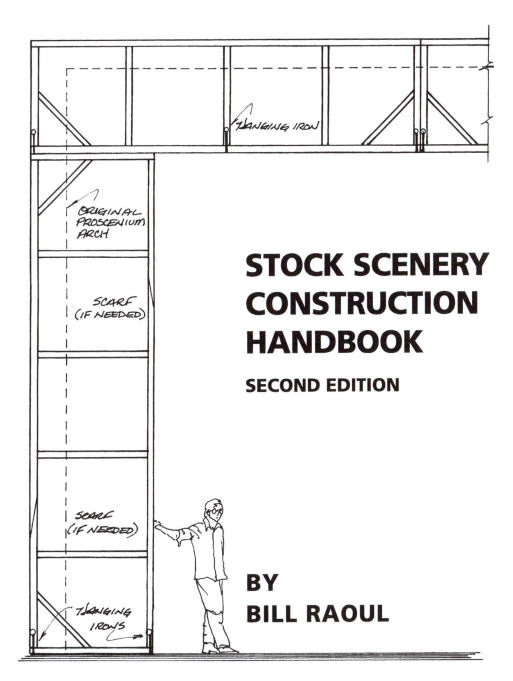

ORIGINAL
PROSCENIUM
ARCH

SCARF
(IF NEEDED)

SCARF
(IF NEEDED)

HANGING
IRONS

HANGING IRON

STOCK SCENERY
CONSTRUCTION
HANDBOOK

SECOND EDITION

BY
BILL RAOUL

BROADWAY PRESS
LOUISVILLE, KY
1999

ISBN: 978-0-911747-38-6

Seventh printing, March 2012.

Manufactured in the United States of America.

Broadway Press
3001 Springcrest Dr.
Louisville, KY 40241
www.broadwaypress.com
800.869.6372

CONTENTS

DRAWINGS

PREFACE

Bores can be divided into two classes: those who have their own particular subject, and those who don't need a subject.

A.A. Milne

Scenery construction must certainly qualify as a subject, but I sincerely hope my digestion of it will not land me in either of Mr. Milne's classes. For more than 35 years I have found scenery construction fascinating, frustrating and even baffling, but, at the same time, exciting and very satisfying. It is a subject in constant change, as is the rest of the theatre. I have also noticed that the more things change, the more they seem to stay the same. That, of course, has changed my thinking.

To some, the techniques and methods presented here will appear old-fashioned and outmoded. I can only counter with an acquiescent nod and hope if they ever need to get back to some of the basics, I don't bore them. There is nothing more instructive than observing the past, and if this handbook becomes something of a history of yesterday's techniques and methods, I have at least succeeded in preserving part of our theatrical heritage. But I truly believe it is more.

In this time of world waste, conspicuous consumption and increasing shortages, we have a responsibility to conserve and reuse. Fortunately, our recycling plant is the theatre, and we all know it must reflect the times.

Before I bore you with my soapbox, let me say my thank yous to the hundreds of talented people who have been my co-workers. Their training methods, skills and thoughts have been diligently collected and stored. Many of their wonderful ideas have metamorphosed to the point of nonrecognition, but, originally, I stole them nonetheless.

This book is now a fourth overhaul of what began as classroom handouts. They were gathered into a slim volume on *Flat Frame Construction*, which, like Topsy, "just grow'd" into an even larger handbook on *Stock Scenery Construction...which* bears some youthful resemblance to the present tome.

Paul Carter, author of the invaluable *Backstage Handbook*, has my thanks for connecting me with publisher David Rodger, whose patience and help have been most appreciated. Stacia Graham, whose fleet fingers typed many a draft, deserves my grateful thanks. Carol Morris whose red pen flowed around many an indefinite pronoun and dangling thought certainly clarified many of the muddier passages. However, none of them knows, as I so gratefully do, how much we must all thank Tim Paul for his uncountable hours as proofreader, gentle suggester and astute critic. The remaining errors must be his, but I will gladly assist him in correcting them if you will be so kind as to point them out.

My thanks ultimately go to my colleagues in the Department of Drama/Dance, and to those within the University of Montana who so graciously granted me the sabbatical leave which enabled me to rework this information.

SECOND EDITION NOTES

Second printings and second editions are both gratifying but while the first is a mark of popularity, the later must admit the need for change. To the many people who have contacted me with kind comments, insightful suggestions and reprimands for omissions, I am extremely grateful. Most users praised (!) the limited scope of this handbook but had specific queries which I have tried to answer in the expanded sections on drops and hardwall scenery with related items. The number of questions specifically about paint and not the techniques of using it per se were surprising and prompted the diatribe which is a new final chapter. To those who wanted a section on steel and metal construction I can only apologize for my lack of knowledge and urge them to seek those answers from a qualified source. However, my limited experience leads me to believe metal shops and wood shops need to be separate areas. The droppings on the floor and particulates and fumes in the air are not compatible. Metal is, however, an excellent scenic material and often perfectly answers the scenery demand of cost vs. weight vs. strength.

Again I must thank those same people who facilitated the first edition for their continued support...with the possible exception of the sabbatical committee...and if reception of this edition is as positive, who knows? They say: "Third's a charm!"

PART I • THE BASICS

AT HOME AND A BOARD

It is really beyond the intent of this handbook to go into great detail on setting up a shop and stocking it with the proper tools and materials. Each theatre situation will create a different set of demands, and available space will adapt differently to those demands. Perhaps it is beyond anybody's scope to describe an adequate scene shop or construction place. In truth, scenery can be built anywhere. A second truism states that "any shop space, no matter how large, is never spacious enough to do the job adequately."

Many theatre groups must build on the stage itself and clear away the shop for rehearsals and performances. Others are fortunate to have separate areas. However, both situations, as well as others, will benefit from careful planning. It is efficient to handle materials as little as possible. Therefore, if the supplies can load in one end and the finished work load out the other, a chain or path for the materials can be created. Each time a board or sheet of plywood must be picked up, turned 90° or 180°, not only is energy lost, but the spinning stock has the potential of interfering with other workers at other tools and jobs. Hollywood long ago exhausted the humor inherent in the situation. Unfortunately most work spaces must compromise this ideal, regardless of the sense of keeping the materials moving through the construction process in a smooth, direct and efficient procedure.

If scenery can be built anywhere, it can also be built with a wide assortment of tools, from the simplest of saws and hammers to the most sophisticated pneumatic fastening tools and saws which automatically feed themselves. Fortunately, there are tools for almost any shop's budget in every area.

Tools can be divided into the following groups: Measuring and Marking Tools, Cutting and Shaping Tools, and Fastening Tools. If you are unfamiliar with a tool, or tools in general, many excellent books are available which cover in detail how each should be safely and correctly used. A call to a high school shop teacher will possibly shake loose an old textbook or the use of one. Some tool dealers will give seminars, especially on products you buy from them, and especially if you specify the demonstration as a condition of the sale. Of course, power tools all come with booklets which explain their use.

Every tool is potentially dangerous, especially if handled improperly, too hurriedly or in less than ideal conditions. Always have tools clean, sharp and working properly. This, combined with the proper safety equipment and proper training, will eliminate accidents. For some it is still necessary to count fingers before and after the day's work. It cannot be stressed enough—always use the correct tool for the job and use the tool correctly.

MEASURING AND MARKING TOOLS

As long as we are living in the last country on earth (except Myanmar and Liberia) to use the English method (versus the metric method) of measuring distances, we can drive the necessary miles to work and drag out our feet and inches in the shop. Available in many sizes, a flexible steel tape is the most common measuring tool for the shop. It should easily measure the longest scenery you normally plan to build. A fifty foot or one-hundred foot tape is most useful for measuring the stage.

A combination square or all-in-one square will greatly aid in many construction situations, in addition to doubling as a marking gauge. The all-faithful of the shop, the steel square or carpenter's square, with its 16″ tongue and 24″ body, is essential for most frame construction. Some of these squares come with a booklet explaining how to build a house, lay out stairs and chart rocket launches to the moon.

Dividers and trammels are useful and can be purchased. A good set of carpenter's trammel points will be most helpful if you plan to do much work with circles. However, these can be made, as shown in the section on Shop Made Tools.

A level is useful. Be certain when purchasing to get one which is long enough to span a surface sufficient to get a correct measurement; usually a four-foot level will do. Unfortunately, experience and use are the best guides. Last, but not least, a chalk-line or snap-line is needed. These can be made by utilizing a good quality mason's line and chalk, which is available in different colors by the cake. Stick charcoal can also be used. A chalk-line in a container which not only allows you to wind it up but charge it with a self-contained chalk supply is also available.

CUTTING AND SHAPING TOOLS

SAWS

Handsaws are over 100,000 years old, and you can often believe it after using a dull one. Like all saws, handsaws must be kept sharp. A dull saw is a dangerous saw. It will slip, skip and stick and throw material at you, or the materials will throw you into the blade. Neither is a pretty sight. All saws work because the teeth on the blade are "set," each alternating in an opposite direction so the kerf or actual cut in the wood is wider than the blade holding the teeth.

Rip-saws, designed to cut along the length of a board, have flat teeth which are usually spaced farther apart than those on a cross-cut blade. This allows the saw to "chisel" away the wood.

Cross-cut saws, as the name implies, cut across the grain and have bevelled teeth to "shear" through the wood. Both saws are becoming extinct, because the portable circular saw has become less expensive and can do the job of both quickly and efficiently. It will also cut plywood and other panel boards. Circular saws are usually electric, but pneumatic ones are also available. A wide choice of blades is available for circular saws.

A sabre saw or portable jigsaw is another electric (and pneumatic) saw which has replaced the coping saw, keyhole saw, and even the metal hacksaw, depending on the style of blade used.

Even in large, non-portable or stationary saws, there is a wide variety of choices. The table saw (or bench saw or contractor's saw) is ideal for ripping lumber and panel materials, although it also cuts accurate dadoes and grooves. It is available in a number of sizes, depending upon the diameter of the circular blade.

The radial arm saw also uses a circular blade; the size of the tool is based upon the diameter of the blade. The saw is used primarily for accurate cross-cutting, but also cuts excellent dadoes and grooves. It can be set to cut both simple and compound angles.

Most theatre work is done on a much less massive scale than the construction industry. Huge versions of power tools, common to some construction sites, are not only unnecessary from a use and cost standpoint, but also can dwarf those using them. Comparing the cost of the different diameters of blades will also be an eye-opener.

A band saw has a continuous blade in an endless loop and has the greatest depth-of-cut of any stationary power saw. Depending upon the blade chosen, the band saw can also rip lumber, but it is most useful for cutting curves and other shapes. Many band saws have gearing to control the speed of the blade, which can be modified to cut plastics and soft metals. Yet, its cost and non-portability make the band saw almost a luxury. A sabre saw can do most of the things a band saw can do, albeit in a much slower and noisier way. However, once you use a band saw, you won't want to live without one.

The miter-box or chop-saw is one of the newer power saws on the market. It is a circular saw, the blade of which is lowered onto the stock to be cut. It will cut angles from a left to right 45° miter. Some shops have opted to use this in place of a radial arm saw, although it will not duplicate all uses, especially cross-cutting boards wider than 1 x 4.

A panel saw is, obviously, designed to cut panels. It can mount against a wall and be out of the way. It will make quick work of a sheet of plywood. However, that is about all it can do, and a table saw or portable circular saw will also perform this task.

KNIVES

Most of the other cutting and shaping tools are hand tools, although a few have been motorized. Perhaps the most useful for scenery work is the utility knife. Made with both fixed and retractable blades, it is advisable to get one with a textured handle to prevent wet or gluey hands from slipping on the grip. Blades are available in packages of five to one hundred. Never use a dull knife.

CHISELS

Chisels are fine woodworking tools which are expensive and difficult to keep sharp or properly honed. They make excellent tools for opening paint cans, cutting through nails or staples and even chopping steel cable… all of which will instantly ruin them. Perhaps a cold chisel designed to cut metal is all a shop needs, becoming an ideal tool to pry up misapplied fasteners and the like.

PLANES

Planes are perhaps more temperamental than chisels and certainly more costly. For most theatre work, the Surform rasp has replaced the plane and indeed will take the "curse" off a sharp corner, chamfer the edge of a plywood fastener or remove a rough surface about as well as a fine plane, but without the excessive replacement cost. The small, hand-held Surform plane and Surform shaver (which is pulled toward you and not pushed) are both very useful and have fairly inexpensive replacement blades.

There are many portable, electric hand planers on the market. And some shops swear by them. But they are not for the careless user. One nail or staple can destroy the expensive blade. Large jointers and planers are, of course, available. Basically, the difference between the two is this: the jointer has short cutters and is used to smooth the edge of a board for joining with glue; the planer uses longer cutters, usually has a power feed, and smooths the face of a board. They both have in common, however, the extreme cost of replacing or sharpening the blades, and the skill needed to reset them properly.

SHEARS

Scissors, shears and snips should be purchased as needed. It is practically hopeless to say that scissors are precision tools and should not be cutting anything but cloth. Shears are big scissors and snips are designed to cut tin and other thin metal, which is normally done with the once usable pair of scissors.

FILES

Files and rasps are useful shaping tools, available in many lengths and shapes. The choice is multiplied by the desired coarseness and kinds of teeth desired. Generally speaking, files are finer and rasps are rougher; files are used on metal (and finger nails) and rasps on wood.

ROUTERS

To most people today, a router is the power tool which has replaced both the hand tool of the same name and the stationary shaper. It is used to form decorative edges and complicated joints, and can carve, incise, pierce and even cut circles. It is an extremely useful portable power tool. The bits can become expensive for theatre work because, like the shaper, jointer and planer, one nick from an overlooked metal fastener or stray nail can ruin it. Also, the more expensive carbide-tipped bits are really necessary for shaping plywood and other panel boards.

LATHES

The last cutting and shaping tool in this discussion is the lathe. This is a luxury tool for most shops and requires some special skills to operate properly. The turning tools it uses are also fairly expensive, and must be kept sharp. You might say a shop has "arrived" when it has a lathe to make its own turnings.

FASTENING TOOLS

HAMMERS

Probably the most common fastening tool is the hammer. It is certainly the most neglected in quality when purchased. Cheap hammers will produce cheap work. Whether the handle is wood (easily replaceable), fiberglass (non rusting and shock absorbing) or metal (nonbreakable), make sure the head is solidly attached to the handle. When you hold the hammer in your hand it should have good balance.

Large, heavy hammers are not made for theatre work. Scenery should be strong but light—so should the hammer. Remember that the force driving the nail is also exerted into the scenery and can knock apart what you're building. A 16-ounce hammer is plenty for any job and some professional shops won't allow any hammer heavier than 13 ounces. It is not the weight of the hammer but the skill of the user which drives the nail.

The claw hammer has a curved claw behind the head for pulling nails easily. A straight claw (or claw arousé) is designed to pry apart previously nailed pieces. Both are useful. Ball peen hammers with their specially tempered heads are designed for pounding metal, something which should never be done with a claw hammer, unless you want to ruin the hammer. Tack hammers, with their magnetic heads, are ideal for light fastening with not only tacks, but also brads and other small nails. Sledge hammers are often used to strike scenery which is going to feed the dumpster. They are rarely used to build it, not being known for inspiring craftsmanship.

Mallets are hammers with nonmetal heads. They should be used when striking another tool, like a chisel or even another hammer, or adjusting (through some friendly persuasion) a finished or polished surface without chipping or damaging it.

While on the subject of hammers, the handiest little tool any shop can have is a nail set. It is designed to set the head of a nail below the surface of the board, but is especially useful because of its cupped tip. Place the tip on a protruding end of a nail or staple and you can drive out the offending fastener enough to reach the head or crown and remove it.

STAPLERS

Many shops have abandoned the hammer for electric or pneumatic staplers and nailers. The fasteners for these speedy and powerful tools, with their coated shafts, have much greater holding power than an ordinary nail and eliminate beating the scenery with a hammer. Certainly if labor and time are considerations, these powered fastening tools will quickly repay their investment. They do not, unfortunately, guarantee better work. There are many hand staplers on the market which are also worth investigating.

SCREWDRIVERS

Screwdrivers are available in many sizes and shapes, but they almost all have a handle, shank and tip. The two most common tips in this country are the flat (or slotted) and the Phillips tip with its cross shape. Be sure to buy the size which fits the screw or bolt head you are using. It is not cheating to take along one of each when shopping for the drivers.

Ratchet screwdrivers will speed up work but be careful of spiral ratchet screwdrivers (also called Yankees). Not only are they expensive, but they can be ruined quickly if not properly stored at all times, can easily slip and plunge through soft scenery, and have been known to eat the palm of the user, removing a most painful pattern of flesh. It is embarrassing, but sounds like the Yankees my mama warned me about.

Electric or pneumatic screw guns and drills with appropriate bits have threatened the existence of the lowly screwdriver. The battery-charged, portable drill may finally do it in. However, many theatre workers will continue to use screwdrivers, especially some of the more specialized ones available.

DRILLS

If the power drill threatens the screwdriver, its ancestors, the hand drill, the push drill, and the brace with its family of beautifully crafted bits, have joined the dinosaurs in the tar pits. Not only are many of the power drills cheaper, they are often much easier to use, and the cordless varieties are quickly gaining. With all tools, you get what you pay for; drills are no exception. Buy good tools which are comfortable to the hand and have the power to do the job. Oversized hand tools are about as useless as undersized ones.

When buying drill bits, remember that wood bits can be used only in wood, but metal bits will do metal, wood and plastics. You might save a little money. Drill bits can be sharpened, either by a professional or skilled worker.

When a drill is mounted into a press, it becomes ideal for drilling perfectly placed holes. There are presses made for portable hand drills, but they are not as good as ones made with the drill permanently mounted. A drill press is particularly useful if you plan to do a lot of metal work. Always be certain to use a V-block (which you can make, see Drawing VII-2) with round stock.

GRIPPING TOOLS

Pliers and wrenches are the last of the fastening tools. Inasmuch as every trade has developed specialized types of wrenches and pliers, the market choice is amazing. Basically, all have handles, a pivot (which slips or not) and jaws which grip or cut. Pliers and wrenches are available as some of the cheapest and worst made tools on the market. Beware! Pliers are meant to grip. Those which also have cutting edges in the jaw are sometimes called "side cutters" or "dikes." There are also end nippers, which are very useful in theatre work because they can grip a barely protruding nail or staple and rock it out of the wood. If you are planning to use piano wire for flying scenery, buy a special pair of cutters for it.

Vise grips will lock onto an object and hold it. Many sizes and jaw designs are available. Open end and box wrenches are sometimes useful. They must be purchased to fit. The "adjustable open end wrench" is a mouthful for a Crescent wrench (from the tool company of the same name). This has replaced most single wrenches for theatre work, but there are times when the others may do a better job. Socket wrenches are often useful tools, though many theatres find a few properly sized nut drivers will often do the job.

There are, of course, many more tools and devices on the market. The best advice I can offer is "go slowly" and wait until demand dictates the purchase, then shop carefully with a reputable dealer. Never, ever, ever buy cheap and shoddy tools.

MATERIALS

The life expectancy of any piece of scenery, stock or not, is directly related to the quality of materials used, the care exercised in construction, proper use and storage. Ideally use only the best materials. Unfortunately, the cost makes that impossible except in a very few of the wealthiest theatres, and then there is the moral question of wasting beautiful wood which could be used elsewhere. We no longer live in a world of unlimited resources, in case you haven't been to a lumberyard lately. Flat frame scenery, more than other types, most clearly demonstrates the importance of a "magic formula"—cost vs. weight vs. strength. The order of importance changes in different situations, but if these three elements are carefully weighed when any scenery is considered, the end product will benefit.

LUMBER

Lumber is the most expensive and variable item in most scenery construction. It will vary in the piece itself, within the tree, with the locale in which the tree grew, and most greatly, of course, with different species.

The two basic types of trees are conifer (softwoods) and deciduous (hardwoods). The actual hardness of the wood is no gauge. Balsa wood, a hardwood, is certainly not as hard as the dense, brittle softwood, yellow pine. Hardwoods such as oak, elm, hickory, ash and birch are used most often in furniture and are not well suited to scenery, even if they were readily available in long, workable lengths.

Of the softwoods, the white pines are the best scenery wood. Both Northern white pine and Idaho white pine are in high demand, but unfortunately, when available, are often very expensive. However, any wood which contains the better characteristics of these pines (good strength through long, straight grain, few knots and light weight) can be substituted. There are many other regional white pines available. Beware of yellow pines because the wood is extremely hard and brittle. There are also redwood, cedar, fir and spruce, but white pine is still by far the best. Study the costs of each plus its characteristics before buying. If a wood doesn't suit the cost vs. weight vs. strength formula, the scenery will suffer.

In order to buy lumber intelligently, you must know some of the vocabulary and methods of a lumberyard. All lumber is graded as to its type and use, in addition to quality. These grades, while standardized by an association, do vary slightly because of interpretation, and it pays to know what each yard has in stock (see Chart I-1, The Grading of White Pine Lumber).

The Drawing I-2 shows some of the many knots and blemishes found in lumber. Knots A, B and C, if small and tight, will usually not affect the strength of a board, especially if they are contained within the edges. However, the next three, because they traverse the width of the stock, will probably weaken the board to the breaking point. Remember that a knot interrupts the grain, and therefore weakens the board.

Also shown in the drawing are six other common flaws. "Wane" occurs when the piece is milled leaving part of the outside of the tree. Sometimes bits of bark remain. The wane in pine stays mainly in the plane. "Split" is an aptly named and obvious flaw, but some lumber yards don't see it. The remainder are commonly grouped as "warps," each having its definite characteristics, although all are caused by uneven drying. "Cupping" is more pronounced in wider boards and, if they are to be ripped into narrower strips, may not affect construction. "Crooks," if not too severe, can be pulled out of most flat frame construction. A slight "bow" can usually be straightened and corrected in on-edge construction, common to hardwall units and platforms. The "twist" is difficult to remove, except to the lumber yard whence it came.

Lumber is either milled or rough, a term which refers to its finish. Milled lumber has been planed smooth. Rough lumber as it is delivered from the first cutting is indeed quite rough. It is in this form that it is given the nominal measurements by which it is computed, and these figures remain, even after the piece is milled. The dimensions, however, will change. An example of the dimension change is seen more clearly when it is understood that a 2 x 4, which rough is 2″ x 4″ (depending upon which side of the splinters one measures), becomes after milling about 1½″ x 3½″. A piece of 1 x 10 is similarly shaved down in the milling process to ¾″ x 9¼″. The milled dimensions are subject to change, but seem only to get smaller each time.

BOARD MEASURE

Lumber can be purchased by the piece (or stick), but it is most commonly sold either by lineal foot (running length) or by board foot (cubic volume) measure. Lumber is usually priced using board measure, with extra charges added for handling small orders.

The board foot is the most common method for measuring lumber. It represents a theoretical board which is 1″ thick, 12″ wide and 12″ long, or 144 cubic inches. This could be a 1 x 12 one foot long or a 1 x 6 two feet long or a 1 x 2 six feet long, etc.

THE GRADING OF WHITE PINE LUMBER   TABLE I-1

GRADE	CHARACTERISTICS
#1 & 2 CLEAR ("B" AND BETTER)	All the best wood falls into this grade. It must be at least 4″ wide. #1 & 2 clear can have slight blemishes (discolorations). It is far too good to use for theatre work.
"C" SELECT	This grade must also be 4″ wide or wider. It resembles #1 & 2 clear, but there are more blemishes. It is an ideal material for building scenery.
"D" SELECT	This grade must also be 4″ wide or wider. "D" select is a borderline grade, and can be considered as the highest grade of common lumber. It can be good on one side with serious defects on the other. It is also excellent for scenery construction.
#1 COMMON	This grade contains sound, tight knots, small pockets, stains, season checks and equivalent characteristics. These are not considered "defects" in common grades but "guides" for grading. The more pronounced the defect, the lower the grade. #1 common is a very good lumber for building scenery.
#2 COMMON	This, of course, has larger and more pronounced defects. It is about as low as you can go and still build scenery, primarily due to the size and number of allowable knots.
#3 COMMON	This lumber is usually cut from a lower part of a log, and the defects are more pronounced. It is also usable for scenery construction if the pieces are carefully selected.
#4 COMMON	Bad.
#5 COMMON	This is the lowest recognized grade, and any defects are allowed as long as the piece will hold together long enough to be taken out of the lumber yard. There have been cases of #5 common accidentally getting mixed in with higher grades. If this happens, a phone call to the lumber yard will often stop this "defect."

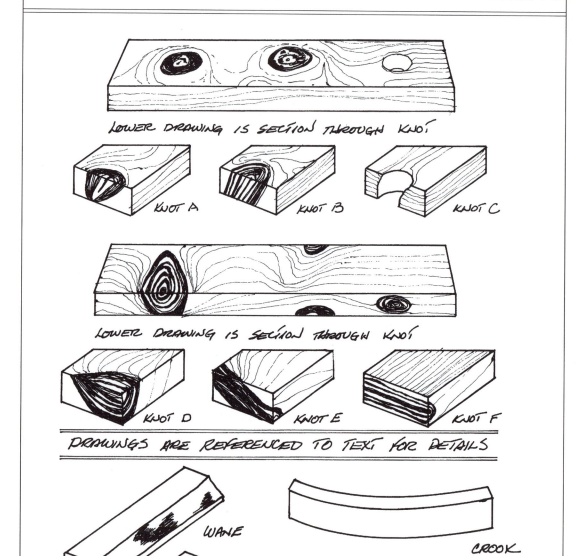

LOWER DRAWING IS SECTION THROUGH KNOT

KNOT A   KNOT B   KNOT C

LOWER DRAWING IS SECTION THROUGH KNOT

KNOT D   KNOT E   KNOT F

DRAWINGS ARE REFERENCED TO TEXT FOR DETAILS

WANE

SPLIT

CUP

CROOK

BOW

TWIST

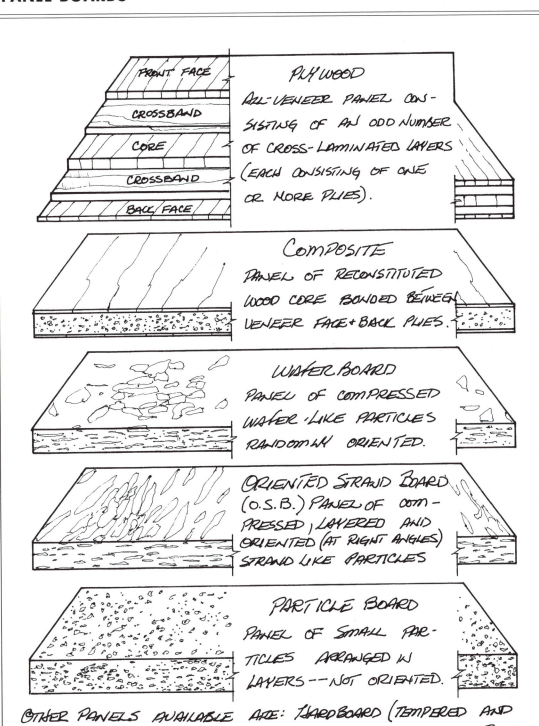

PLYWOOD
ALL-VENEER PANEL CON-
SISTING OF AN ODD NUMBER
OF CROSS-LAMINATED LAYERS
(EACH CONSISTING OF ONE
OR MORE PLIES).

FRONT FACE
CROSSBAND
CORE
CROSSBAND
BACK FACE

COMPOSITE
PANEL OF RECONSTITUTED
WOOD CORE BONDED BETWEEN
VENEER FACE + BACK PLIES.

WAFER BOARD
PANEL OF COMPRESSED
WAFER-LIKE PARTICLES
RANDOMLY ORIENTED.

ORIENTED STRAND BOARD
(O.S.B.) PANEL OF COM-
PRESSED, LAYERED AND
ORIENTED (AT RIGHT ANGLES)
STRAND LIKE PARTICLES

PARTICLE BOARD
PANEL OF SMALL PAR-
TICLES ARRANGED IN
LAYERS -- NOT ORIENTED.

OTHER PANELS AVAILABLE ARE: HARDBOARD (TEMPERED AND
UNTEMPERED) FIBER BOARD, COMPRESSED AND CORRUGATED PAPER.

For computing lumber, any board less than one inch thick is figured at one inch. Any width is figured in even numbers, with the exception of 3″ and 5″, and partial amounts are computed as the next highest number. White pine is sawed to 3″, 4″, 5″, 6″, 8″, 10″ and 12″ widths. A 3″ board is figured as 3″, but 3½″ is figured as 4″ wide and 5¼″ is figured as 6″ wide.

To calculate board feet when all dimensions are in inches, use the following formula:

$$\frac{T'' \times W'' \times L''}{144}$$

If the length is in feet, use the following formula:

$$\frac{T'' \times W'' \times L''}{12}$$

(T = Thickness, W = Width, L = Length)

Strip lumber, such as moulding, full round, etc., is sold by the lineal foot. The important thing to remember in ordering lumber is that if you order either lineal or board measure, you will get a delivery of random lengths from the yard unless you specify a length or lengths necessary (i.e., 650′ of 1 x 10 in 16′-0″ lengths would be 40.6 pieces of 16′-0″ long stock, and you will received either 40, 41, or 40 plus a piece, and be charged accordingly).

If the length is important, be sure to specify. If you have computed the materials needed for construction, be sure to add 20% to the amount figured for waste. In an educational situation, 25% or even 30% should be added to make sure there will be sufficient material on hand to complete the job after the learning experience has taken place.

There are two schools of thought on ordering 1 x stock for a shop. One is to order dimensioned lumber (1 x 3, 1 x 6, etc.) as needed and store each width. The other method is to order 1 x 10 and 1 x 12 only and rip the stock into narrower sticks as needed. There are advantages to each!

If you bulk order and store a stock of lumberyard pieces (1 x 3, 1 x 6, 1 x 8, etc.) in the shop, there is little time spent in selecting each as needed and little chance of varying width differences, assuming the mill is accurate. The edges are all planed smooth and the quality of the wood is often quite good. A major disadvantage is the necessity of storing each width separately. This is partially avoided if you order only enough to complete a specific job, but that requires careful planning. Another problem can be the limitations a designer might encounter in the width sizes available, inasmuch as ordering anything other than what is commonly stocked at the yard is cost-prohibitive.

If you stock 1 x 10 and 1 x 12 and rip your own narrower pieces, you can build with any width called for by the designer at that moment and not have to order it from the yard. By stocking wide lumber, you can take advantage of price breaks which come from large orders of single sizes. Another advantage is a more compact storage area. However, a table saw is necessary to rip the lumber. The fact that the ripped edges are not as smooth is usually of little importance, and they can be smoothed if need be.

Often a slightly lower grade of lumber may be ordered in the narrower widths. Wide widths have been known to have large knots which are structurally sound in the original board but, when ripped into narrower pieces, cause the lumber to break. This is often the deciding factor for ordering narrower stock. Check the lumber yard.

LUMBER STORAGE

Regardless of the size of lumber ordered, it must be stored evenly and with its own length and width to prevent warping. The most common method is to store it in horizontal racks with supports about every four feet. Do not mix lengths and widths on the same shelf, or warping will occur. The 1 x 10s and 1 x 12s can also be stored on end in vertical racks if there is little floor space and sufficient height. Try not to store stock narrower than 1 x 10 on end, because it tends to warp.

PLYWOOD

Plywood is one of the oldest manufactured wood products. The Egyptians and Greeks did veneer work, but it was not until the latter part of the nineteenth century that plywood became a commercial material for furniture. Perhaps the negative connotations of "veneer" (and perhaps the faulty glues) prevented widespread use. In 1905 the first commercial plywood plant opened in Portland, Oregon. The standardized 3'-0" x 6'-0" sheet was almost immediately replaced by the still common 4'-0" x 8'-0" panel. Plywood quickly became widely used in many industries and trades. The introduction of synthetic resin adhesives about 1935, which greatly shortened production time and increased strength, assured a permanent place for plywood in all the building trades.

Plywood manufacturing steps are basically the same for all types of ply. Plywood is made with an odd number of layers of wood, each consisting of one (or more) sheets of veneer. These veneers are laid up and glued together with the adjacent layers at right angles. Therefore, the two outside veneers have their grain running in the same direction, almost always parallel with the 8'-0" length (see Drawing I-3).

Plywood is most commonly manufactured from logs which are placed in a giant lathe and rotated against a long knife. This peels the wood off in a long, continuous sheet of veneer. The veneer is next cut to desired widths, dried and graded. It is then spread with glue and the plywood panel is laid up.

The freshly glued panel is put into a hydraulic press and subjected to intense heat and pressure, which cures the glue in minutes. From the press it is trimmed to size, finished with filler, and sanded to a predetermined grade.

VENEER CLASSIFICATIONS

The grade classification refers to the outer veneers of the sheet of plywood. There is a face (or front) veneer and a back veneer. When a sheet of plywood is given two letters in its classification, the first refers to the front of the sheet and the second to the back.

Grade	Description
N and **A**	The highest grade with no knots and restricted patches. N is intended for natural finishes (staining, varnishing, etc.) and A is a good, smooth painting surface.
B	A solid surface. Small knots, patches and round plugs are allowed.
C plugged	This is a C grade all dolled up. This "high-drag" of plywood is only cosmetic, and designed for underlayment.
C	Small knots, knotholes and patches. This is the lowest grade in exterior-type plywood.
D	Aaaah! Home again. Larger knots, knotholes and some limited white pocket in sheeting grades are allowed. This is the most common back veneer grade for interior plywood.

INTERIOR / EXTERIOR

Plywood is available in INTERIOR and EXTERIOR types. The plywood varies little in appearance. The major difference is the resistance of the glue to water, and that exterior plywood allows no veneer grade below C. However, in manufacturing some mistakes slip by and are then relabeled "Interior plywood with exterior glue," or with some other telling, and quite catchy, little phrase.

AVAILABILITY

Plywood is available in many thicknesses in a standard 4'-0" x 8'-0" sheet. Both narrower and longer sheets are made and can sometimes be had through special order, although the cost is generally prohibitive. One exception is the 5'-0" x 9'-0" x ⅝" thick plywood made for ping-pong tables. However, despite the enthusiasm of the Chinese for the game, this size is becoming rare. Isn't tradition a wonderful thing?

Thicknesses for plywood commonly stocked by most yards are ¼", ⅜", ½", ⅝", ¾", ⅞", 1" and 1⅛". Some other sizes are available, but would probably need to be special ordered. After all, if they don't build houses with it, it is not common. It behooves one to seriously consider bribery or at least the cultivation of the person who runs the lumberyard. That can usually be done with complimentary tickets. If more is expected, check with a lawyer.

BENDING PLYWOOD

Plywood, especially in the thinner sheets, can be bent into curves. Narrower strips will bend more easily than full sheets and, as the following chart shows, strips cut across the grain will bend more easily than those cut parallel to the grain.

MINIMUM RADIUS FOR BENDING FULL SHEETS OF PLYWOOD

Thickness	Across Grain	Parallel to Grain
1/4″	2 ft.	5 ft.
3/8″	3 ft.	8 ft.
1/2″	6 ft.	12 ft.
5/8″	8 ft.	16 ft.
3/4″	12 ft.	20 ft.

PLYWOOD STORAGE

Plywood will warp if not stored properly. It can be placed in vertical racks which do not allow it to lean and bend, or it can be stored flat, if space allows. Often there is room to incorporate a plywood storage area under a large work table in the shop.

APPROXIMATE WEIGHTS OF SHEET PRODUCTS (4′-0″ X 8′-0″)

	1/8″	1/4″	3/8″	1/2″	5/8″	3/4″
plywood[1]	13 lbs.	26 lbs.	35 lbs.	48 lbs.	58 lbs.	70 lbs.
hardboard[2]	19 lbs.	38 lbs.				
particle board[3]		24 lbs.	48 lbs.	62 lbs.	78 lbs.	94 lbs.
Thermoply[4]	13 lbs.					

NOTES:

1   Plywood weights will vary, depending on the type of wood used in veneers as well as on grade and type. Mahogany veneer (⅛″) is available in 4′-0″ x 8′-0″ sheets and 3′-0″ x 7′-0″ sheets (door skins). It is reasonably priced, but often must be a special order.

2   Hardboard is available in many sheet sizes and thicknesses up to 12′-0″ long. Masonite is a common trade name for hardboard. It is available in untempered (easier to nail) and tempered with an oil substance which makes it quite hard and brittle. The tempered sheet makes an excellent "tap-dance"

surface when laminated over stock platforms. A "rough" screened surface is available on one side if ordered. This is a good texture for facings and floors.

3   Particle board varies greatly in weight, density, and strength, depending upon manufacturing techniques.

4   Thermoply is a trade name for a paper board with a silver foil laminated to both surfaces. It is light, readily available and not too expensive. The foil does not like to take paint or glue to wood framing.

APPROXIMATE WEIGHTS OF DIMENSIONED LUMBER

	8'-0"	12'-0"	16'-0"
2 x 4	10 lbs.	16 lbs.	21 lbs.
1 x 4	4 lbs.	6 lbs.	8 lbs.
1 x 10	12 lbs.	18 lbs.	24 lbs.
1 x 12	14 lbs.	21 lbs.	28 lbs.

Note: weights will vary greatly depending on the amount of moisture in the wood (how well it has been dried). Typically, "two-by" stock is fir and "one-by" stock is white wood (white pine, spruce, hemlock, etc.).

JOINTS

Some knowledge of the common wood joints used in scenery construction is helpful. Drawing I-3 shows how basic they are. All boards have narrow edges, a wider face (both front and back), and ends (so named because the ends of the wood's cellular structure are exposed). The edges and faces give good surfaces for holding nails, screws and staples, but the ends have no real holding power.

Two pieces of wood are butted together to make a butt joint. This is the most common joint in scenery construction and can be described in more detail by naming the parts of the boards which are touching.

A scarf joint is used to create a longer board than is on hand. As can be seen, the face scarf is stronger than the edge scarf because the surfaces to be glued together are greater. However, the edge scarf is faster and easier to make and often more accurate, which gives it some advantage. Until the board stretcher is perfected, the scarf joint is the best solution to create extra-long lengths.

Lap joints are quick and, when properly attached, quite strong. The half-lap has the same good strength, with the added advantage of keeping the wood pieces in the same plane.

Make sure all joints fit tightly and that scarf and lap joints are well glued.

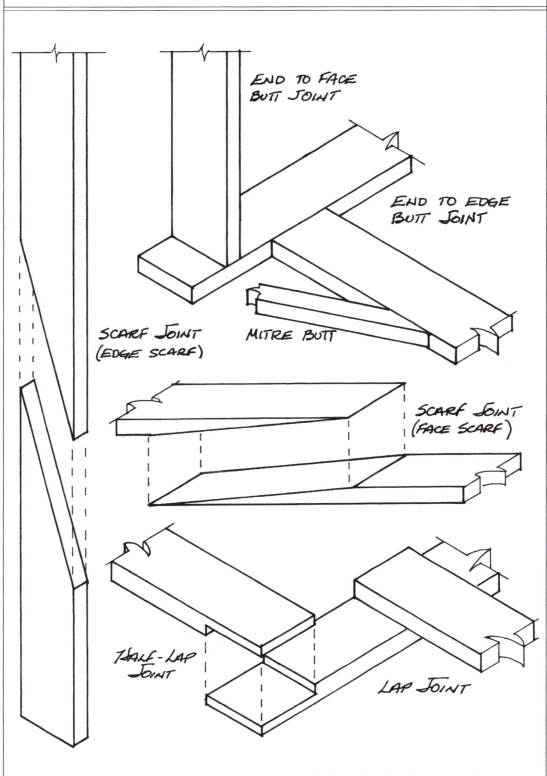

END TO FACE BUTT JOINT

END TO EDGE BUTT JOINT

SCARF JOINT (EDGE SCARF)

MITRE BUTT

SCARF JOINT (FACE SCARF)

HALF-LAP JOINT

LAP JOINT

PART II • FLATS

"STOCK" SCENERY

What is stock? Mr. Webster defines it as something "used or employed for constant service; kept in stock; as a stock size." If we may define "in stock" as meaning "on hand" and "stock size" as a "standardized size," we are close to a good definition for stock scenery. Indeed, stock scenery is designed with the specific goal of being able to keep it on hand and re-use it, thus gaining significant savings of time, money and personnel.

When scenery becomes stock, we have combined more than nouns, verbs and adjectives—we have consolidated our thinking. Scenery can no longer be designed for a specific production and then be discarded so the process may begin anew. This type of wanton consumerism is rapidly becoming outmoded in all aspects of our society. This does not mean designs for a production must be compromised or be inappropriate, but in the design process some practical restrictions must be applied. No designer quibbles about the director, the script, shape of the theatre, the building period, size of crew, budget, limited tech and dress period or the many other restrictions he inherits. Bitch and moan, yes, but quibble, never! Asking a designer to work with and utilize stock scenery is but one more "limitation" added to the stack. If we believe that nothing is more detrimental to an artist than total freedom, it stands to reason that stock limitations should help the design. But in all seriousness, working with stock scenery does not have to be a limitation. The creative recycling can actually assist a clever designer, and allow more time for other aspects of the production. This, of course, assumes the stock is well planned.

The stock scenery discussed in this book breaks down into four basic categories: flats, draperies (or soft scenery), platforms (with ramps) and stairs. Obviously, theatre-in-the-round has little use for flats, per se, but a proscenium theatre would, as might the thrust. All three utilize platforms and steps. Unfortunately, for those not needing flats, I have included in the section on flats some of the determining factors for building stock scenery for all three categories... alas!

Stock scenery takes time and money to build. It is a crucial step for a theatre to take because it affects many aspects of production. Make sure the theatre is going to produce the types of plays which benefit from settings made from stock flats. I do not necessarily mean "box sets," even though that is the most common type. If a good percentage of the production can utilize stock flats, the chances are also good that you can save in the long run by building a stock of flats. If the decision to build is made, be sure that the director, designer and technical staff are in agreement and will cooperate in using the flats. Make sure all are aware of the limitations, as well as the advantages.

There are many factors to consider if a stock is going to be built. The first is the theatre itself. What is the proscenium width, height, and its relationship to the floor space? A flat which works proportionately to these should be determined (see Drawing II-1). What is the depth of the stage and what is its wing space? What is the access to the stage (shop door, winding stairs, etc.) and where is the offstage storage area? Some theatres have very low ceilings over the stage or they have draperies which are dead hung to a very low trim. Often the draperies can be raised, but usually not the ceiling.

Equally important is the storage space. Stock flats spend more time offstage than on. To be effective, storage must handle many times the number of flats which could be used in a single production. If space does not exist, seriously reconsider building a stock of flats. Storage is a major limitation of stock.

The shop area is important. As discussed earlier, flats require a certain amount of "floor space" to be built. Though it is true that stock flats can relieve the burden upon a shop, this is true only after they are built. There are few shows, also, which will not have additional flats built for them, which could then become a part of the stock. It is, however, a rare shop which cannot build a flat! A reasonable collection of power tools greatly facilitates flat construction, but is not necessary.

Budget is often considered all important. Remember that a budget is nothing but priorities with backing. Shift accordingly. Stock scenery is not cheap to build. It only becomes economical after it has been paid for and can be used again. Because a well built flat can be utilized dozens of times before it needs recovering and the frame can last many coverings, the possibilities of reuse are great. But, the initial outlay is large.

Manpower must be considered. If there is a skilled crew in the shop, they would probably rather build most shows from scratch, as is usually done in professional situations. However, in the nonprofessional theatre, the designer, technical director and crews would often rather spend their time on a few detail pieces and are more than willing to accept the "shell" of a box set, already built and ready to paint. But is there sufficient manpower to build the stock, handle the stock in set-ups, shifts, and strikes? Is there manpower to properly return the stock to storage? Don't get discouraged, the worst is yet to come.

Time, of course, is decidedly related to using stock flats. Like money, it takes a lot of time to build a good stock, but little to use it afterwards. This gives the paint crews more time to do a better job, and frees the designer and set dressers to spend extra hours adding the finishing touches. The technical crew can concentrate on building those elements which will be added to the set or which will play in conjunction with it. The tired old song, "Time is Money," hits the ear with a sour bleat to any exhausted technician who knows a truer lyric, "Money is Time."

Stock scenery is also affected by the age of the people using it and (God forbid)

BELOW IS AN EXAMPLE OF A 4'-0" STANDARD FLAT SHOWN IN SIX COMMON HEIGHTS. THE PLACEMENT OF THE CORNER BRACES REMAINS CONSTANT. THE MAJOR CHANGES CONCERN TOGGLE PLACEMENT... AND THE NUMBER USED. IN THE 8'-0" FLAT (AND POSSIBLY IN THE 10'-0" FLAT), ONE TOGGLE IS CENTERED. IN THE 10'-0", 12'-0" AND 14'-0" FLATS, THE TWO TOGGLES ARE CENTERED AT INTERVALS ONE-THIRD THE HEIGHT. THE TALLER FLATS (16'-0" + 18'-0") HAVE TOGGLES WHICH CENTER ON INTERVALS ONE-FOURTH THE TOTAL HEIGHT.

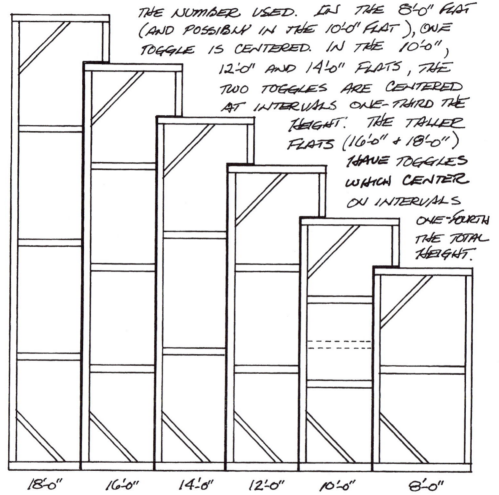

18'-0"   16'-0"   14'-0"   12'-0"   10'-0"   8'-0"

THE <u>FOUR TO SIX RULE</u>

GENERAL RULE OF THUMB FOR TOGGLE PLACEMENT:

HORIZONTAL MEMBERS DO NOT NEED TO BE CLOSER THAN 4'-0" APART BUT SHOULD NOT BE FARTHER APART THAN 6'-0". SPECIFIC OR UNUSUAL USE CAN VARY THE "RULES."

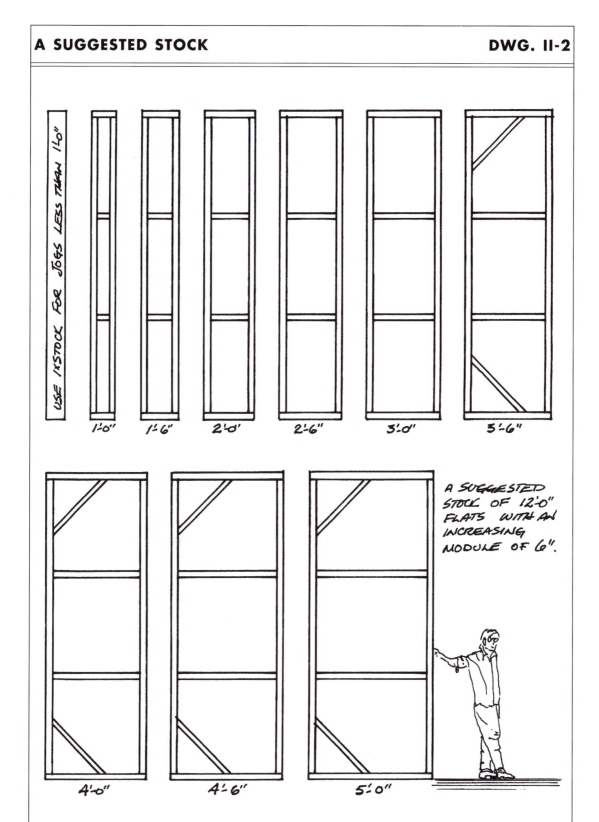

USE 1x STOCK FOR JOGS LESS THAN 1'-0"

1'-0" 1'-6" 2'-0' 2'-6" 3'-0' 3'-6"

4'-0" 4'-6" 5'-0"

A SUGGESTED STOCK OF 12'-0" FLATS WITH AN INCREASING MODULE OF 6".

sex. Grade school children certainly cannot be expected to handle stock flats which are 16'-0" high. They shouldn't handle any scenery if they have not developed good reflexes and coordination; it is not only dangerous, but shortens the life of the scenery. Girls' schools might not have the same size of flats as boys' schools. Though this difference is often slight, it still determines the effectiveness of a usable stock. Just be careful to use sex in a discriminating manner.

Another important factor is the availability of materials. Lumber is commonly available in lengths up to 16'-0" long. It is possible to get longer pieces, but the cost is usually prohibitive. Another factor is the very popular 4'-0" x 8'-0" size of plywood. If platforms are being planned with the stock flats, 4'-0" (or divisions and multiples of it) is a common size. Some of the more subtle determining factors are door openings, which are 28-36" wide by 6'-9" to 7'-0" high. This affects movement of the scenery and will also affect the flat which contains a door opening.

In summary, the determination of the sizes for stock flats, platforms and stairs is one which must come from weighing all the factors and setting priorities. Some common flat heights usually start at 8'-0" and continue (often in 1'-0" intervals) to 16'-0" (see Drawing II-1). The most common flats seem to be 12'-0" or 14'-0" high. Widths are usually based on a module (see Drawing II-2); 6" seems to give a satisfactory width change, although 3", 8" and 9" are also used. Some theatres have no width restrictions. Widths usually start with flats which are 1'-0" wide and increase on the module chosen. 4'-0" seems to be the most common width, probably because many people choose to build wider flats from a combination of two or more smaller ones. Flats much wider than 5'-0" often create a storage problem. The old "law" of no-wider-than 5'-9" still holds, but for different reasons. We seldom need to clear the opening in a boxcar door while touring, but an economical muslin width is 72", and the problems in handling flats increase as they get wider.

It is a rare theatre indeed which can afford to have more than one height of stock flats. Theatres usually pick the most practical height and occasionally will have a small "stock" of shorter flats which serve as backings for doors, windows, etc. Platforms and stairs also need to be saddled with specific regulations, which will be discussed later.

FLAT FRAME COMPONENT PIECES

There are only four basic parts to a standard flat frame (see Drawing II-3). They are the rails, stiles, toggles (sometimes called toggle boards or toggle rails) and the corner braces.

The rails are the horizontal top and bottom pieces in the frame. The stiles (note spelling) are the outside vertical members of the frame. The names come from architectural frames like doors and windows into which secondary members are tenoned. On older doors, the stiles go from the bottom to the top. This gives a strong edge and prevents the bottom rail of the door from being broken off when it is kicked. The stiles in a standard flat frame are always inside the rails. If this were not so, the end grain of the stiles would split apart when the frame is dragged on the floor. Therefore the length of the protected stiles is the height of the frame minus the width of two rails.

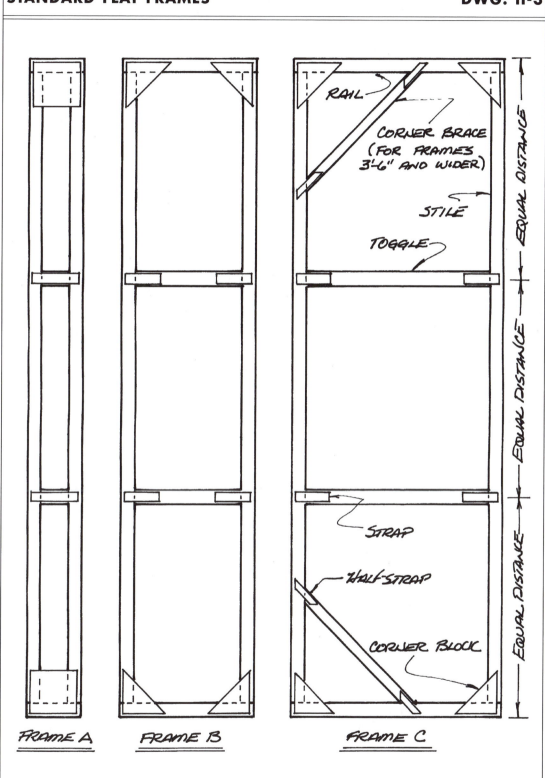

RAIL

CORNER BRACE
(FOR FRAMES
3'-6" AND WIDER)

STILE

TOGGLE

EQUAL DISTANCE

EQUAL DISTANCE

EQUAL DISTANCE

STRAP

HALF-STRAP

CORNER BLOCK

FRAME A　　　　FRAME B　　　　FRAME C

The toggles are placed in the frame to keep the stiles at their prescribed distance. They were originally tenoned also, but today with the widespread use of plywood blocks to fasten flat pieces together, there are very few shops left which still use these exacting methods (see Drawing II-6). The derivation of the word "toggle" is unclear, but it probably comes from the verb "to toggle," which means to fix or fasten in the manner of a pin (like the toggle bar on the end of a watch chain, which is inserted into the button hole). Don't ask how it got to be an internal "rail."

Toggles are always fixed in the same place in the same height of stock (see Drawings II-1, II-2 and II-3). Usually, they are centered on some specific measurement which is determined by the height of the flat. However, exceptions do exist. For example, when hanging a cornice on a set, an additional toggle could be placed near the top rail to help hold it. If there are often chair rails on sets, a toggle at the necessary height from the floor could be added. These "odd" toggles could affect the placement of the other toggles. A good rule of thumb for toggle placement is to have one at least every six feet from another horizontal member, but it is not necessary to have one any closer than 3'-0" from another horizontal member. Close to 4'-0" is a safe choice, but, again, need is often a deciding factor (see Drawing II-1).

Rails, stiles and toggles are made of 3" wide stock. The corner brace is a piece of 2" stock which is 3'-0" long with a 45° cut placed on each end, like part of a picture frame. The corner brace is used to help hold larger flat frames square. Two corner braces are placed in every flat that will accept them. The braces are always contiguous to one stile. It does not matter which stile, as long as they remain consistent within one height of stock. For the sake of sanity, in this book braces are always placed touching the left stile. Corner braces can be made ahead of time in quantity, often from tailing strips remaining from 1 x stock after it has been ripped down for another piece. This will use up scrap, cut down on waste and speed construction.

PLYWOOD FASTENERS

Rails, stiles, toggles and corner braces butt up against each other in the frame. The butt joint is held together by specially made ¼" 3-ply fasteners. There are three stock shapes made up in quantity and stored for use as needed (see Drawings II-4 and II-5). The corner block ("block" is a large piece of material laid over a joint) holds the corners of the frame. The strap (a narrow piece laid over a joint) holds the toggle to the stile, and the half-strap holds the corner brace to the rail and stile. All plywood pieces should have their grain running at a right angle to the joint for maximum strength. Never have a joint fastened with the grain running parallel to it, because it will probably break.

CORNER BLOCK

The corner block is best made by ripping a 6½" x 8'-0" strip of ¼" 3-ply. Then, with the arm on the radial arm saw set for 45°, cut across this strip. Flip the strip over and move it along the fence until the first cut reaches the blade. Pull the saw again and the result will be a corner block (see Drawing II-5). Repeat the cut, flipping the strip each time, until it is all cut into corner blocks.

STRAP

The strap is a piece of ¼" 3-ply which is 8" long and as wide as the toggle stock minus ¼". The minus ¼" prevents the edge from overhanging the toggle and snagging anything. In this book, because toggles are 3" wide, straps are 2¾" wide. The grain must run the length of the strap, so rip a piece of ¼" 3-ply 2¾" x 8'-0" long. Set the radial arm saw for a straight cut (90°), and cut the strip into 8" straps. A "stop block" clamped to the fence eight inches from the blade will speed up this step by allowing you to move the plywood quickly to the stop and not measure each time. Don't bang the stop or it could move. Do not try to cut more than one strap at a time The cut pieces can flip up into the blade, or slip and slide and create inaccurate cuts.

HALF-STRAP

The half-strap is as wide as the corner brace stock minus ¼". Therefore, in this book, they are 1¾" wide. The half-strap measures 8" on the long side and has a 45° angle cut on each end. A stop block clamped to the fence of the radial arm saw (with the arm swung over to a 45° angle) will aid in cutting these pieces also.

KEYSTONES

Keystones are seldom used today, though their added strength might sometimes warrant it. They are more time-consuming to make and the yield per sheet of plywood is less than that of the strap. Strength loses to cost and weight.

CHAMFERING FASTENERS

All plywood fasteners should have a ⅛" chamfer on the face edge (see Drawing II-6). This is a bevel cut which eliminates splinters and lessens the chance of snagging costumes or soft scenery. The chamfer also makes the flat frame easier to handle because the edges are smooth and eliminate any danger of tearing the covering when the flats are stored.

Chamfering the fasteners, while a tedious process, is well worth the time. A small plane is ideal to chamfer irregular blocks and straps made for special applications or adaptations to stock fasteners, but it is far too time-consuming for the thousands of pieces necessary to build a stock of flats. An easy method is to use the table saw. Clamp or bolt a piece of 1 x stock to the fence on the saw. Put a veneer blade in the saw. Crank the blade to a 45° angle and lower it below the table's surface. Move the fence, with the 1 x stock on it, up to the blade opening. Turn on the saw. Carefully raise the blade and cut into the 1 x stock on the fence. By adjusting the fence and the blade, a relationship can be established which will allow you to pass a piece of ¼" 3-ply across the angle blade and get an ⅛" chamfer. Workers doing the chamfering should switch duties periodically, because the work can become hypnotizing and therefore dangerous. Chamfering also ties up the saw, so this work should be done when there is a lull in the schedule. A what? In the what?

Rule of Thumb: Always hold the plywood fasteners back ¾" (or stock thickness) from the outside edge of the frame. This clearance allows one flat to butt flush against another and make a smooth corner (see Drawing II-48). The fasteners can also act as stops. On the inside openings (like doors and windows), you should also hold the

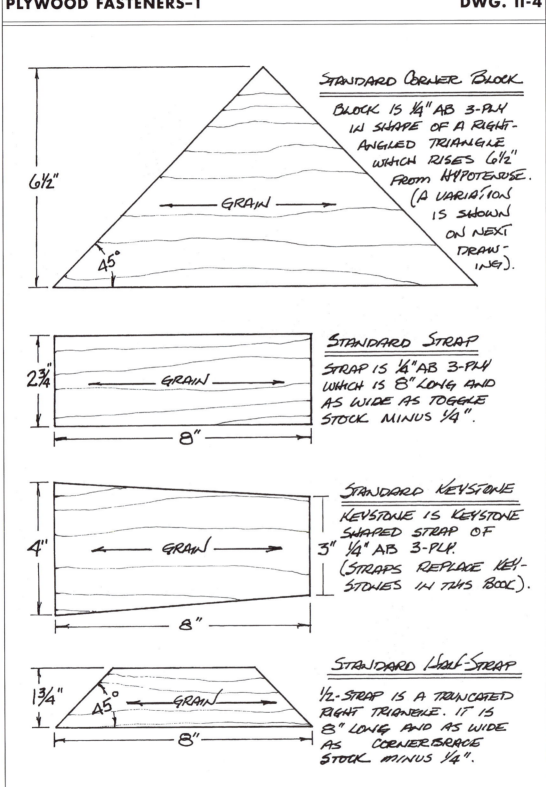

STANDARD CORNER BLOCK

BLOCK IS ¼" AB 3-PLY IN SHAPE OF A RIGHT-ANGLED TRIANGLE WHICH RISES 6½" FROM HYPOTENUSE. (A VARIATION IS SHOWN ON NEXT DRAWING).

6½"

GRAIN

45°

STANDARD STRAP

STRAP IS ¼" AB 3-PLY WHICH IS 8" LONG AND AS WIDE AS TOGGLE STOCK MINUS ¼".

2¾"

GRAIN

8"

STANDARD KEYSTONE

KEYSTONE IS KEYSTONE SHAPED STRAP OF ¼" AB 3-PLY. (STRAPS REPLACE KEYSTONES IN THIS BOOK).

4"

GRAIN

3"

8"

STANDARD HALF-STRAP

½-STRAP IS A TRUNCATED RIGHT TRIANGLE. IT IS 8" LONG AND AS WIDE AS CORNER-BRACE STOCK MINUS ¼".

1¾"

45°

GRAIN

8"

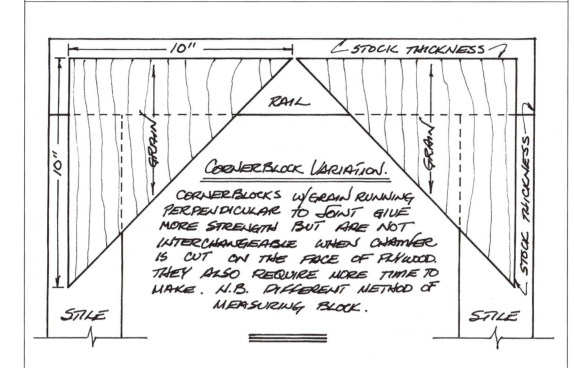

10"

STOCK THICKNESS

RAIL

GRAIN

10"

GRAIN

STOCK THICKNESS

CornerBlock Variation.

CornerBlocks w/grain running perpendicular to joint give more strength but are not interchangeable when chamfer is cut on the face of plywood. They also require more time to make. N.B. Different method of measuring block.

STILE   STILE

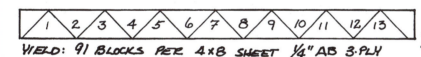

| 1 | 2 | 3 | 4 | 5 | 6 | 7 | 8 | 9 | 10 | 11 | 12 | 13 |

YIELD: 91 BLOCKS PER 4×8 SHEET ¼" AB 3-PLY

CORNER BLOCKS:
RIP 6½" × 8'-0" STRIP OF PLY AND CUT AS DRAWN.

| 1 | 2 | 3 | 4 | 5 | 6 | 7 | 8 | 9 | 10 | 11 | 12 |

YIELD: 192 STRAPS PER 4×8 SHEET ¼" AB 3-PLY

STRAPS:
RIP 2¾" × 8'-0" STRIP OF PLY AND CUT AS DRAWN.

| 1 | 2 | 3 | 4 | 5 | 6 | 7 | 8 | 9 | 10 | 11 | 12 | 13 | 14 |

YIELD: 350 ½-STRAPS PER 4×8 SHEET ¼" AB 3-PLY

HALF STRAPS:
RIP 1¾" × 8'-0" STRIP OF PLY AND CUT AS DRAWN.

KEYSTONES:
RIP 8" × 4'-0" STRIP OF PLY. N.B. GRAIN MUST RUN PERPENDICULAR TO THE 4'-0" CUT. CUT AS DRAWN.

| 1 | 2 | 3 | 4 | 5 | 6 | 7 | 8 | 9 | 10 | 11 | 12 | 13 |

YIELD: 143 KEYSTONES PER 4×8 SHEET ¼" AB 3-PLY.

LAYOUT AND CUTTING METHODS FOR PLYWOOD FASTENERS—

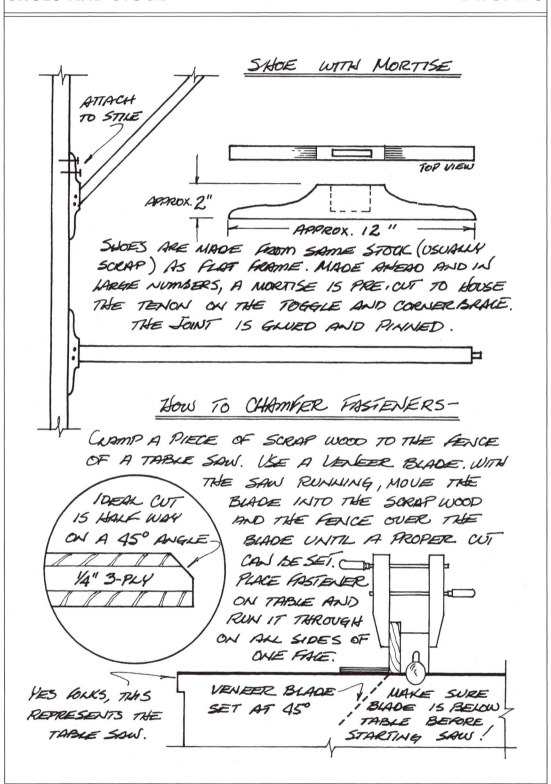

SHOE WITH MORTISE

ATTACH TO STILE

TOP VIEW

APPROX. 2"

APPROX. 12"

SHOES ARE MADE FROM SAME STOCK (USUALLY SCRAP) AS FLAT FRAME. MADE AHEAD AND IN LARGE NUMBERS, A MORTISE IS PRE-CUT TO HOUSE THE TENON ON THE TOGGLE AND CORNER BRACE. THE JOINT IS GLUED AND PINNED.

How TO CHAMFER FASTENERS-

CLAMP A PIECE OF SCRAP WOOD TO THE FENCE OF A TABLE SAW. USE A VENEER BLADE. WITH THE SAW RUNNING, MOVE THE BLADE INTO THE SCRAP WOOD AND THE FENCE OVER THE BLADE UNTIL A PROPER CUT CAN BE SET. PLACE FASTENER ON TABLE AND RUN IT THROUGH ON ALL SIDES OF ONE FACE.

IDEAL CUT IS HALF WAY ON A 45° ANGLE

1/4" 3-PLY

YES FOLKS, THIS REPRESENTS THE TABLE SAW.

VENEER BLADE SET AT 45°

MAKE SURE BLADE IS BELOW TABLE BEFORE STARTING SAW!

fasteners back to allow a piece of 1 x stock to be placed on edge for a thickness or reveal if desired (see Drawings II-13 and II-19).

It is interesting to know that before the age of plywood, scenic carpenters made their fasteners of thin wood which had linen duck glued to both sides to strengthen it. They were then nailed over the frame joints, which were usually mortised and tenoned or doweled.

STANDARD FLAT CONSTRUCTION

All flat construction is based on the standard flat (see Drawing II-3). This is one of the best examples of cost vs. weight vs. strength. When vertical, the flat frame is very strong. It is weaker when placed on its side because the ends of the rails are exposed to the floor and can be split apart. When leaning or suspended horizontally, the frame is at its weakest because the plywood fasteners are taking the stress. Flats should be used vertically, if possible.

To build a 4'-0" x 12'-0" flat like Frame C on Drawing II-3, follow this procedure: Rip the stock to a true 3" and cut two stiles 11'-6" long. Unless you are using perfect wood, it is advisable to test each piece as it is ripped. Hold the piece at one end and raise it up. Allow it to drop down. This should put enough "bounce" and "shock" through the piece to break it at any weak place. It is better to find weaknesses at this point and not after the frame is complete. Always cut the longest pieces first, and then the shorter ones can be cut from the scrap. Next cut two rails 4'-0" long, and then two toggles 3'-6" long. Pull two corner braces from the stockpile and get four corner blocks, four straps and four half-straps.

A large work table is ideal for building flat frames, but the floor will do. Place the pieces in approximate position. Take one rail and butt it against the end of one stile. Drive two ¼" or ⅜" long corrugated fasteners against the joint (these are available at any hardware store). This will temporarily hold the pieces together until the plywood fasteners can be applied. (See later comment on corrugated fasteners also known as corrugators.) Move around the frame. Measure up 4'-0" from the bottom of the rail and make a mark on the stile. Center one of the toggles on it. Butt it tightly and hold it with a corrugator. Measure up 8'-0" from the bottom of the rail and center the second toggle. Set it with a corrugator also . Now put the second rail to the stile. Hold it to the stile with two corrugators. Place the second stile in place and attach it to the rail, measure 4'-0" and set the toggle, measure 8'-0" and set the second toggle, and then tie the stile to the rail. The frame is now completed with toggles in place.

Now take a marking gauge (see Drawing II-8) and, with it securely against the edge of the frame, scribe a pencil line along the outside of the frame. This will leave a line ¾" in from the outside edge on the face of the 1 x 3" stock. This line determines the placement of the plywood fasteners. If they were closer to the edge, another frame could not butt smoothly against the 1 x 3, and if they were farther away, they would not act as stops for the butted flat.

Next, take a framing square and place it at the corner of the flat frame (see Drawing II-8). Even if the frame is held together with corrugators, it can still "rack" slightly because there are not corner braces to hold it square. If the flat is square,

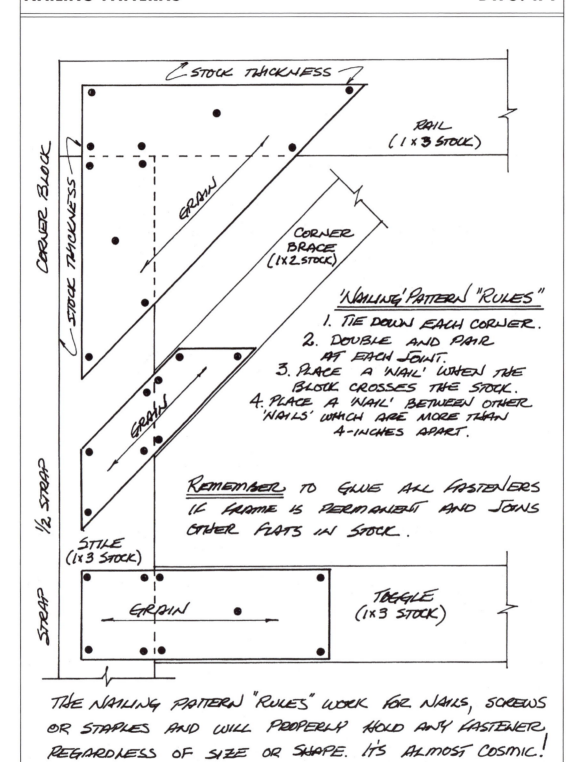

STOCK THICKNESS

RAIL
(1 x 3 STOCK)

CORNER BLOCK

STOCK THICKNESS

GRAIN

CORNER BRACE
(1 x 2 STOCK)

'NAILING' PATTERN "RULES"

1. TIE DOWN EACH CORNER.
2. DOUBLE AND PAIR AT EACH JOINT.
3. PLACE A 'NAIL' WHEN THE BLOCK CROSSES THE STOCK.
4. PLACE A 'NAIL' BETWEEN OTHER 'NAILS' WHICH ARE MORE THAN 4-INCHES APART.

GRAIN

REMEMBER TO GLUE ALL FASTENERS IF FRAME IS PERMANENT AND JOINS OTHER FLATS IN STOCK.

½ STRAP

STILE
(1 x 3 STOCK)

STRAP

GRAIN

TOGGLE
(1 x 3 STOCK)

THE NAILING PATTERN "RULES" WORK FOR NAILS, SCREWS OR STAPLES AND WILL PROPERLY HOLD ANY FASTENER, REGARDLESS OF SIZE OR SHAPE. IT'S ALMOST COSMIC!

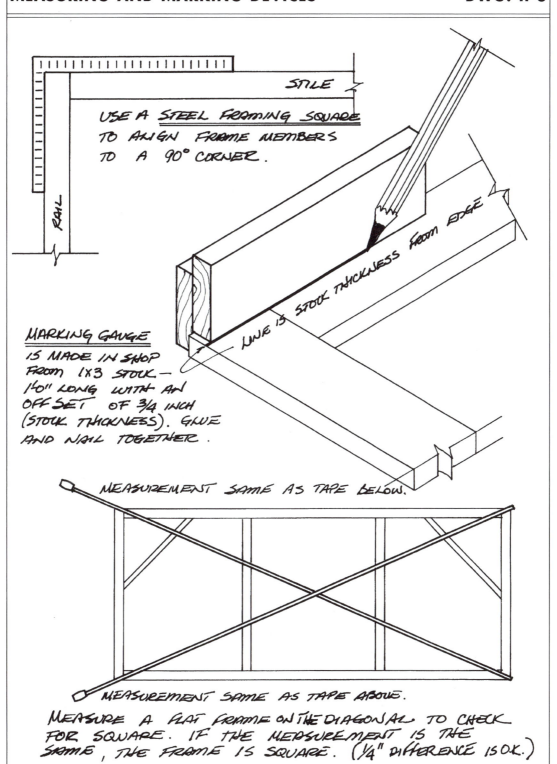

STILE

USE A STEEL FRAMING SQUARE TO ALIGN FRAME MEMBERS TO A 90° CORNER.

RAIL

LINE IS STOCK THICKNESS FROM EDGE

MARKING GAUGE
IS MADE IN SHOP FROM 1X3 STOCK — 1'-0" LONG WITH AN OFFSET OF 3/4 INCH (STOCK THICKNESS). GLUE AND NAIL TOGETHER.

MEASUREMENT SAME AS TAPE BELOW.

MEASUREMENT SAME AS TAPE ABOVE.

MEASURE A FLAT FRAME ON THE DIAGONAL TO CHECK FOR SQUARE. IF THE MEASUREMENT IS THE SAME, THE FRAME IS SQUARE. (1/4" DIFFERENCE IS O.K.)

which it probably will be if all cuts were square and all joints tightly butted, proceed. If it is not square, rack it into square and hold it square by driving a few 6d duplex nails through the frame and into the work table or floor.

When the frame is squared, place the two corner braces on the left stile. Make sure the braces are equally spaced from the edge of the flat. This will assure a tight butt. Hold each by driving a corrugator across the joint. The frame will not rack out of square now unless it is jarred with great force.

Note: Corrugators are certainly not necessary for good flat construction. They slow the building process, but in many situations, especially learning ones, there is an advantage in knowing the frame is accurate before it is fixed with the plywood fasteners.

Place a corner block with glue applied on its back over the butt joint of the stile and rail. Align it to the penciled line ¾" from the edge. Drive nails or staple it using the proper pattern (see Drawing II-7). Again, moving in a circle around the flat, place a glued half-strap on the corner brace joint and nail it down. Move to the toggle and glue a strap and nail it down to that butt joint. Make sure that all the plywood fasteners are held back the ¾" stock thickness. Continue around the frame until all the joints are fixed.

Double-check the frame to make sure it is square. The fastest way to do this is to measure it diagonally (see Drawing II-8). Take a steel tape and place one end on the corner of the frame. Move to the opposite end of the frame and take a diagonal measurement. Repeat the process on the other diagonal. The measurement should be the same if the frame is square. If the difference is no more than ⅛", it is probably not worth trying to correct. However, if it is more, take the framing square and check the corners of the square. When you find the error, it is still not too late to correct because the glue has not set up yet. Remove the necessary fasteners and throw them away. Knock the frame into square and put new fasteners down because they will hold better, not having been banged up in removal. It is advisable, if using nails, to drive them in only part way, leaving the head about ¼" up until the frame has been checked on the diagonal. Any error is easier to repair if you can pull out the nails. If an electric or air powered stapler is being used, there is no such thing as "half-driven," but the hold is still easy enough to break before the glue sets.

As can be seen in standard flat frames (see Drawing II-3), the methods for Frame B would be the same as for Frame C except that there are no corner braces. Frame A would require special blocks be made for it, top and bottom. Make sure the grain on the ¼" 3-ply runs across the joint and that stock thickness is allowed on the edges. Chamfer the block before attaching it. Use the same nailing pattern "rules" for tying it down (see Drawing II-7). The straps can be specially made and chamfered, or stock straps could be cut to butt together in the center of the toggle.

As simple and basic as the steps are for building standard flat frames, they must be mastered. Everything else in flat frame construction (stair carriages, parallel platforms, et al.) is based on them, either as they exist or in a variation.

EXTRA TALL FLATS

There are situations when oversize flats are needed (see Drawings II-9 and II-10). Some theatres, indeed, have decided on set stock heights which necessitate flat construction using scarf-jointed stiles, but the most common uses are probably tormentors, hard-legs or masking, and false proscenia.

Construction methods are the same for these tall buggers as for the shorter flats. The exception is the flat with tapered stiles (see Drawing II-10) This involves the thinning or narrowing of the stile, which removes excess weight at the top of the flat and thus lessens "wobbling" when the frames are moved.

When tapering a stile, use a portable circular saw or carefully feed the stile through the table saw. Cut the taper on the inside edge of the stile. Make sure that there are no metal fasteners (nails, staples, screws) holding the scarf joint until the tapering is completed, or you will be replacing saw blades. It is possible to attach the scarf after the line has been snapped to determine the cut.

Either a face scarf joint or an edge scarf joint (see Drawing I-3) can be used for making the long stile. The edge joint is easier to cut but does not have quite as much strength as the face joint because there is not as much surface to glue together. Both joints can be reinforced with a plywood block held back stock thickness from the outside edge.

Rails can be scarfed in a similar way for headers or the tops of a false proscenium. For "one-shot" uses, it is sometimes advantageous to build a plug and batten it to a stock flat for extended height (or length). A dutchman (see Drawing II-53) will hide this indiscretion. Details follow.

THE FALSE PROSCENIUM

When the theatre's proscenium, the architectural frame which separates the auditorium from the stage proper, is quite large, designers will often choose to decrease the opening with a smaller inner (or even outer) framework and thus decrease the amount of scenery needed to fill each setting. This "false proscenium" commonly echoes the original, but could be shaped or decorated for a special production. Regardless, the false proscenium usually requires oversized flats. The two drawings (II-11 and II-12) show false proscenia created with specially built flats and created from stock flats and plugs.

If a performance space is being created in a room and a proscenium is being made, perhaps one of hardwall construction (see Drawing II-61) would be a preferable solution.

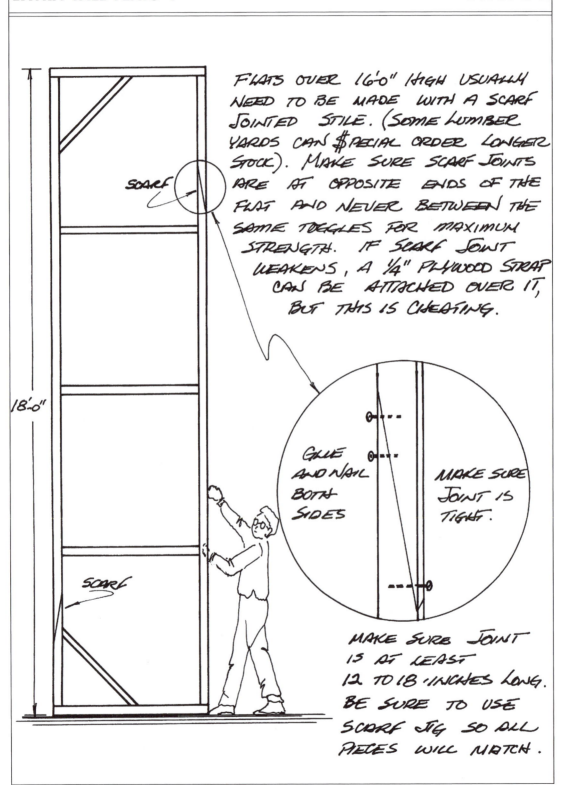

FLATS OVER 16'0" HIGH USUALLY NEED TO BE MADE WITH A SCARF JOINTED STILE. (SOME LUMBER YARDS CAN $PECIAL ORDER LONGER STOCK). MAKE SURE SCARF JOINTS ARE AT OPPOSITE ENDS OF THE FLAT AND NEVER BETWEEN THE SAME TOGGLES FOR MAXIMUM STRENGTH. IF SCARF JOINT WEAKENS, A ¼" PLYWOOD STRAP CAN BE ATTACHED OVER IT, BUT THIS IS CHEATING.

SCARF

18'-0"

SCARF

GLUE AND NAIL BOTH SIDES

MAKE SURE JOINT IS TIGHT.

MAKE SURE JOINT IS AT LEAST 12 TO 18 INCHES LONG. BE SURE TO USE SCARF JIG SO ALL PIECES WILL MATCH.

BE SURE TO USE A JIG TO CUT SCARF TAPERS. A DRAWING CAN BE FOUND IN THE SECTION ON 'SHOP-MADE HELPERS'.

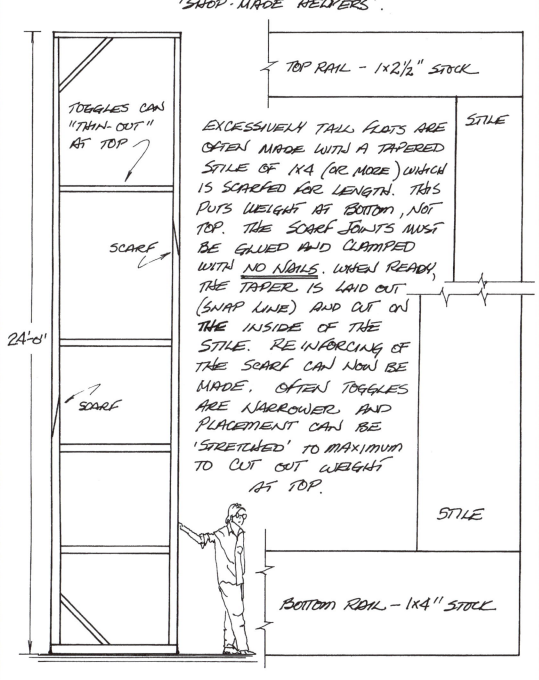

TOP RAIL – 1×2½" STOCK

TOGGLES CAN "THIN-OUT" AT TOP

SCARF

SCARF

24'-0"

STILE

EXCESSIVELY TALL FLATS ARE OFTEN MADE WITH A TAPERED STILE OF 1×4 (OR MORE) WHICH IS SCARFED FOR LENGTH. THIS PUTS WEIGHT AT BOTTOM, NOT TOP. THE SCARF JOINTS MUST BE GLUED AND CLAMPED WITH NO NAILS. WHEN READY, THE TAPER IS LAID OUT (SNAP LINE) AND CUT ON THE INSIDE OF THE STILE. REINFORCING OF THE SCARF CAN NOW BE MADE. OFTEN TOGGLES ARE NARROWER AND PLACEMENT CAN BE 'STRETCHED' TO MAXIMUM TO CUT OUT WEIGHT AT TOP.

STILE

BOTTOM RAIL – 1×4" STOCK

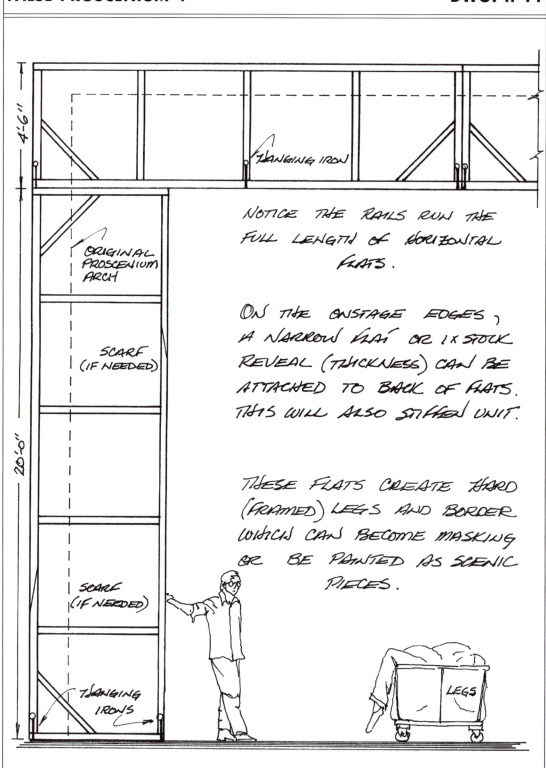

4'-6"

HANGING IRON

ORIGINAL PROSCENIUM ARCH

SCARF (IF NEEDED)

20'-0"

SCARF (IF NEEDED)

HANGING IRONS

NOTICE THE RAILS RUN THE FULL LENGTH OF HORIZONTAL FLATS.

ON THE ONSTAGE EDGES, A NARROW FLAT OR 1× STOCK REVEAL (THICKNESS) CAN BE ATTACHED TO BACK OF FLATS. THIS WILL ALSO STIFFEN UNIT.

THESE FLATS CREATE HARD (FRAMED) LEGS AND BORDER WHICH CAN BECOME MASKING OR BE PAINTED AS SCENIC PIECES.

LEGS

STOCK 12-FOOT FLATS FORM THE BASIC UNIT — PLUGS ARE ADDED TO ACHIEVE DESIRED HEIGHT & WIDTH.

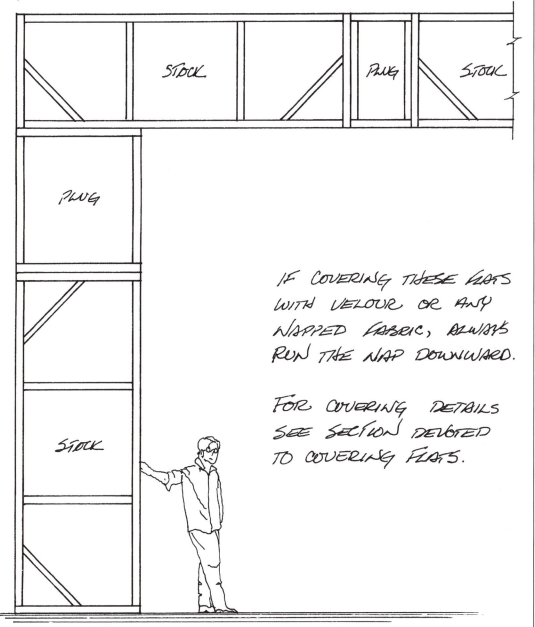

IF COVERING THESE FLATS WITH VELOUR OR ANY NAPPED FABRIC, ALWAYS RUN THE NAP DOWNWARD.

FOR COVERING DETAILS SEE SECTION DEVOTED TO COVERING FLATS.

WINDOW FLAT

Flat frames designed to house windows (see Drawing II-13) are built on the same principles as standard frames. The drawing shows the most basic of window openings. Notice the placement of the horizontal battens which determine the opening. For this example, special blocks must be cut to tie the upper window batten and the toggle to the stiles. Cut these from ¼" 3-ply and chamfer the edges. Make sure that the grain runs perpendicular to the joints. The lower window batten can be fastened using corner blocks because it is necessary to hold the blocks back ¾" (or stock thickness) from the edge of the opening as well as from the outside of the flat frame. This eliminates making a special narrow strap. The additional vertical batten below the window will take the added weight of the actors climbing through this opening. Notice that only the top corner brace will fit this particular frame; therefore, only one brace is used, but it is still on the agreed side.

A variation on the window flat (see Drawing II-14) is the hinged two-fold window. This type is built when large picture windows are needed, not an uncommon occurrence in modern plays. The stiles are broken in the single flats, but when the unit is hinged together with 2" backflap hinges on the face, it is again quite strong. This "two-fold" can be folded for storage, requiring less space. Note that the toggles are set to align with standard flats of the same height. This helps the open two-fold to be attached to other flats. In the Drawing II-14 the lower corner braces will just fit if they are set under the corner blocks. They can be glued and nailed through the block with an additional strap needed for that joint. The Drawing II-16 shows another window variation.

Windows can also be created using standard stock flats and building plugs to go between them (see Drawing II-15). This is often a good solution when an unusual opening is demanded, because it takes less time to build a plug than a whole flat. Plugs can be saved to be reused, but they can also multiply and bury you. The major disadvantage to building openings with plugs is that it takes more time to assemble the unit, batten it together with standard flats, and conceal the additional cracks where they butt.

The window itself can, like a door, be either dependent or independent, depending on whether or not it is a framework which is removable from the flat. The construction of the removable frame is like that of an independent door unit (II-25 and II-26). The shape should adjust. The variety of windows in this world makes it more difficult to standardize their size and shape than for doors, but certainly some common dimensions should be predeterminable to limit stock.

ARCH FLATS

The arch flat (see Drawings II-15 through II-20) differs in construction only in setting the sweeps into the frame. Great care must be taken to have the sweep fit tightly into the space cut away to receive it. The more slop there is in the fit, the weaker the joint.

Try to cut the sweeps from 1 x stock if possible, because it is the same thickness and weight and will have the same working quality as the rest of the frame. However,

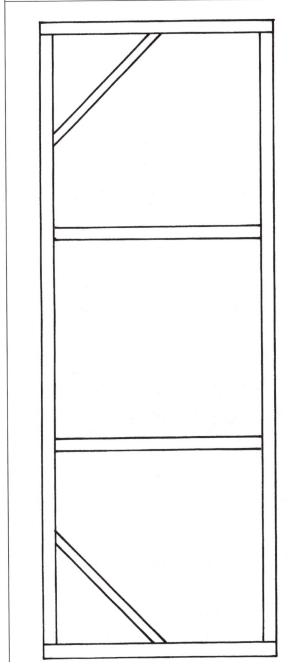

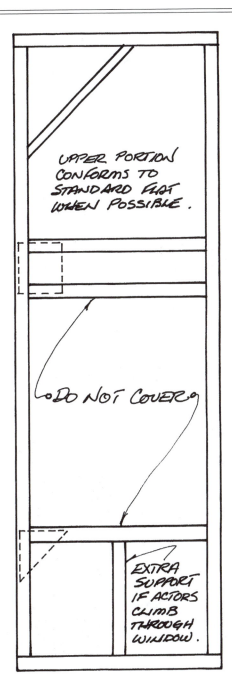

UPPER PORTION CONFORMS TO STANDARD FLAT WHEN POSSIBLE.

DO NOT COVER

EXTRA SUPPORT IF ACTORS CLIMB THROUGH WINDOW.

STANDARD FLAT

SIMPLE WINDOW FLAT

NOTICE THE FASTENERS ARE HELD BACK STOCK THICKNESS FROM INSIDE OF OPENING TO FACILITATE LATER ADDITION OF REVEAL IF SO DESIRED.

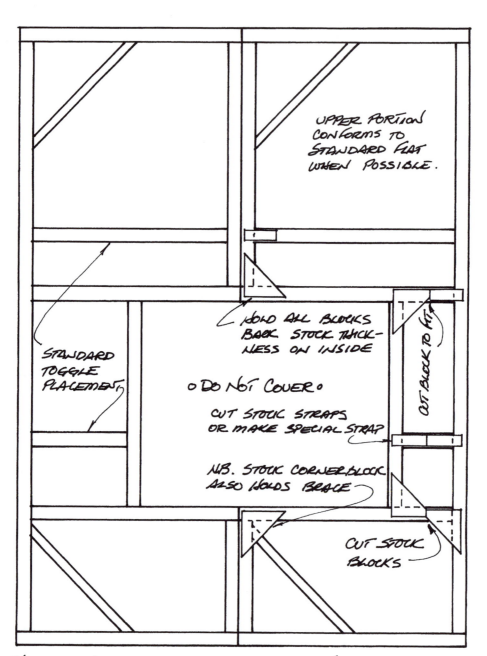

UPPER PORTION CONFORMS TO STANDARD FLAT WHEN POSSIBLE.

HOLD ALL BLOCKS BACK STOCK THICKNESS ON INSIDE

CUT BLOCK TO FIT

STANDARD TOGGLE PLACEMENT

• DO NOT COVER •

CUT STOCK STRAPS OR MAKE SPECIAL STRAP

N.B. STOCK CORNER BLOCK ALSO HOLDS BRACE

CUT STOCK BLOCKS

THESE FLATS WOULD PROBABLY HINGE TOGETHER ON FRONT AND FOLD FOR STORAGE. WHEN OPEN THEY WOULD STIFFEN W/KEEPER HOOKS AND BATTEN.

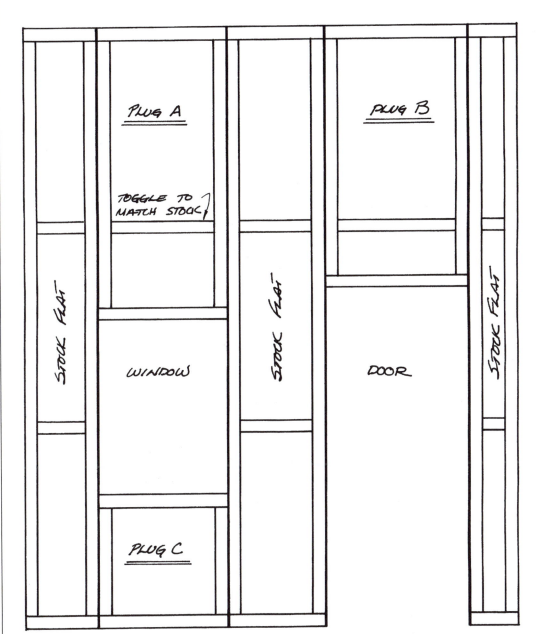

THIS WALL IS CREATED WITH STOCK FLATS AND
THREE SMALL FLAT PLUGS. THE WALL WOULD
BE DIFFICULT TO MOVE, ESPECIALLY THE DOOR,
UNLESS A TEMPORARY SILL WERE HINGED INSIDE.

N.B. ARCH SWEEPS NOTCH INTO VERTICALS.

o DO NOT COVER.

N.B. HOLD ALL BLOCKS BACK STOCK THICKNESS INSIDE OPENING.

LOWER PORTION CONFORMS TO STANDARD FLAT WHEN POSSIBLE.

STANDARD FLAT   ARCH WINDOW FLAT

METHODS FOR DEALING WITH SWEEPS IS DETAILED IN NEXT PAGE OF DRAWINGS.

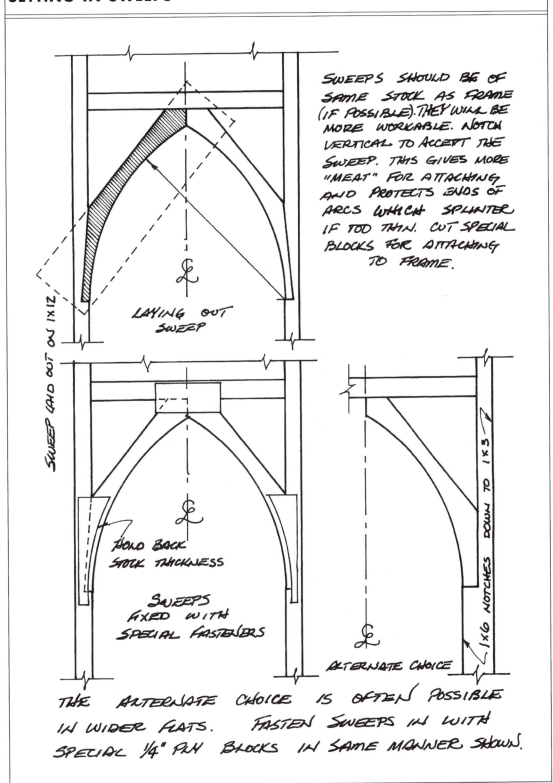

SWEEPS SHOULD BE OF SAME STOCK AS FRAME (IF POSSIBLE). THEY WILL BE MORE WORKABLE. NOTCH VERTICAL TO ACCEPT THE SWEEP. THIS GIVES MORE "MEAT" FOR ATTACHING AND PROTECTS ENDS OF ARCS WHICH SPLINTER IF TOO THIN. CUT SPECIAL BLOCKS FOR ATTACHING TO FRAME.

LAYING OUT SWEEP

SWEEP LAID OUT ON 1×12

HOLD BACK STOCK THICKNESS

SWEEPS FIXED WITH SPECIAL FASTENERS

1×6 NOTCHES DOWN TO 1×3

ALTERNATE CHOICE

THE ALTERNATE CHOICE IS OFTEN POSSIBLE IN WIDER FLATS. FASTEN SWEEPS IN WITH SPECIAL ¼" PLY BLOCKS IN SAME MANNER SHOWN.

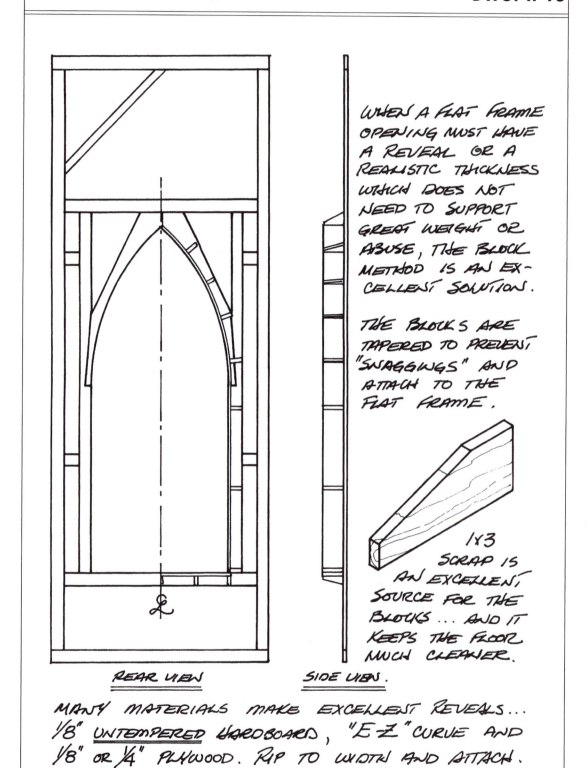

WHEN A FLAT FRAME OPENING MUST HAVE A REVEAL OR A REALISTIC THICKNESS WHICH DOES NOT NEED TO SUPPORT GREAT WEIGHT OR ABUSE, THE BLOCK METHOD IS AN EXCELLENT SOLUTION.

THE BLOCKS ARE TAPERED TO PREVENT "SNAGGINGS" AND ATTACH TO THE FLAT FRAME.

1×3 SCRAP IS AN EXCELLENT SOURCE FOR THE BLOCKS ... AND IT KEEPS THE FLOOR MUCH CLEANER.

REAR VIEW   SIDE VIEW.

MANY MATERIALS MAKE EXCELLENT REVEALS... 1/8" UNTEMPERED HARDBOARD, "E-Z" CURVE AND 1/8" OR 1/4" PLYWOOD. RIP TO WIDTH AND ATTACH.

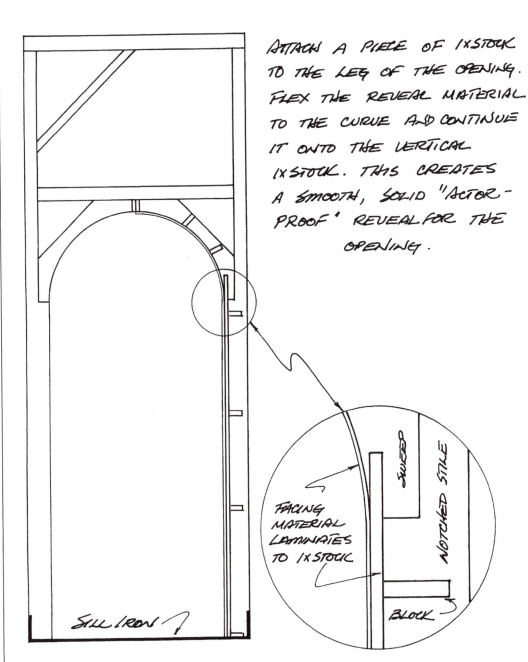

ATTACH A PIECE OF 1×STOCK
TO THE LEG OF THE OPENING.
FLEX THE REVEAL MATERIAL
TO THE CURVE AND CONTINUE
IT ONTO THE VERTICAL
1×STOCK. THIS CREATES
A SMOOTH, SOLID "ACTOR-
PROOF" REVEAL FOR THE
OPENING.

SWEEP

NOTCHED STILE

FACING
MATERIAL
LAMINATES
TO 1×STOCK

BLOCK

SILL IRON

SOME SHOPS WILL TAKE THE 1×REVEAL TO THE
TOGGLE ABOVE THE ARCH AND BOX ACROSS THE
TOP PROVIDING GREATER PROTECTION FOR THE CURVE.

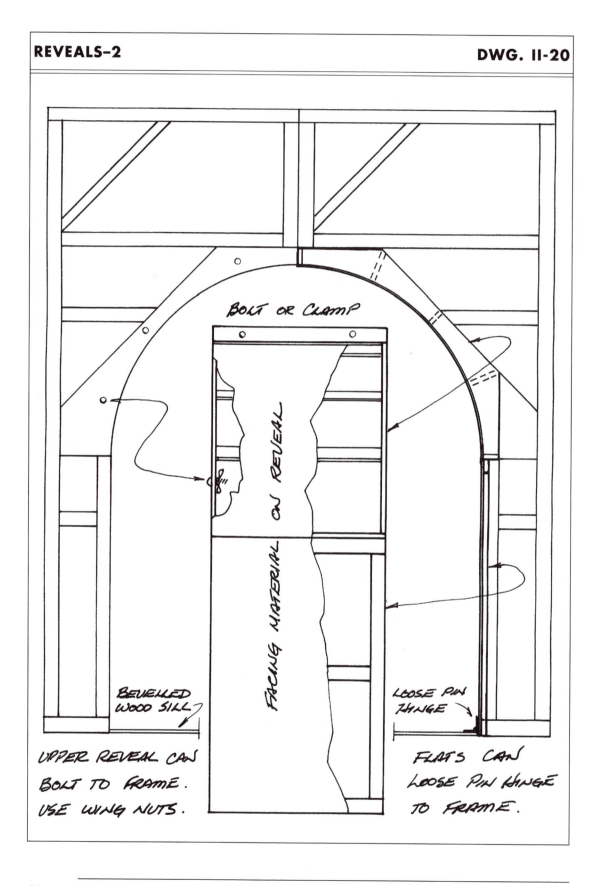

BOLT OR CLAMP

FACING MATERIAL ON REVEAL

BEVELLED WOOD SILL

LOOSE PIN HINGE

UPPER REVEAL CAN BOLT TO FRAME. USE WING NUTS.

FLATS CAN LOOSE PIN HINGE TO FRAME.

¾″ plywood can be used if the sweep will not fit on 1 x stock, but it is much heavier and the plys tend to separate when cut into narrow strips.

For best results build the frame of the flat first and then loft up the sweeps full scale for a pattern (see Drawing II-17). You can adjust a paper pattern far more easily and cheaply than you can wood.

Notice that the sweep is set into the stiles with an angled cut. This cut gives maximum strength and surface area to attach the special blocks. Never cut into the stile more than halfway or you will be building a collapsing flat with irregular fold-lines. It is always better to increase the width of the stile if the sweep is being set into it, but this is not always possible.

DOOR FLATS

The door flat (see Drawings II-19, II-22 through II-24) involves additional planning and care in execution. Because the bottom rail of the flat is "broken" or removed completely, allowing the stiles to extend to the floor, a piece of strap iron must be fixed to the bottom. This not only protects the end of the stiles but prevents the "legs" of the frame from pulling apart when the flat is moved (see Drawing II-19, II-21 through II-24). The best iron to use is ³⁄₁₆″ or ¼″ thick by ¾″ or 1″ wide flat steel. This mild steel is available from most hardware companies or a local steel yard and is sold in 20′-0″ lengths. It can be worked with a hacksaw, drill and metal bits.

DOOR SIZES

Rule of thumb for doors: The average modern door opening is about 6′-9″ high and ranges from 2′-4″ to 3′-0″ wide. If you are building stock flats and will use independent doors which set into the openings (see Drawing II-25 and II-26), the heights and width of the frame opening must be increased to accept it.

The height of the door flat is affected by the thickness of the sill iron and must be adjusted accordingly at the bottom of the frame so the toggles and top will match the other frames in the stock. If a bent sill iron or a saddle iron is used, remember to drill and countersink the holes before bending or welding. Working the irons is very difficult once they are bent. Both the bent and saddle iron must be let-in (notched into) the frame. This is done most easily with a sabre saw. If you do not shorten the stiles, the bottom rail pieces need to be ripped narrower for the straight sill iron. The saddle iron is the easiest to make accurately, but you must have welding equipment or access to a place that can do it for you, such as a machine shop or auto repair garage. The bent sill iron must be accurately measured and carefully bent. This takes no special equipment except a vise, but requires considerable care to keep the bends in the same plane as the rest of the iron and to maintain the correct measurements. If the iron is the wrong size or twisted, it will probably warp the flat frame and make it difficult to fit doors into it. If an iron bends or becomes twisted once it is installed, replace it, or actors will trip on it.

It is best to center a door opening in a flat frame. This equalizes the stress in the frame (see Drawing II-22). It is also better to avoid using the same 1 x 3 for the stile of the flat and the door (see Drawing II-23). This stile takes quite a beating and the 1 x 3

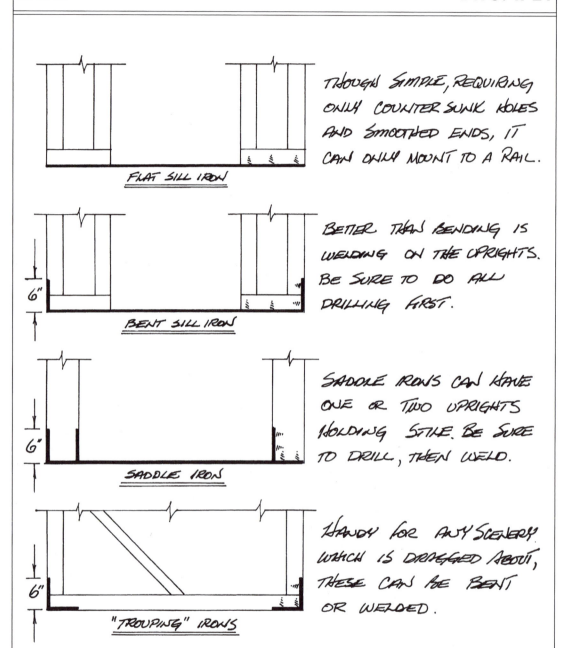

FLAT SILL IRON

THOUGH SIMPLE, REQUIRING
ONLY COUNTER SUNK HOLES
AND SMOOTHED ENDS, IT
CAN ONLY MOUNT TO A RAIL.

BENT SILL IRON

BETTER THAN BENDING IS
WELDING ON THE UPRIGHTS.
BE SURE TO DO ALL
DRILLING FIRST.

SADDLE IRON

SADDLE IRONS CAN HAVE
ONE OR TWO UPRIGHTS
HOLDING STILE. BE SURE
TO DRILL, THEN WELD.

"TROUPING" IRONS

HANDY FOR ANY SCENERY
WHICH IS DRAGGED ABOUT,
THESE CAN BE BENT
OR WELDED.

OF COURSE THE EXAMPLES ABOVE CAN, AND ARE,
USED IN VARIOUS COMBINATIONS AS DEMANDED
BY THE SITUATION. ALWAYS BE SURE TO DRILL
AND COUNTERSINK SCREW HOLES FIRST, THEN WELD.

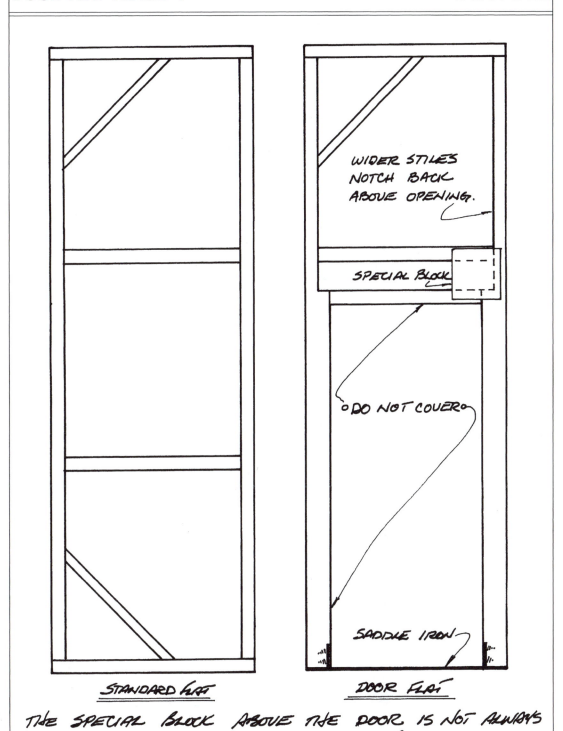

WIDER STILES
NOTCH BACK
ABOVE OPENING.

SPECIAL BLOCK

DO NOT COVER

SADDLE IRON

STANDARD FLAT   DOOR FLAT

THE SPECIAL BLOCK ABOVE THE DOOR IS NOT ALWAYS
NECESSARY. IT DEPENDS ON STANDARDIZED TOGGLE PLACEMENT.

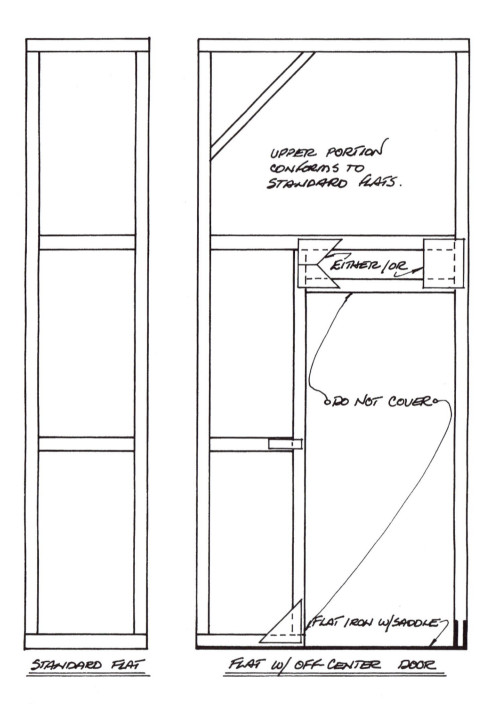

UPPER PORTION CONFORMS TO STANDARD FLATS.

EITHER/OR

◦ DO NOT COVER ◦

⌐FLAT IRON W/SADDLE⌐

STANDARD FLAT

FLAT W/ OFF-CENTER DOOR

N.B. FASTENERS ARE HELD BACK STOCK THICKNESS IN OPENING.

A STANDARDIZED 3×7 DOOR OPENING IN A 10'0" AND 14'0" FLAT SHOWS OTHER VARIATIONS USING BOTH STOCK FASTENERS + SPECIAL BLOCKS.

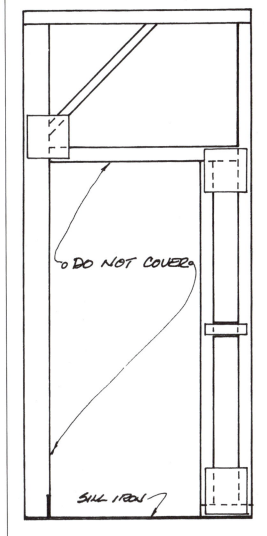

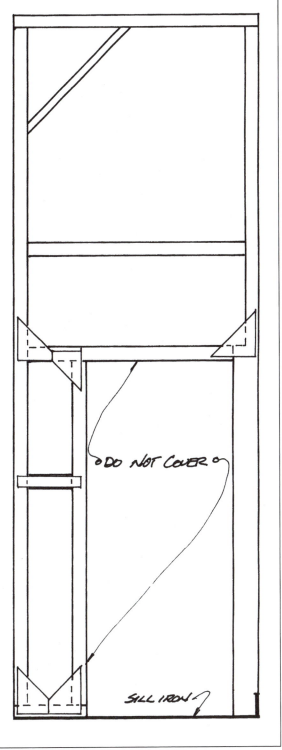

°DO NOT COVER°

SILL IRON

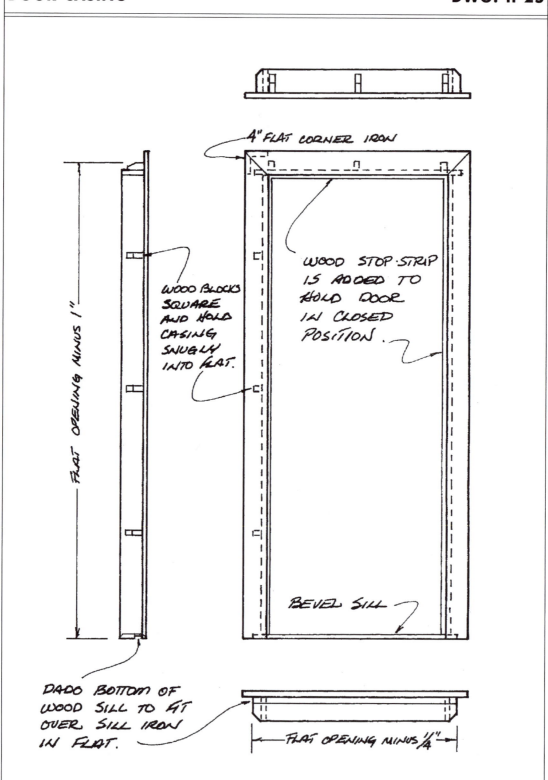

4" FLAT CORNER IRON

WOOD STOP·STRIP IS ADDED TO HOLD DOOR IN CLOSED POSITION.

WOOD BLOCKS SQUARE AND HOLD CASING SNUGLY INTO FLAT.

FLAT OPENING MINUS 1"

BEVEL SILL

DADO BOTTOM OF WOOD SILL TO FIT OVER SILL IRON IN FLAT.

FLAT OPENING MINUS 1/4"

STOCK DOOR UNIT

DWG. II-26

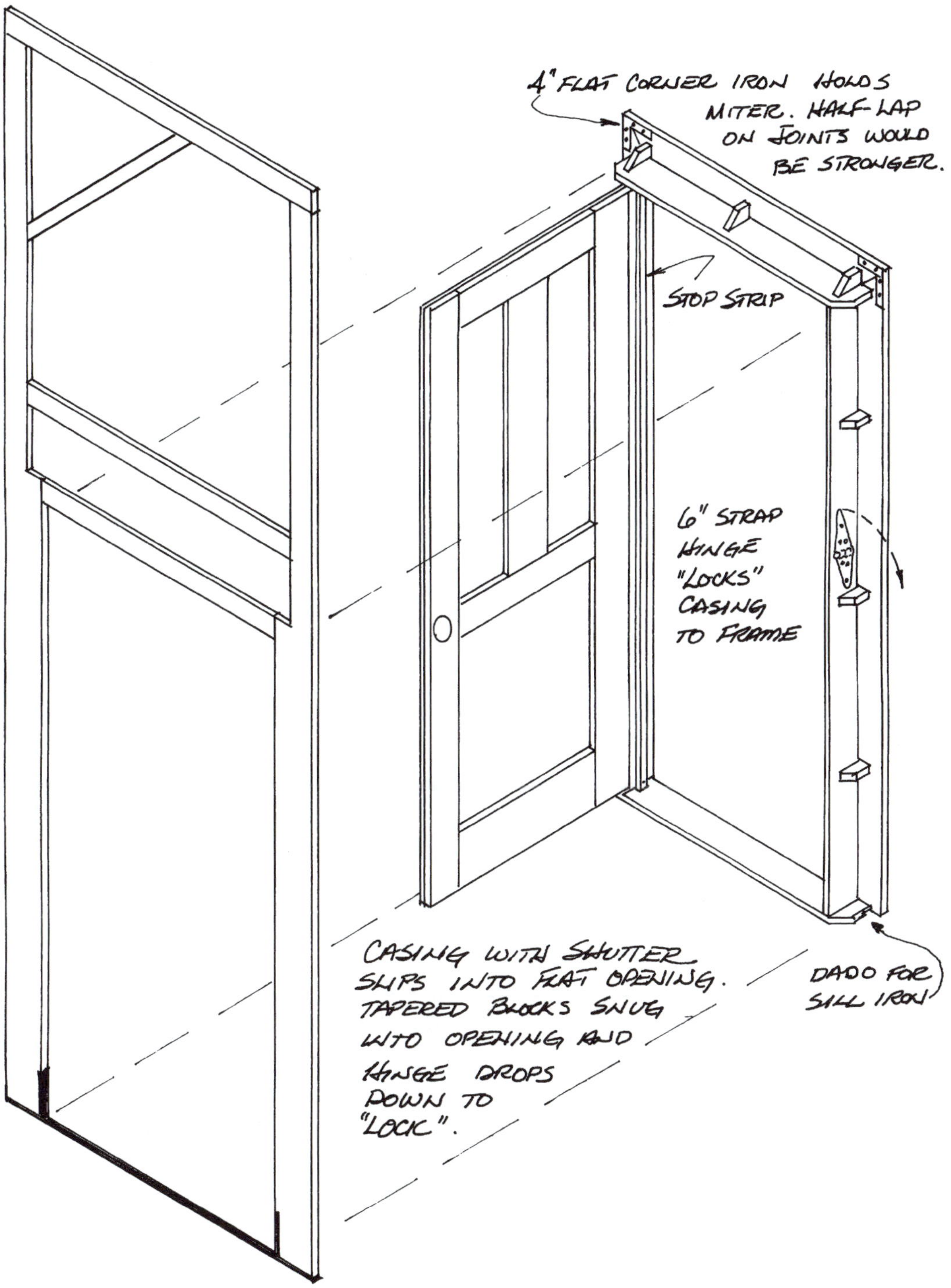

4" FLAT CORNER IRON HOLDS MITER. HALF-LAP ON JOINTS WOULD BE STRONGER.
STOP STRIP
6" STRAP HINGE "LOCKS" CASING TO FRAME
CASING WITH SHUTTER SLIPS INTO FLAT OPENING. TAPERED BLOCKS SNUG INTO OPENING AND HINGE DROPS DOWN TO "LOCK".
DADO FOR SILL IRON

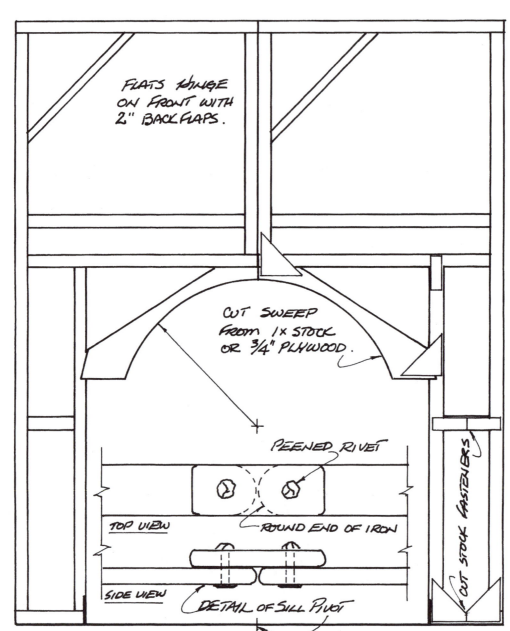

FLATS HINGE ON FRONT WITH 2" BACK FLAPS.

CUT SWEEP FROM 1x STOCK OR 3/4" PLYWOOD.

PEENED RIVET

TOP VIEW

ROUND END OF IRON

SIDE VIEW

DETAIL OF SILL PIVOT

CUT STOCK FASTENERS

IT MIGHT BE POSSIBLE NOT TO USE A SILL IRON AT ALL. REPLACE IT WITH A PIECE OF 1x3 WHICH IS HINGED IN THE CENTER AND TEMPORARILY ATTACHES TO THE LEGS OF THE FLAT WITH LOOSE-PIN HINGES.

leaves little "meat" for attaching a door casing or trim (see Drawing II-25). However, when neither can be done, the strength of the frame is not affected too greatly. Notice how, though not structurally necessary, the wider stile is notched back above the additional batten in the Drawing II-22. The wide stile could continue to the top rail (see Drawing II-24). It is notched back primarily to keep the top of the frame consistent with the other flats and to cut down on additional weight. Top-heavy flats are difficult to move. The special ¼" plywood blocks (see Drawings II-23, -24 and -28) should have the grain perpendicular to the joints butting to the outside frame.

The door opening in Drawing II-27 presents a combination of interesting problems. Like the hinged window flats, this unit is face-hinged with 2" backflaps. Because the "legs" of the opening could break if there were no sill iron, a modified saddle iron is placed at the bottom. Note that there are pivots in the iron so it can fold with the flat. Extra care must be taken when this unit is folded for storage, because undue pressure on the iron can bend it out of shape. Because of this weakness, these flats are often stored upside down.

Note how the corner block is used on this particular sweep, thus saving the time required to make special fasteners. The corner blocks at the bottom of the frame are cut so they butt together in the center and save the addition of a special block there also. The rest of the construction on the frames is quite standard.

Door openings can also be made with flat frame plugs (see Drawing II-15). Indeed, this is sometimes the best solution for openings of unusual size or design. For normal stock use, however, a door flat is preferable because as it is in one piece, and therefore stronger.

FIREPLACE FLATS

The fireplace flat (see Drawing II-28) is a variation on the door flat. Usually an elaborate mantel piece is placed before the opening in front of the flat and a backing made of plugs is placed behind (see Drawing II-42). However, make sure to hold all blocks back from the edge around the opening, in case a reveal is necessary. Sometimes fireplace flats are made by placing a plug in the upper part of a door frame. This is a workable solution if you don't need many fireplaces in shows. The plug can be lowered and become a window, if budget constraints force you to build a minimal number of pieces.

IRREGULAR FLATS

Irregular flats are built using the same principles as standard flats. They have rails on the floor, stiles rising off them, and toggles and corner braces as necessary. The major difference is that the rectangular shape is often tossed to the wind. Thus, angles must be cut in the 1 x stock and that the plywood fasteners must be specially made and chamfered for many of the joints (see Drawing II-29).

Any time you deviate from using standard flat frame components, you increase the construction time. Building an entire show of irregular flats takes tremendous time and, because such flats are rarely reusable, there is no way to prorate the resulting

SPECIAL BLOCKS ARE NECESSARY FOR THESE AREAS

CUT STOCK OR MAKE

DO NOT COVER

SILL IRONS

STANDARD FLAT   FIREPLACE FLAT

HOLD BACK FASTENERS FROM OPENING FOR REVEAL.
SILL IRON KEEPS LEGS TOGETHER WHICH IS MORE THAN...

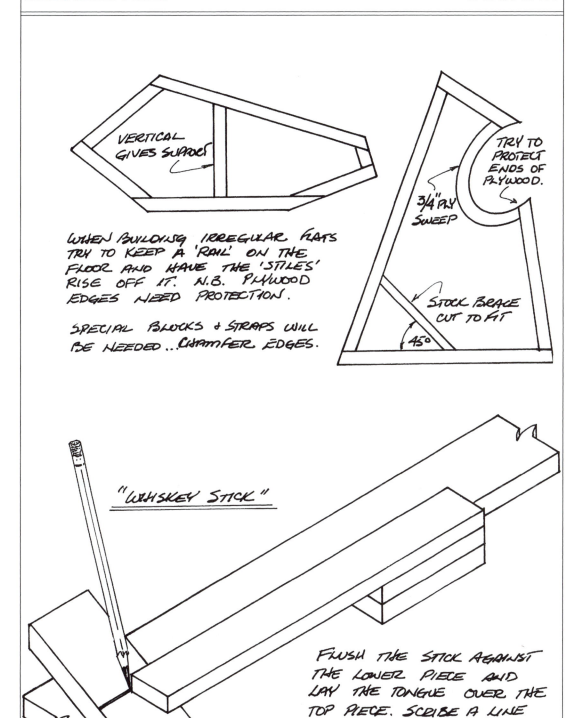

VERTICAL GIVES SUPPORT

TRY TO PROTECT ENDS OF PLYWOOD.

3/4" PLY SWEEP

STOCK BRACE CUT TO FIT

45°

WHEN BUILDING IRREGULAR FLATS TRY TO KEEP A 'RAIL' ON THE FLOOR AND HAVE THE 'STILES' RISE OFF IT. N.B. PLYWOOD EDGES NEED PROTECTION.

SPECIAL BLOCKS & STRAPS WILL BE NEEDED... CHAMFER EDGES.

"WHISKEY STICK"

FLUSH THE STICK AGAINST THE LOWER PIECE AND LAY THE TONGUE OVER THE TOP PIECE. SCRIBE A LINE TO MARK CUT.

expenditure. The cost of building this "disposable" scenery is great, so don't say you haven't been warned!

WHISKEY STICK

The whiskey stick (see Drawing II-29) will greatly aid in making and cutting unusual angles. It is made of three pieces of 1 x stock carefully laminated so the edges are all flush. The base should be about 8″ long and the tongue about 16″ long. Vary the size to suit your needs. To mark the cutting line, overlap the 1 x stock at the desired position. Place the stick's base against the bottom piece of wood and the tongue on the top piece to be marked. Scribe a line and cut the piece on the mark.

PROFILE FLATS

Any flat which has its edge altered to mock a given shape is a profile flat (see Drawings II-30 and II-31). The easiest way to achieve this effect is to use ¼″ 3-ply, which is still called "profile board" in some shops, though in days of old a profile flat was made with thin pieces of wood scrimmed with linen. Whenever possible, adjust a profile piece so a standard flat can be incorporated to save time and money. If not possible, irregular flats can be built.

Some profile flats are worth keeping in stock, especially skylines and trees. These can be used as backing to give a finished touch to the set.

To build a profile flat it is necessary to place a rabbet (note spelling) in the face of the 1 x 3 (see Drawing II-30). A rabbet is a groove or slot which is designed to accept another piece of material, in this case the ¼″ 3-ply. The rabbet is set halfway into the 1 x 3 stock allowing the plywood to be flush with the face of it. Build the frame with the rabbeted stock on the edges to be profiled, using plywood fasteners on the back as required. Then set in the profile pieces of ¼″ 3-ply. When the unit is completed, cover the entire face with muslin and glue it down to all edges and around all openings which will be cut away. The surface now has the same qualities as a standard flat, and can be painted as desired. If holes need to be cut into the muslin, be certain to do this after the unit is painted. Large holes may need netting (see Drawing III-8).

SAWHORSES

I have included this section on sawhorses here (rather than in the Shop Made Tools section) because these sawhorses are so handy when covering flat frames. These are the greatest horses a shop could own. They weigh very little, open easily, and collapse quickly for storage. They are not good building surfaces for heavy hammering. But for just about everything else they are ideal.

As indicated in the Drawings (II-32 and II-33), the frame is a variation of the standard flat. The dimensions given in the drawing are for a useful horse, but can be adapted to suit need.

The top rail is like any top rail (though extended) but the stiles do vary. Inasmuch as the stiles go to the floor and the end grain is against it, the ends are nipped off at a 45° angle (see Drawing II-34). This prevents any splitting of the stile when the horse is

X = CUT OUT

FRONT ELEVATION

STOCK hAT

HINGE ON
FACE WITH
2" BACKFLAPS
OR CLEAT
WITH BATTEN

MUSLIN

1/4" 3-PLY

1/4" 3-PLY

MUSLIN

REAR ELEVATION

CONSTRUCT PROFILE FRAME USING STANDARD METHODS BUT
UTILIZE 1XSTOCK WITH A 1/4" x 1 1/2" RABBET (A STEP-SHAPED
RECTANGULAR RECESS CUT IN EDGE). WITH FRAME TOGETHER
INSERT 1/4" 3-PLY PROFILE INTO RABBET. COVER WITH MUSLIN.

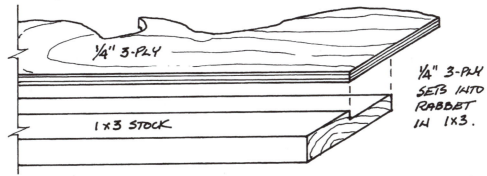

1/4" 3-PLY

1/4" 3-PLY
SETS INTO
RABBET
IN 1X3.

1X3 STOCK

IT IS CHEATING, OF COURSE, BUT YOU COULD   LAMINATE
1/2" STOCK (PLANE DOWN TO SIZE) OR WORSE, 1/2" PLYWOOD
TO THE BACK OF THE PROFILE AND CLEAT IT TO THE FLAT.

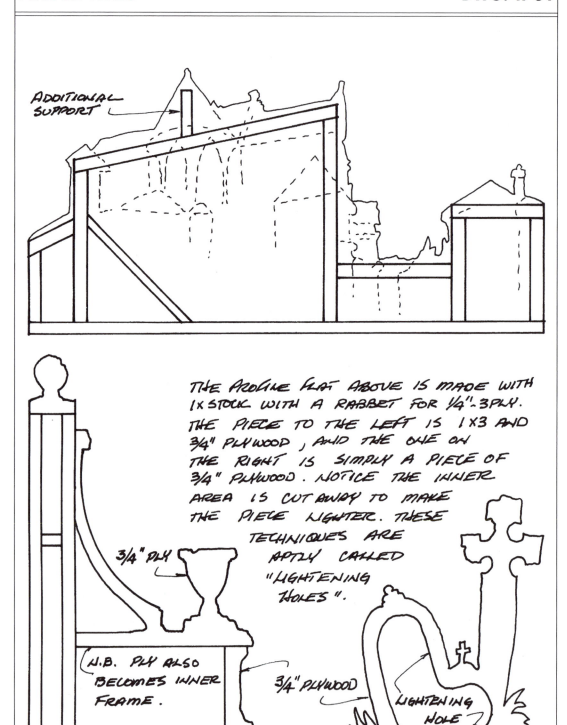

ADDITIONAL SUPPORT

THE PROFILE FLAT ABOVE IS MADE WITH 1X STOCK WITH A RABBET FOR 1/4"-3PLY. THE PIECE TO THE LEFT IS 1X3 AND 3/4" PLYWOOD, AND THE ONE ON THE RIGHT IS SIMPLY A PIECE OF 3/4" PLYWOOD. NOTICE THE INNER AREA IS CUT AWAY TO MAKE THE PIECE LIGHTER. THESE TECHNIQUES ARE APTLY CALLED "LIGHTENING HOLES".

3/4" PLY

N.B. PLY ALSO BECOMES INNER FRAME.

3/4" PLYWOOD

LIGHTENING HOLE

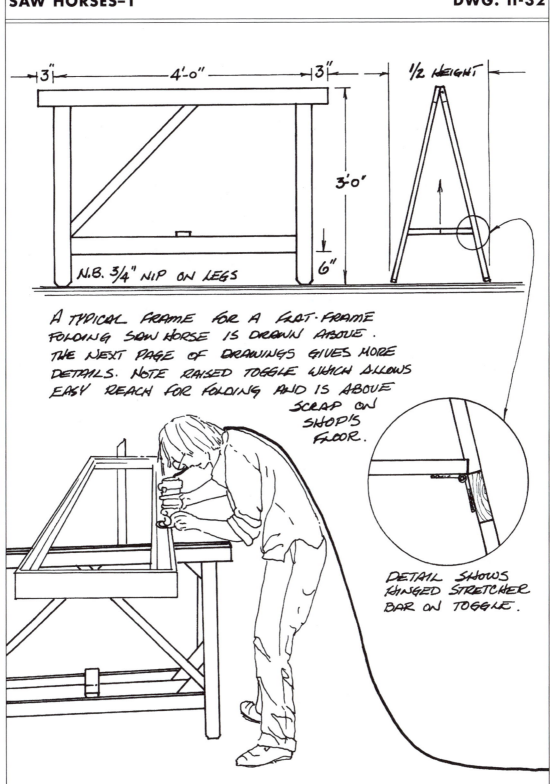

3" | 4'-0" | 3" | ½ HEIGHT

3'0"

6"

N.B. 3/4" NIP ON LEGS

A TYPICAL FRAME FOR A FLAT-FRAME
FOLDING SAW HORSE IS DRAWN ABOVE.
THE NEXT PAGE OF DRAWINGS GIVES MORE
DETAILS. NOTE RAISED TOGGLE WHICH ALLOWS
EASY REACH FOR FOLDING AND IS ABOVE
SCRAP ON
SHOP'S
FLOOR.

DETAIL SHOWS
HINGED STRETCHER
BAR ON TOGGLE.

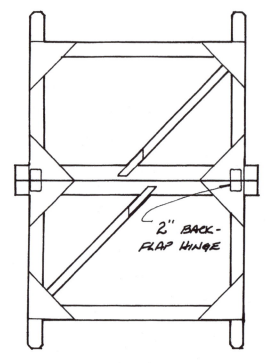

TO ASSEMBLE SAW HORSE, BUTT TWO FLAT FRAMES TOGETHER. PLACE A 2"- BACK FLAP HINGE (CENTERED ON STILE) OVER BLOCKS AND SCREW IT DOWN. ONE 3/16" STOVE BOLT IN EACH FLAP WILL ADD EXTRA STRENGTH IF HORSES ARE GOING TO BE "RODE HARD AND PUT UP WET." WHEN HINGED, STAND UP AND OPEN LEGS (ONE-HALF HEIGHT IS STANDARD) TO MEASURE FOR HINGED SPREADER.

2" BACK-FLAP HINGE

OTHER SIZES CAN BE BUILT AND ARE OFTEN VERY USEFUL. SHOP USE AND PRODUCTION DEMANDS WILL CERTAINLY DICTATE SOME NEEDS

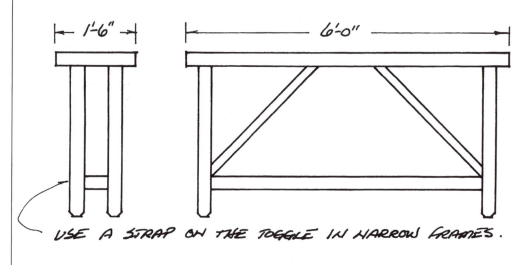

1'-6"   6'-0"

USE A STRAP ON THE TOGGLE IN NARROW FRAMES.

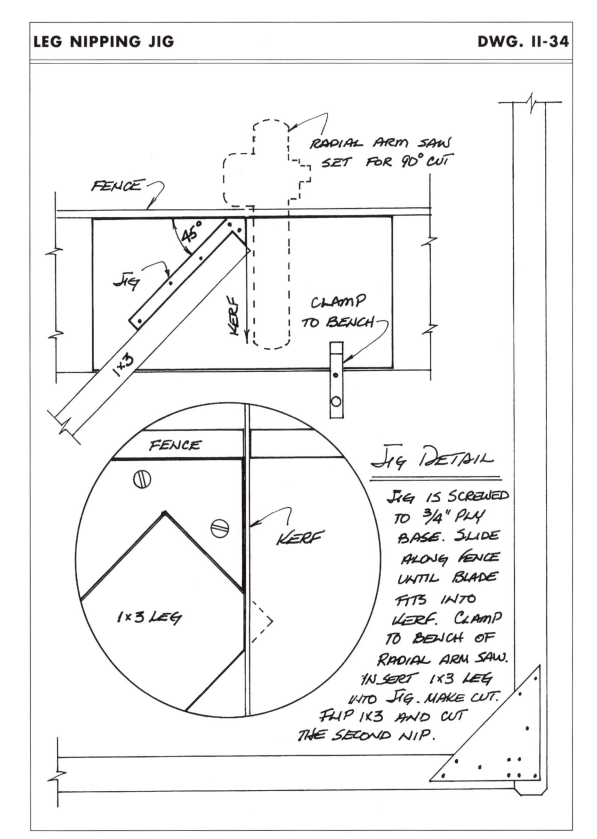

RADIAL ARM SAW
SET FOR 90° CUT

FENCE

45°

JIG

KERF

1x3

CLAMP
TO BENCH

FENCE

KERF

1X3 LEG

JIG DETAIL

JIG IS SCREWED
TO ¾" PLY
BASE. SLIDE
ALONG FENCE
UNTIL BLADE
FITS INTO
KERF. CLAMP
TO BENCH OF
RADIAL ARM SAW.
INSERT 1X3 LEG
INTO JIG. MAKE CUT.
FLIP 1X3 AND CUT
THE SECOND NIP.

dragged along the floor. The toggle is placed 6″ off the floor, to be clear of scrap and make it easier to reach under the stretcher bar with your foot to lift and close the horse. The corner brace can be a stock one which is cut down to fit.

The corner blocks are flushed to the edge because it is not necessary to butt anything to these frames. Note that the toggle is held with corner blocks as well. One end of the corner brace is also attached this way. The blocks give a stronger joint and reduce frame sway.

To put a horse together, build two frames as drawn. Use glue under all plywood pieces. Lay out the two finished frames, rail against rail, with the plywood fasteners up (see Drawing II-33). When completed, the corner braces will automatically go in opposite directions to give maximum support. Place a 2″ backflap hinge on the rail, centered over the stiles. Center the barrel of the hinge on the crack. If the corner blocks are correctly beveled, the barrel will nestle down into the "valley" between them. Attach the hinge with two 1″ #8 or #9 flat-head wood screws. One ³⁄₁₆″ flat-head stove bolt in each flap will really make it strong. Place the nut on the outside of the frame and pull it into the wood until it is flush, then break or cut off the excess bolt. File down any rough remains.

After the top hinges are mounted, stand the horse up on its feet and spread the frames apart until the distance is half the height of the frame. Now, measure the inside distance between the two toggles; this will determine how long the stretcher bar will be. Halve the distance and cut two pieces of 1 x 3 this length. Hinge the stretcher bar together with a 1½″ backflap hinge. Place another 1½″ backflap at each end of the stretcher bar on the same side as the first hinge, with the barrel centered on the end of the 1 x 3. Attach them in the same way. Now, center the stretcher bar between the toggles. Raise the 1 x 3 on the stretcher so the bottom of it is flush with the top of the toggle and the flap of the hinge is resting on the inside of the toggle. Attach the other flap of the hinges temporarily (small clamps or duct tape work well). Make sure the horse will close by lifting up in the center of the stretcher bar and moving the frames together. If it doesn't fold smoothly, adjust the stretcher bar to allow it to do so. Bolt the hinges in place when it folds correctly.

Eight to twelve horses should suffice for starters, but they are easy to build if more are needed.

COVERING FLAT FRAMES

Covering the flat frame is the final step in construction. The task is neither difficult nor tricky, but it requires practice because you must work quickly. There was a time when it was necessary to tack or staple the flat covering (originally linen, then cotton duck, and now medium-weight unbleached muslin (alas)). This tacking was necessary because the glues were very water-sensitive, and when the flats were scrubbed after each show to remove the old scene paint, the glue would soften on the frame and only the tacks held the covering until the glue could reset.

THE MYSTERIES OF MUSLIN... UNRAVELED

Muslin is an undyed, plain-weave fabric made with carded cotton yarns containing

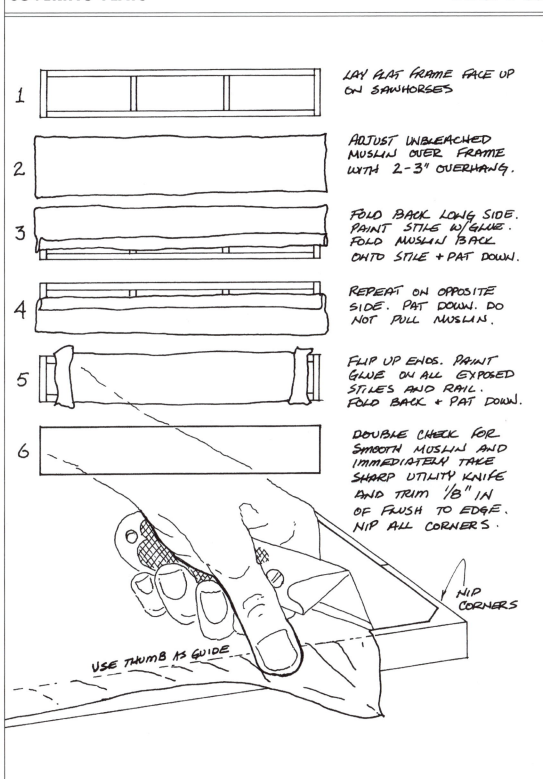

1.   LAY FLAT FRAME FACE UP ON SAWHORSES

2.   ADJUST UNBLEACHED MUSLIN OVER FRAME WITH 2-3" OVERHANG.

3.   FOLD BACK LONG SIDE. PAINT STILE W/GLUE. FOLD MUSLIN BACK ONTO STILE + PAT DOWN.

4.   REPEAT ON OPPOSITE SIDE. PAT DOWN. DO NOT PULL MUSLIN.

5.   FLIP UP ENDS. PAINT GLUE ON ALL EXPOSED STILES AND RAIL. FOLD BACK + PAT DOWN.

6.   DOUBLE CHECK FOR SMOOTH MUSLIN AND IMMEDIATELY TAKE SHARP UTILITY KNIFE AND TRIM 1/8" IN OF FLUSH TO EDGE. NIP ALL CORNERS.

NIP CORNERS

USE THUMB AS GUIDE

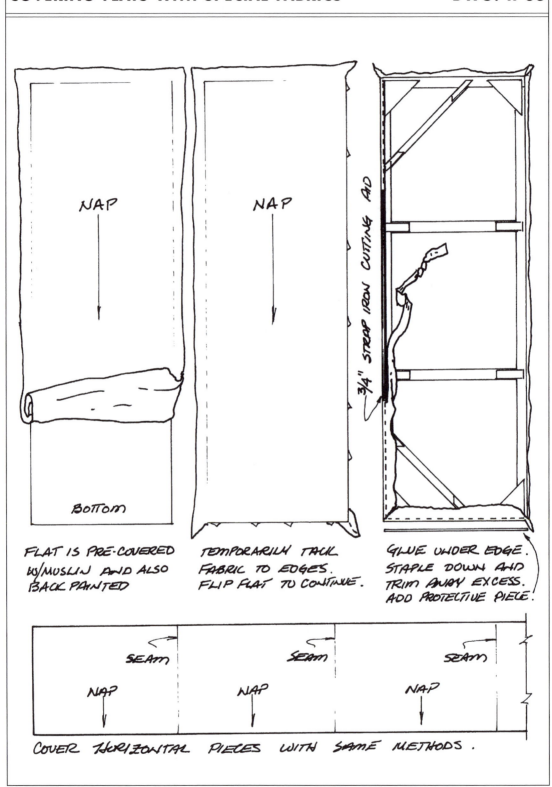

NAP

NAP

¾" STRAP IRON CUTTING AID

BOTTOM

FLAT IS PRE-COVERED
W/MUSLIN AND ALSO
BACK PAINTED

TEMPORARILY TACK
FABRIC TO EDGES.
FLIP FLAT TO CONTINUE.

GLUE UNDER EDGE.
STAPLE DOWN AND
TRIM AWAY EXCESS.
ADD PROTECTIVE PIECE.

SEAM   SEAM   SEAM

NAP   NAP   NAP

COVER HORIZONTAL PIECES WITH SAME METHODS.

characteristic slubs, specks and impurities. Muslin for covering flats must also be unbleached and not flameproofed when purchased or it will not shrink properly.

Because muslin is unbleached and undyed, the cotton fibers have been subjected to a minimum of shrinkage, but when sized will, therefore, shrink on the flat frame, forming a tight "skin" of cloth.

Plain-weave fabrics are the simplest of woven goods. The warp threads (those parallel to the woven edge of the cloth or selvage) and the weft threads (those passing from selvage to selvage) are alternately passed over one another. This weave makes a cloth which has good, stable strength both parallel and perpendicular to the selvages. It also will stretch easily and greatly on the bias, or diagonal of the weave, a trait which makes it useful for covering spherical surfaces.

Carding is done after cleaning and picking the raw cotton. It is the first step used in aligning the fibers into a loose strand which will become the spun yarn used in weaving the muslin. The yarn could be further refined by combing which removes shorter fibers, aligns the remaining fibers and creates a smoother and stronger yarn.

Muslin is sold by weight in ounces per yard and by the thread count. The textile industry has divided cloth into four main categories: light, medium, heavy and very heavy. The weight of one square yard of fabric is the determining factor. Most muslin is a medium weight fabric (heavier than 3.5 ounces but less than 8 ounces). The thread count ranges from 112 to 200 threads per square inch. Sizing, of various glutinous materials, is added to muslin with lower thread counts to fill the voids in the weave. This greatly increases the muslin's weight, but not its strength or ability to hold paint and become opaque.

Muslin sheeting with higher thread counts is often called percale and is usually woven with the more refined combed yarns, which allow a closer weave.

Unbleached muslin is available in various widths. Narrow pieces 39½ inches wide (that dreaded meter we won't recognize) are not uncommon in fabric stores. Theatrical supply houses commonly carry muslin in widths of 60, 72 and 80 inches. Wider pieces are also available, and at one time could be found in 30'-0" widths, ideal for translucent drops. The cost usually increases dramatically in extra-wide pieces.

GLUE

Today's synthetic glues, such as the popular white glues (Elmer's, Wilhold, etc.) are aliphatic resin. They are much stronger, easier to use and much more "water-proof" than the older, animal compound glues. These factors, combined with declining use of powdered scene paint with a water soluble binder, have practically eliminated the need for tacking or stapling.

LAYING OUT THE MUSLIN

The actual covering job is quite simple (see Drawing II-35). Use white glue (as above) to which enough water has been added to allow it to "tack through" the muslin. To test, paint some glue onto a board and take a scrap of the covering muslin and pat it down on the glued surface. Just a bit of the glue should seep through. If you feel no tackiness, add a bit more water. Continue testing until you feel the glue. No formula can really be given because the glue will vary as will the weave of the muslin. Place the frame on the sawhorses; make sure it is dust-free. Lay the muslin on the frame, allowing 2″ to 3″ overhang on all sides. Never use the woven edge or selvage because it will shrink differently and show. Smooth out the muslin and get rid of any large ripples or "puddles." On some irregular flats it helps to place a few temporary staples at strategic spots to hold the unbleached muslin in place while working. Tear off all excess muslin leaving only a few inches overhang. This makes it easier to manage and avoids getting the glue on the excess fabric, keeping it usable for future projects.

GLUING THE FRAME

Glue one edge at a time. Start with a long side of the frame and flip back the muslin, exposing the wood. Using a 3″ brush, quickly apply a liberal amount of the thinned glue to the frame. Make sure the frame is covered and the glue is evenly spread. Now flip the muslin back onto the glued frame and pat it down with your hand. You should be able to feel the glue just start to seep through the muslin. This "tack-through" assures you that the muslin will bond, because the glue is now into it. It should not be necessary to stretch the muslin tightly or pull it in any way. In fact, if unbleached muslin is too tight, it can warp the frame when it shrinks after it is sized. If you must lift the muslin to correct a bubble or some mistake, make sure there is fresh glue under the spot when you put it back down. Also, make sure that the muslin glued to the frame is smooth and flat. With patience you can flatten almost any ripple or bump on the frame. If there are ripples or slight pulls in the center of the flat, ignore them, because they will disappear when the flat is sized. In fact, the unbleached muslin can sag many inches and still shrink tight.

When the first side is glued and patted smooth, go to the opposite side, smooth out the muslin, flip it back and glue away. Flip it back onto the glued frame, pat it down and smooth it out. Next do the ends of the frame. Do not glue the covering to the toggles or corner braces, only to the outside members of the frame. This allows the muslin to shrink into a smooth surface over the entire frame. Never apply glue to the top of the muslin. It can cause "shiners" and "glue burns," which will affect the painted surface.

TRIMMING THE MUSLIN

As soon as the muslin is smoothed down on all members of the frame, get a sharp utility knife and trim away the excess materials (see Drawing II-35). Hold the knife firmly in your hand and, with your thumb as a guide along the edge of the 1 x 3, cut in ⅛″ from the edge. This is done to protect the covering from being rubbed and peeled off. With your other hand, gently pull away the waste strip as it is cut. Be sure to nip the muslin in the corners because the corner of the frame wears down more quickly and is more likely to expose the fabric to friction. This trimming must be done before the glue dries so that the cloth will bend into the groove in the 1 x 3 left by the knife. It is also easier to release the excess scrap before it has dried to the frame.

There are shops which prefer to trim the muslin flush with the edge of the frame. The argument for this is that with proper handling, edges of the frame are not abused and the muslin will not lift. It is also stressed that the ⅛″ indented cut shows in smaller theatres and is ugly. It is debatable which method is preferable, inasmuch as both do the job, but still nip the corners.

When covering flat frames with openings such as windows or doors, three different methods can be used!

The first is to lay the muslin on the entire frame as with a standard flat and glue a long side down. Now ease the rest of the muslin toward the glued edge by gathering it up accordion fashion until it has exposed the internal parts of the frame which need to be glued. Glue them and quickly and carefully lift the muslin and lay it over the newly glued parts. A second person can make this step easier. Once the internal pieces are glued and patted smooth, proceed as with a standard flat.

The second method is to cover the outside of the frame first and then cut away the muslin inside the opening, allowing some overhang. Lift the muslin around the opening carefully and apply glue to the frame. Lower it and pat it smooth.

The third method is to use smaller pieces of muslin and glue them to the frame around the opening. This often requires some overlapping of muslin, which might show from the front row, but it is certainly economical. It is often the best way to cover the legs on door flats. Purists will shudder at the third method, but they are notoriously wealthy.

Irregular or profile flats present no new problems. Just remember to try to glue down the long side first and then the shorter ones. In working with irregular shapes, be careful not to pull the muslin on the bias to smooth it down or it will ripple. Bias ripples tend to increase instead of tightening up when the frame is sized. Trim irregular flats in the same manner as standard frames.

Once the frame is trimmed, let it sit until the glue has set. If you must move it, carefully lift the flat and store it vertically until the glue has dried. The glue "sets" in about 15 minutes. Store the frame with the muslin side out and exposed to the air. Don't stack newly covered flats together or they may stick. Drying takes several hours, depending on the weather and who has applied the glue. It is best to wait overnight before sizing, because if the glue is still wet, the sizing will shrink the muslin and it will pull off the frames! It must then be recovered . Store muslin scraps for covering narrow pieces and making dutchmen (see Drawing II-54).

SIZING

When completely dry, the flat is ready to be sized. Sizing will remove any looseness in the covering, draw it tight, and prepare the surface for painting. The best size to use is wall size. It is also the cheapest! Wall size is available from paint and hardware stores and is sold as a primer for walls which will be papered. Make doubly sure you get a 100% natural wall size and not one which is vinyl or plastic or "new and magic." Using the instructions on the package, mix the size with cold water. When mixed, add additional water equal to the amount already used. This will dilute the size to a workable solution. It is best to let the size sit and "cook" for several hours before using. This does not mean to heat it. A few dollops of paint can be added to color the size to help see it when it is on the muslin. If the size is too "hot" (thick and sticky), add a little more water. Paint in on with a large brush, forcing the solution into the fabric, and, as if by magic, the muslin will shrink up. After it has dried, the flat is ready to be flame-proofed, back-painted and primed. Will this never end?

Be sure to "clear" the toggles and corner braces before back-painting. Clearing refers to unsticking the covering from the frame members which are not glued to it, but which are stuck because of the binder in the size or paint.

BACK-PAINTING

Back-painting serves many purposes. It opaques the muslin and stops light from bleeding through from behind and silhouetting the frame. Back-painting also helps stop "bounce light" backstage because of its dark value. It also acts as an additional flame retardant. A back-painted flat looks better, which is important, but aesthetics are difficult to defend.

Back-paint should be a medium to dark grey and can be mixed specially or made by boxing together all the leftover paint from previous shows and tinting or shading this scrap paint to approximate the desired grey.

Back-painting is the final step necessary to give the flat, and all scenery, a finished and professional touch. When the back-paint is dry, again clear the toggles. This will leave horrendous bumps on the front, but they will re-tighten when the front is primed. The primer coat fills the muslin and prepares a workable surface for the scenic artist. When dry, the flat is ready.

For additional flame retardation treatment, some suggestions are offered in the section on Soft Scenery.

The pride of accomplishment in delivering a well-built flat cannot be stressed enough. Simple as it may seem, you will earn the undying gratitude of the painters who will transform the surface, as well as other technicians who will handle it later.

HARD COVERED FLATS

Just to add to the confusion, sometimes it is advantageous to build hard-covered flats. These are standard flat frames which are covered with solid, rigid material like plywood, paneling, plastic, etc. (Drawing II-37). Perhaps the flat needs the rigidity for moulding or perhaps it must realistically take the abuse of having objects thrown at it, or can't jiggle when someone climbs through a window. Regardless of the intended abuse, the flat thus made is now "hard-covered" with a board and not "soft" as with muslin. The surface is often treated with the same covering material as the standard flats with which it is being used, so it will blend in. The hard-covered flat is often marginally thicker than the standard flat.

Some shops make hard-covered flats without plywood fasteners. The frame is built face up and held to shape with corrugated fasteners. A covering sheet of ¼" panel (plywood, hardboard, etc.) is then glued and attached to the front. When finished, it is the same thickness as the flat.

Hard covered flats should not be confused with hardwall flats (see Drawings II-55-61), which are constructed differently.

ALIGN TOGGLE FOR PLYWOOD JOIN

HARD COVERED FLATS ARE
USUALLY COVERED WITH
A PANEL BOARD OF SOME
SORT, OFTEN 1/8" OR 1/4"
PLYWOOD. THIS MAKES A
THIN FLAT WHICH WILL
ACCEPT 3-D TRIMS.
THE COVERING IS USUALLY
SCRIMMED WITH MUSLIN
TO MATCH SURFACES OF
OTHER FLATS.

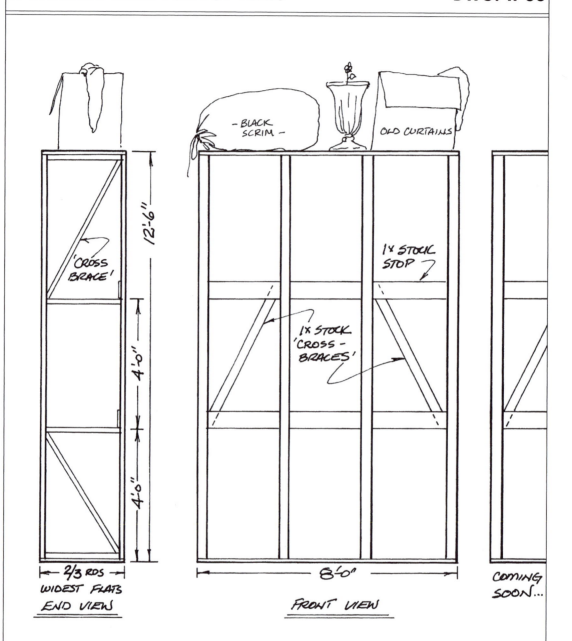

'CROSS BRACE'

12'-6"

4'-0"

4'-0"

2/3 RDS WIDEST FLATS
END VIEW

BLACK SCRIM

OLD CURTAINS

1× STOCK STOP

1× STOCK 'CROSS-BRACES'

8'-0"

FRONT VIEW

COMING SOON...

THIS DRAWING IS BUT A SUGGESTION FOR A SELF-STANDING, EASY-TO-CONSTRUCT STORAGE RACK FOR A STOCK OF 12'-0" FLATS. THE BASIC UNIT IS MADE FROM 2×4 S (UGLY STUFF) WITH A 3/4" PLY BASE AND TOP. ADJUST TO FIT YOUR STOCK NEEDS.

STORAGE

As mentioned before, flat storage is extremely important. Install a good storage rack for the flats. The finished frames should be stored vertically, face-to-face and back-to-back. This lessens warping and protects the covering. A flat which leans at an angle too long will permanently warp and is then difficult to use effectively.

The rack illustrated in the Drawing II-38 is a simple design and can easily be adapted for any height or width stock. It is only a suggested design and any suitable rack could be built. Constructed of 2 x 4, 1 x stock and plywood, this particular rack is independent (self-supporting and self-standing) and eliminates the need to anchor into the wall or floor. However, it could easily be adjusted and modified to a permanent installation.

Note that there is less than 2'-8" between the verticals forming the "storage bays." This prevents too many flats from leaning and resting against themselves, making it difficult to move them without a great deal of shuffling. Flats of the same height and width should be stored next to each other. This eliminates any unnecessary stress in their frames and allows easy inventory of stock. It is also advisable to store flats "face-to-face" and "back-to-back."

Again, let me stress that sufficient storage facilities be built along with the stock flats. The best flats can be ruined and rendered useless if not stored properly.

MOVING FLATS

It is always safer to move scenery, especially flats, with one person unless it is easier and safer to use two. Phew! If you think that is confusing, try three people.

Flats are more awkward than heavy; one person can easily raise a flat (Drawing II-39). Start by lifting from the center to relieve some of the strain in the frame. By moving to the rail and placing a toe at the base, you can grab forward as far as it is comfortable and then lift and (sorta) sit back. A second person can help with the initial take-off by lifting the other end. Once the flat is standing, and assuming the sit was only "sorta," move to the edge. Stand to the side of the flat. Grab with one hand high and the other low. Be sure this is comfortable and the stretch is not too great. Next, lift the frame a bit from the floor and walk as normally as possible, keeping the side of your body to the flat. Because your hands and the back corner of the flat form a triangle, you can easily maneuver the piece. You will soon learn to stoutly refuse offers of help as workers try to raise the back corner, disengaging your control. With a bit of practice, moving flats becomes a bravura performance of technical expertise. It's easy, too.

On excessively tall flats, a second person can help steady the unit by attaching an adjustable stage brace through an eye near the top of the frame.

To lower flats, simply let them float to the floor (see Drawing II-39). This assumes a clean floor, flats without openings (they "float" damn fast) and a courtesy call of "Clear, please." Be sure to "foot" the bottom. Always float a flat so its face lands on the floor.

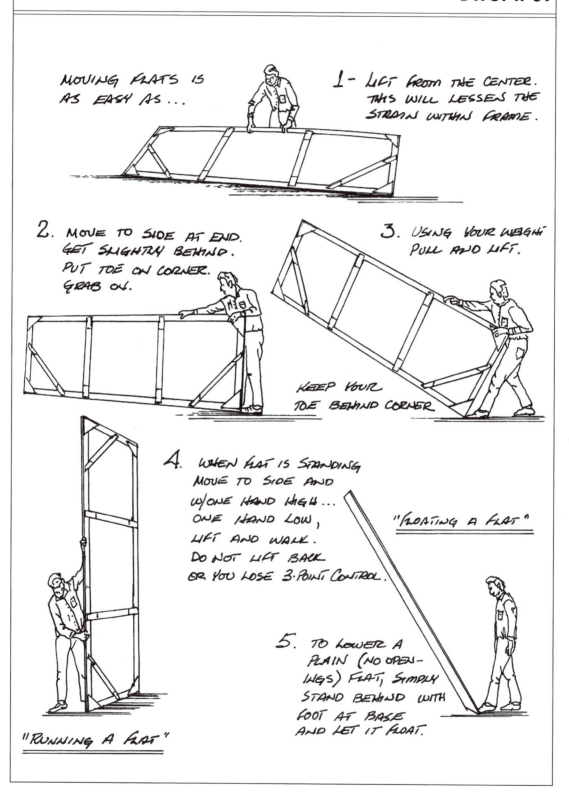

MOVING FLATS IS AS EASY AS...

1- LIFT FROM THE CENTER. THIS WILL LESSEN THE STRAIN WITHIN FRAME.

2. MOVE TO SIDE AT END. GET SLIGHTLY BEHIND. PUT TOE ON CORNER. GRAB ON.

3. USING YOUR WEIGHT PULL AND LIFT.

KEEP YOUR TOE BEHIND CORNER

4. WHEN FLAT IS STANDING MOVE TO SIDE AND W/ONE HAND HIGH... ONE HAND LOW, LIFT AND WALK. DO NOT LIFT BACK OR YOU LOSE 3-POINT CONTROL.

"FLOATING A FLAT"

5. TO LOWER A PLAIN (NO OPENINGS) FLAT, SIMPLY STAND BEHIND WITH FOOT AT BASE AND LET IT FLOAT.

"RUNNING A FLAT"

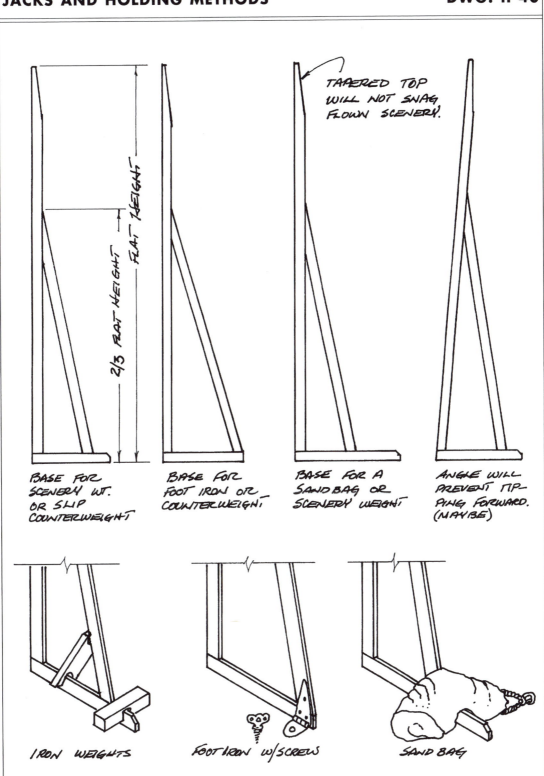

TAPERED TOP
WILL NOT SNAG
FLOWN SCENERY.

2/3 FLAT HEIGHT

FLAT HEIGHT

BASE FOR
SCENERY WT.
OR SLIP
COUNTERWEIGHT

BASE FOR
FOOT IRON OR
COUNTERWEIGHT

BASE FOR A
SAND BAG OR
SCENERY WEIGHT

ANGLE WILL
PREVENT TIP-
PING FORWARD.
(MAYBE)

IRON WEIGHTS

FOOT IRON W/SCREW

SAND BAG

JACKS

A jack is a flat frame brace which, when attached to a piece of scenery, holds and stabilizes it, usually by anchoring it to the floor (see Drawing II-40). Jacks can vary in size as needed, but should continue to the top of the piece of scenery in case there is need of bracing there. The rail seldom needs to be more than one-quarter the stile's height, and can usually be somewhat less. The drawing shows that the vertical stile and horizontal rail are both 1 x 3, as is the "corner brace." The brace need only extend about two-thirds the height of the stile, as the 1 x 3 is on edge and will not bend easily. 1 x 2 can be used for the "corner brace" in smaller jacks.

It is recommended that the stile and rail be nipped off on the exposed end (as shown) to lessen the chances of catching or snagging either actors or other scenery—particularly scenery—because it is expensive to replace.

A good rule of thumb is to hold the plywood fasteners back the stock thickness (¾″) to allow for the possibility of butting the jack to the edge of a flat. Hold the fasteners back on the rail also, so you can attach a 1 x stock cleat to the floor and butt up against either side of the jack. Attaching the jack to the cleat on the floor results in a secure brace.

The Drawing II-40 shows a few of the many common and often ingeniously simple ways of securing jacks to the floor if you cannot use screws.

When building several jacks for a long unit, remember to R & R (reverse and repeat) the jack during construction so the plywood fasteners will alternate sides and allow flush fits as desired.

Jacks are usually attached to scenery with 2″ backflap hinges. These can be either tight-pin or loose-pin hinges. However, jacks can also be anchored with screws or, if necessary, nailed to the scenery.

FASTENING FLATS

There are several methods of joining flats together. The most useful are battening, hinging and lashing.

BATTENING

Battening flats assures a certain amount of rigidity and is the most common way of creating a wall of more than one flat. When the derivation of "batten" is known, it can be more easily understood. "Batten" originally meant a strip of sawed lumber used for flooring or nailing across other pieces to cover a crack. We still have board-and-batten houses and can batten-down-the-hatches. Battens in the theatre can mean many things, including a small piece of 1 x 3 inserted between toggles or stiles for holding pictures (see Drawing II-45). It can be a piece of 1 x stock or a laminated 1 x 3 used to hang drops on (hence any pipe which has scenery, draperies or lights hanging on it). It is also a strip of 1 x 3 attached across a wall of flats to hold and stiffen them together. This particular batten, usually 1 x 3, is either "permanently" or temporarily held against the flats. If it is "permanent," it is best screwed across the flats over the rails and toggles (see Drawings II-41, II-43 and II-44).

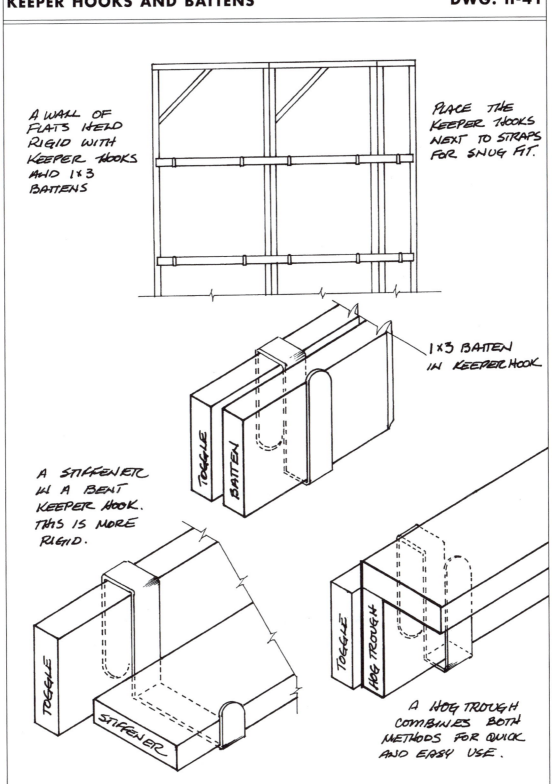

A WALL OF FLATS HELD RIGID WITH KEEPER HOOKS AND 1×3 BATTENS

PLACE THE KEEPER HOOKS NEXT TO STRAPS FOR SNUG FIT.

1×3 BATTEN IN KEEPER HOOK

TOGGLE

BATTEN

A STIFFENER IN A BENT KEEPER HOOK. THIS IS MORE RIGID.

TOGGLE

STIFFENER

TOGGLE

HOG TROUGH

A HOG TROUGH COMBINES BOTH METHODS FOR QUICK AND EASY USE.

To batten flats, place them face down on a well-swept floor. Align the bottom rails. Place 1 x 3 battens face down across the rails and toggles. The batten should be at least 1″ shorter than the flats on each end to allow another flat to butt against the wall or to attach a jack. This clearance also moves the end of the batten onto the plywood fastener and eliminates a possible protruding "hook" which could snag on something. The batten can be screwed down with 1-½″ #8 or #9 flat-head screws or with self-starting sheet-rock screws with their "nonslip" Phillips head. There should be two screws secured into each end of the batten and at least one screw secured into each stile the batten crosses. If the batten is not able to be attached over a plywood fastener at some point, a block of ¼″ plywood should be inserted between the flat frame and batten to eliminate the chance of warping by keeping the batten on the same plane.

When a wall is battened, carefully raise it by using sufficient workers to "walk it up" so it is standing vertically. Have one or more persons at the bottom to foot the unit and enough people to lift the top and "walk" along the stiles with their hands, raising the unit. Do not let too much bend occur, or the battens can loosen.

Duplex nails can be used to attach the battens, but they do not hold as well as screws. The second head of the nail also protrudes, and this can snag scenery or costumes. In addition to these problems, the abuse given to the frame when the nails are hammered in weakens it. Duplex nails are, however, very fast to drive and the second head facilitates quick removal.

Flats which are battened should be tightly lashed first (details follow) to help hold them in place while the battens are being applied. If there is no lash hardware, clamps can be used as needed, and removed after battens are affixed.

Battens can also be hinged on the flats. This allows the 1 x 3 to be on edge or at a right angle to the frame, and it gives greater stiffening power. When this is done, either 2″ tight-pin or loose-pin backflaps can be used. The 2″ backflaps are placed on the top of the batten with at least one hinge per flat. The weight of the batten will hold it at a right angle to the frames. Again, it is best if the battens can run over the rails or toggles (see Drawing II-44).

Battens are also temporarily placed on the back of flats to stiffen them (see Drawings II-41 and II-44). This is usually done for sets which must shift and strike quickly. When temporary battens are used, the flats should be face-hinged with 2″ backflaps. This hinged joint is covered with a dutchman when the flats are painted (see Drawings II-55 and II-56). The batten is now held in place with keeper hooks on the toggle and often on the top rail. These hooks are available from theatrical supply houses, or they can be homemade if you have a metal shop and lots of patience.

HINGING

Hinges are used to connect flats into large wall units which must fold for strike or storage. The flats can be hinged on the face or back.

When the flats are hinged on the front, they can easily fold into compact units. However, when they are back hinged there must be ¼″ blocks under the hinges if folding is desired. This prevents the flats binding against the plywood fasteners, which causes the hinges to bend, the screws to pull out and the frame to split.

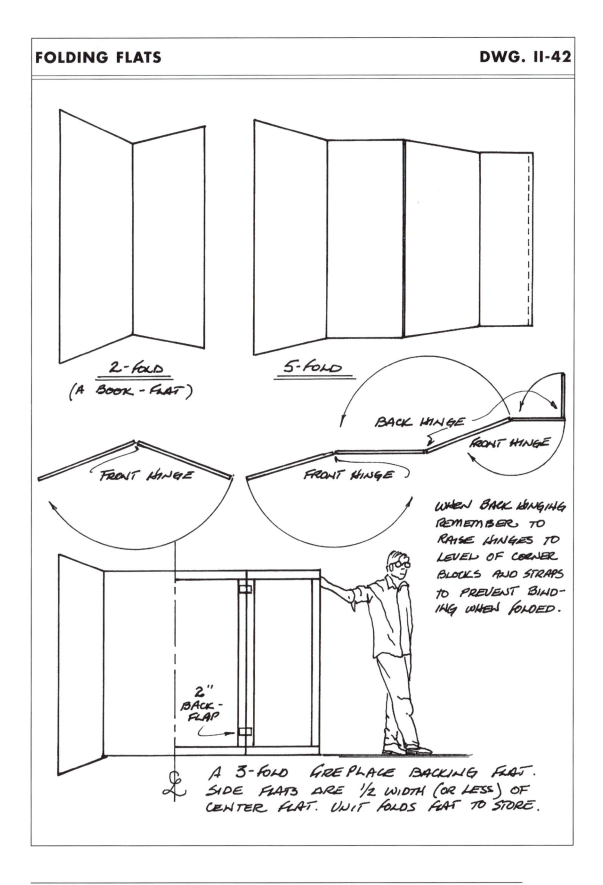

2-FOLD
(A BOOK-FLAT)

5-FOLD

FRONT HINGE

BACK HINGE

FRONT HINGE

FRONT HINGE

WHEN BACK HINGING
REMEMBER TO
RAISE HINGES TO
LEVEL OF CORNER
BLOCKS AND STRAPS
TO PREVENT BIND-
ING WHEN FOLDED.

2"
BACK-
FLAP

A 3-FOLD FIREPLACE BACKING FLAT.
SIDE FLATS ARE ½ WIDTH (OR LESS) OF
CENTER FLAT. UNIT FOLDS FLAT TO STORE.

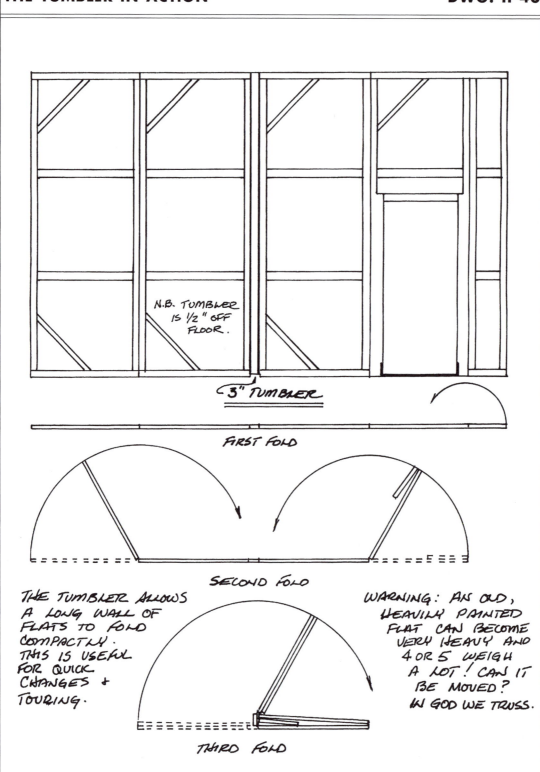

N.B. TUMBLER
IS ½" OFF
FLOOR.

3" TUMBLER

FIRST FOLD

SECOND FOLD

THE TUMBLER ALLOWS
A LONG WALL OF
FLATS TO FOLD
COMPACTLY.
THIS IS USEFUL
FOR QUICK
CHANGES &
TOURING.

THIRD FOLD

WARNING: AN OLD,
HEAVILY PAINTED
FLAT CAN BECOME
VERY HEAVY AND
4 OR 5 WEIGH
A LOT! CAN IT
BE MOVED?
IN GOD WE TRUSS.

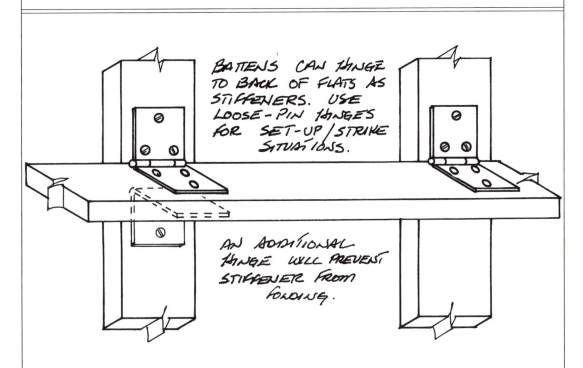

BATTENS CAN HINGE TO BACK OF FLATS AS STIFFENERS. USE LOOSE-PIN HINGES FOR SET-UP/STRIKE SITUATIONS.

AN ADDITIONAL HINGE WILL PREVENT STIFFENER FROM FOLDING.

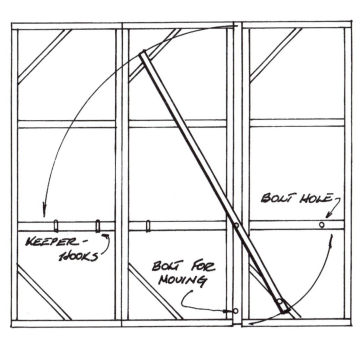

BOLT HOLE

KEEPER-HOOKS

BOLT FOR MOVING

A "PERMANENT" BATTEN IS BOLTED ONTO TUMBLER. IT PIVOTS INTO KEEPER HOOKS AND IS FIXED WITH A BOLT.

Always use enough hinges to keep the flats together and to prevent them from warping away from each other. Usually, if hinges are placed about 6″ from the top and bottom rails, the ends of the flat are securely held and there is little chance of splitting the ends of the wood in the frame with the screws. Additional hinges on the stiles aligned to the toggles are usually sufficient. The toggles also distribute any stress throughout the frame. As a bonus, this automatically places all hinges in line with the others, which makes them less offensive if they show.

When two flats are hinged (usually on the face) and the unit folds together, it is called a two-fold. A three-fold contains three hinged flats, a four-fold, four, and so on. Remember that a 4′-0″ x 12′-0″ flat with several coats of paint can easily weigh 30-40 pounds. The total weight, if too great, can seriously hamper striking an "easy to move" wall section.

A two-fold unit of stock flats can always fold face-to-face if hinged properly. However, on three-folds and larger groupings, the flats can force a bind on the hinges when they try to fold together. To prevent this, a tumbler (sometimes called a wooden dutchman or jigger) is inserted between the flats to create an area for the thickness of the folded flats and prevent binding (see Drawings II-43 and II-44).

A tumbler is a piece of 1 x stock (usually 1 x 3) as wide as needed to clear the thickness of all the folded flats and to hold the flap of the hinge. It is inserted between the two flats where bind would occur. The tumbler is hinged with 2″ backflaps to each of the flats, using the same hinge placement as the regular folding pieces as much as possible.

Important! Remember to make the tumbler ½″ shorter than the flats and to raise it that much from the floor. This prevents it from dragging when the folded flats are moved, which could split the tumbler and "shudder" the unit so much that the hinges could loosen. Remember also that the tumbler adds extra width to the wall of flats and that this difference will possibly need to be compensated for elsewhere.

PICTURE BATTENS

Picture battens (see Drawing II-45) are necessary when an object needs to be attached to the front of a muslin-covered flat. It is a vertical piece which can be standardized because toggle placement is standardized. Simply slip it between the two toggles and screw it into place. It will not only hold the picture, but support the bottom of it and keep it from denting into the flat.

If you are attaching anything which must be electrified (a sconce, clock, plug box, etc.) which must pass through the flat, make sure it passes through the picture batten also. This will hold the weight and prevent any tearing of the muslin. If possible, cut an "X" shape in the muslin and pass the cable or plug through to the back. If the muslin must have a large hole cut into it, tape the piece removed onto the back of the flat so it can be replaced after the production has completed its run (see Drawing II-54 and related text for details)

LASH HARDWARE

The principle of lashing flats is quite basic. It involves temporarily tying two flats together by criss-crossing a lightweight line around metal cleats and fixing the taut line in a knot (see Drawings II-46, 47 and 48).

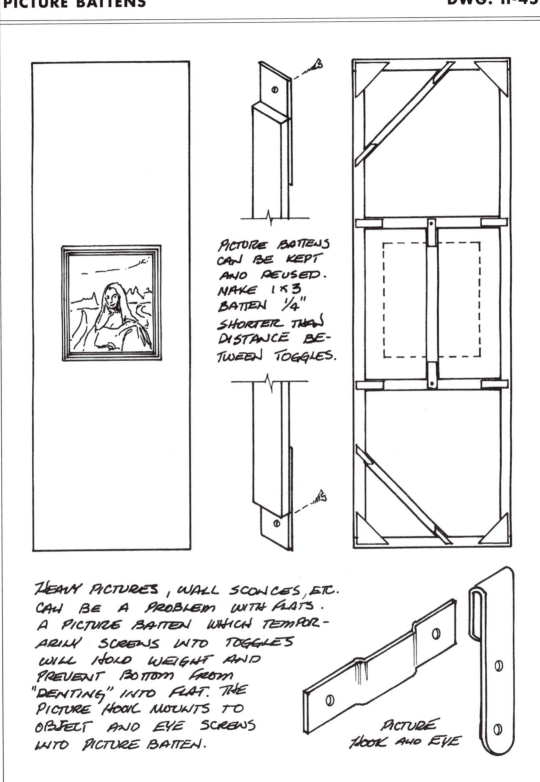

PICTURE BATTENS CAN BE KEPT AND REUSED. MAKE 1×3 BATTEN ¼" SHORTER THAN DISTANCE BE- TWEEN TOGGLES.

HEAVY PICTURES, WALL SCONCES, ETC. CAN BE A PROBLEM WITH FLATS. A PICTURE BATTEN WHICH TEMPOR- ARILY SCREWS INTO TOGGLES WILL HOLD WEIGHT AND PREVENT BOTTOM FROM "DENTING" INTO FLAT. THE PICTURE HOOK MOUNTS TO OBJECT AND EYE SCREWS INTO PICTURE BATTEN.

PICTURE HOOK AND EYE

Placing lash hardware on a set of stock flats allows quick, easy makeup of wall areas to match a floor plan. It is also one of the fastest methods of striking one set and erecting another for a multi-set show. Lash hardware is, however, expensive. If cost is a problem, determine for each individual show whether or not lash hardware would be advantageous to use. However, whether or not the hardware is permanently placed on the stock flats (an ideal situation), it is an indispensable aid to the technical staff. A certain amount of each type of hardware should be stocked for those occasions when its use will more than pay for itself.

Usually a worker can "throw" a lashline and fix the two flats without assistance (see Drawing II-49), although sometimes awkward or oversized flats require help. Lashing may seem an impossible task at first, but with a little practice the job becomes easy. To lash, align the two flats and hold them with your left hand. In your right hand take the lash line and pull it taut. Then quickly whip the line to the left with a flick of the wrist, releasing the tension on it so it can bow out and slip behind the top lash cleat. Almost immediately, as the line slips behind the cleat, pull it tight and the line will drop behind the cleat and hold in place. Then whip the line behind the next cleat down and pull it tight. Repeat until you have passed the line behind each cleat. Now pass it around the tie-off cleat, continuing the criss-crossing, and pull the line tight with both hands. Place it around the second tie-off cleat and tie it off (see Drawing II-47). A good lashing is done quickly and quietly (and after a lot of practice). If you're left-handed, I'm sorry.

THE LASHLINE

The best lashline is ¼" braided cotton rope (#8 sash cord). It can be purchased at any hardware store. The line is anchored at the top of the flat on the same side as the corner brace. This is important because the first throw of the line is the most difficult and the first lash cleat is opposite the starting point of the line, which would place it away from the corner brace and free of any additional obstructions which could hinder the throw.

The lashline is attached through the corner block. To make the hole for doing this, place a block of 1 x stock under the corner block and drill a ⅜" hole about one inch from the butt of the stile and rail. The 1 x stock block will prevent the plywood from splintering when the drill passes through it and also will protect the covering of the flat. After the hole is in, pass the line through it and pull the end out from behind the corner block. Tie a figure eight knot (see Drawing II-51) and then pull the rope back to snug the knot behind the hole. In the event there is no corner block, a Wise lash eye cleat can be used (see Drawing II-50).

The lashline should be pulled to the bottom of the flat and then cut off. It should never be longer than the flat, to prevent tripping on it when the flat is moved. If the line is shorter than the flat's length, it will be difficult (often impossible) to make the lash and have enough rope to tie it off.

CLEAT PLACEMENT

A good and workable "rule" is to place lash cleats 1'-0" above and 1'-0" below each toggle (see Drawing II-46). Attaching the cleat with this pattern, starting with the first cleat opposite the corner brace and the next opposite it, etc., places the lash cleats between two and three feet apart. This makes a good solid lash (see Drawings II-47 and II-48). This rule would, of course, have to be adjusted if there is unusual toggle placement or none at all.

If you are placing lash hardware as a permanent part of your stock, you should exchange a stage brace cleat for the lash cleat which is about two-thirds of the way up the flat. This brace cleat allows any flat to be braced instantly with an adjustable stage brace without adding a cleat. The brace cleat is a workable substitute for the lash cleat, and also saves money by not doubling up on hardware (see Drawing II-48). Make sure that the lash cleats work down the flat on alternate stiles. Once the pattern is established, the placement becomes "stock" in order to interchange flats and still make the lash. Do not allow variations without a specific reason.

The tie-off cleats are placed on each stile of each flat. They are the same height. They should be at a height which is conducive to tying the knot; 3'-0" from the floor is a good height. However, if short people will be using the stock, you could drop to 2'-8", but no lower or the lashline runs out before the knot can be tied.

Hammering large nails (or driving screws) into the inside edge of the stiles to make inexpensive lash hardware is a poor practice. The muslin is constantly bruised when the line is passed around the nail, but a bigger problem is the tendency for the frame to self-destruct when lashed. The nails and screws often split the stiles because of tension from the lash. This occurrence is not economically sound and the extra dollars for the lash hardware are better spent here than for other purposes. It is also expensive to rebuild flats constantly.

Regardless of whether or not you plan to place lash hardware on your stock, make sure that all corner braces are on the same stile and all toggles are at the same height within your chosen size of stock, because they are also used for other types of fastening.

TYPES OF LASH HARDWARE (see drawing II-50)

A *Wise Lashline Eye Cleat* is more expensive than a hole in the corner block. To attach the Wise cleat to the stile, lay it on the inside edge and with a hammer drive the chisel-pointed extension into the edge of the stile and then screw it down to the face with a ¾" #8 or #9 screw. This cleat is used when there is no corner block which can anchor the lashline, most commonly when a short piece of scenery is lashed to a taller one. It is not advisable to nail the lashline to the stile because the wood may split and weaken the frame. The lashline is attached by passing it through the eye and tying a figure-eight knot in the end (see Drawing II-51).

Lashline Cleat. This is the least expensive of all lash cleats and also the least sophisticated. The cleat sits on the back face of the stile and is screwed down with four ¾" #8 or #9 screws. Make sure it is at least flat stock thickness (¾") from the outside edge, so it won't interfere with another flat abutting . This cleat tends to fray the lashline and is not a good permanent installation.

The *Improved Lashline Cleat* is just that; it will not fray the rope because its edges are rounded, although it can stick up and possibly scar other flats in storage. It is applied in the same manner as the unimproved lashline cleat, but is more expensive.

Wise Lashline Cleat. This is perhaps the best and, of course, the most expensive cleat. Place it on the inside edge of the stile and pound with a hammer until the chiseled point underneath is driven into the stile. Then screw one ¾" #8 or #9 screw into the countersunk hole, It is the fastest lash cleat to install and it is easiest to whip the lashline around. This lash cleat is quite strong and secure.

The *Round Lashline Cleat* is a good buy. It can be attached to the flat with ¾" #8 or #9 screws. It can be used for lash cleats and, if slanted downward at 30°, it makes an excellent tie-off cleat (see Drawing II-51). There is the added advantage of having to stock only one item for both jobs. It is available in two lengths, but the longer cleat is generally more useful.

The *Offset Round Lashline Cleat.* This is used when there is no flat frame to allow the lashline to pass behind the cleat. This is most commonly used with jogs made of 1 x stock and with stiles on some door flats or on certain window flats (see Drawing II-48).

The *Towel Lashline Hook* is designed to be screwed into the edge of the stile and become a tie-off cleat. It can also be used in some situations where the offset round lashline cleat (above) is used, but it is difficult to throw the line around the hook. The hook will snag on other flats if mounted on the face of the stiles, because it does protrude.

The *Tie-off Cleat.* It is placed on the back face of the stile. It faces inward and is matched on the opposite stile. It is screwed down with two ¾" #8 or #9 screws.

It is possible to make all your own hardware from ¼" x ¾" sill iron. Cut the iron into 4" pieces and round off all edges on a bench grinder. Drill two ³⁄₁₆" holes about 1" apart near one end and countersink them for a #8 or #9 screw. Mount the hardware on the stile for lash cleats and tie-off cleats. However, unless you have a great deal of time and energy, it is not practical to construct your own hardware because commercially manufactured hardware is usually superior to homemade.

The brace cleats in Drawing II-50, J, K, L and M are all basically the same. However, the Scheel Brace Cleat (M) is the best and well worth the extra money. It allows the stage brace hook to easily slip into the hole and then "lock" the other hook into the slot. Attach this cleat (and the others) to the back of the stile with ¾" #8 or #9 screws. Make sure all cleats are set back stock thickness (¾") from the outside of the stile to allow one flat to butt smoothly against another.

The *Wise Brace Cleat.* This cleat is driven into the edge of the stile like other Wise cleats. Unlike the other Wise cleats, the brace cleat does not seem to be superior to its competitors' products.

The *Stop Cleat.* It is screwed to the back of a flat with the rounded edge extending past the flat approximately ¾". It acts as a stop for another flat which will butt up against it (see Drawing II-48). To prevent a potential snagging problem, the stop cleats should be removed when the show is struck and the flat is put back into storage.

The *Flat Cleat* is used when nothing else is available or nothing else will do. It can be a lash cleat, stop cleat of sorts, and is useful to help temporarily hold step units to platforms. It is not necessary to own a single flat cleat.

Stop Blocks (see Drawing II-48) are made in the shop of 1 x 1 stock. They are usually about 1'-0" long and are temporarily screwed to a flat to prevent it from

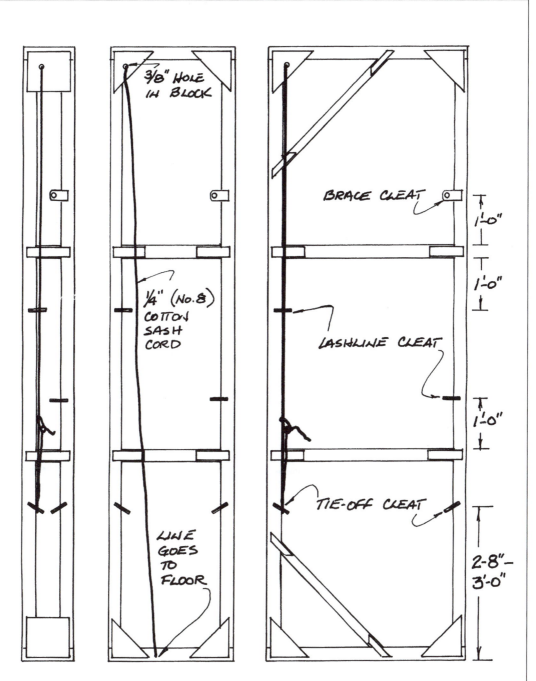

3/8" HOLE IN BLOCK

BRACE CLEAT

1'-0"

1'-0"

1/4" (NO.8) COTTON SASH CORD

LASHLINE CLEAT

1'-0"

LINE GOES TO FLOOR

TIE-OFF CLEAT

2-8"– 3'-0"

THE "FOOT ABOVE/FOOT BELOW" RULE WORKS WELL FOR ALL FLATS WHICH HAVE TWO OR MORE TOGGLES. FOR FLATS WITH ONE TOGGLE ADDITIONAL CLEATS ARE USED.

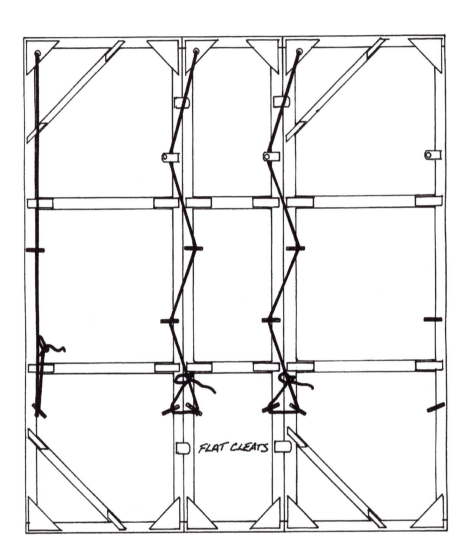

FLAT CLEATS

ONCE THE FLATS ARE LASHED TOGETHER, THEY NEED A BATTEN ON EACH TOGGLE. THESE MAY BE HELD IN PLACE WITH KEEPER HOOKS. NOTE THE FLAT CLEATS WHICH HELP PREVENT THE FLATS FROM SLIPPING. OF COURSE, IT IS MUCH EASIER TO SIMPLY SCREW BATTENS OR HOG TROUGHS TO THE TOGGLES OR RAILS, BUT LASHING WORKS WELL FOR QUICK CHANGES.

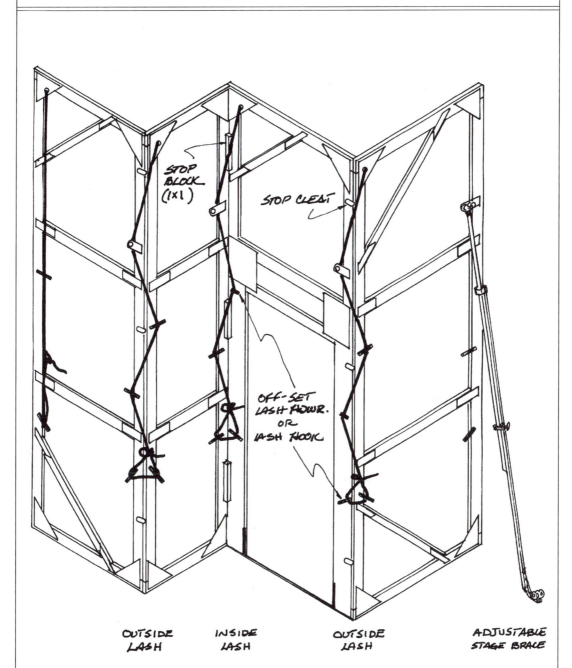

STOP
BLOCK
(1×1)

STOP CLEAT

OFF-SET
LASH FIXTUR.
OR
LASH HOOK

OUTSIDE
LASH

INSIDE
LASH

OUTSIDE
LASH

ADJUSTABLE
STAGE BRACE

AN OUTSIDE LASH CAN BE DONE WITHOUT STOP CLEATS BUT
THEY DO HELP HOLD THE CORNER FIRM. THE STOP BLOCKS
ARE NECESSARY FOR AN INSIDE LASH BECAUSE THE FLAT
TENDS TO RIDE OVER THE CORNER BLOCKS. NOTE: THE WIDE
STILE OF THE DOOR REQUIRES SPECIAL LASH HARDWARE.

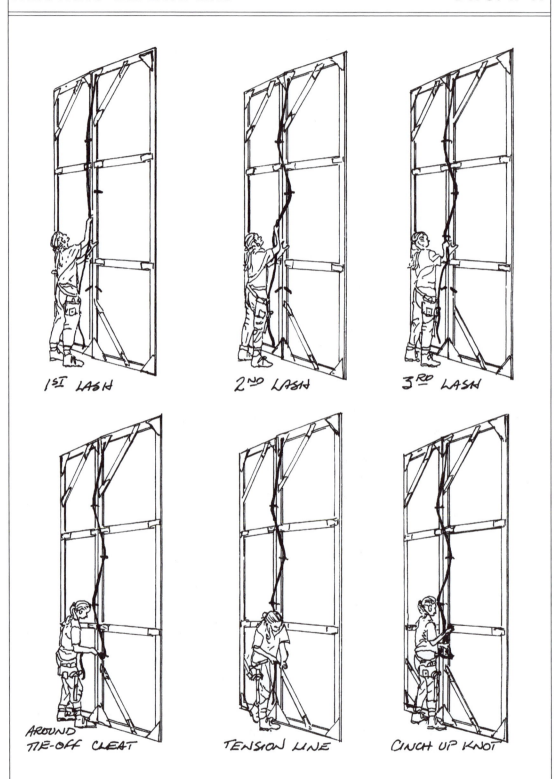

1ST LASH

2ND LASH

3RD LASH

AROUND TIE-OFF CLEAT

TENSION LINE

CINCH UP KNOT

LASH CLEATS

A. WISE LASHLINE EYE

B. LASHLINE CLEAT

C. IMPROVED LASH CLEAT

D. WISE LASHLINE CLEAT

(AN EXCELLENT CLEAT)

E. ROUND LASHLINE CLEAT

F. OFF SET LASHLINE CLEAT

G. TOWEL LASH HOOK
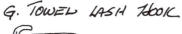

H. TIE-OFF CLEAT

ADJUSTABLE
STAGE BRACE

BRACE CLEATS

J. LARGE BRACE CLEAT

K. SMALL BRACE CLEAT

L. IMPROVED BRACE C.

M. SCHEEL BRACE C.

N. WISE BRACE C.

OTHER CLEATS

O. STOP CLEAT

P. FLAT CLEAT
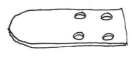
STAGE SCREW

USE IN THE TOP END OF
THE LASH LINE TO HOLD
ROPE BEHIND 3/8" HOLE
IN CORNER BLOCK OR
IN LASH EYE.

FIGURE 8 KNOT

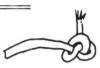

TIE-OFF KNOT

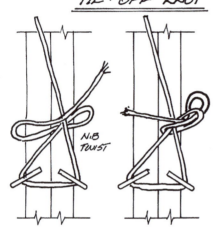

NIB
TWIST

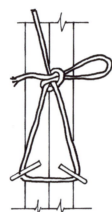

THIS KNOT WILL GIVE
GREAT TENSION ON
THE LASH LINE BUT
WHEN THE END IS
PULLED WILL QUICKLY
AND COMPLETELY
UNTIE. NOTE TWIST
IN FIRST LOOP.

THIS KEEPS THE LOOSE
LASH LINE AT WAIST
HEIGHT AND OFF THE
FLOOR OR FROM FALLING
ABOUT. IT COMPLETELY
UNTIES WHEN PULLED.

LASH LINE STORAGE KNOT

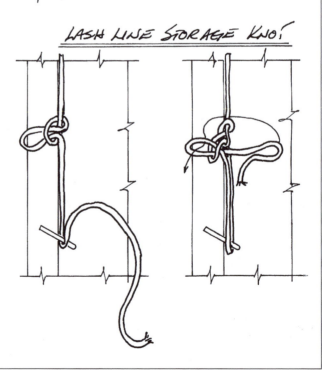

slipping when butted with another. There is no reason why these blocks can't be saved and reused like other hardware.

NAILING FLATS

The 6d duplex nail seems excellent for temporarily attaching flats in a rigid position. However, constant use of these nails (or any nails) will eventually weaken the wood. Try to use nails only when essential and not as a quick solution which could be better handled with screws, hinges or lash hardware. The flat frames will last longer and remain stronger without nails.

FRENCH FLATS

French flats are only a battened wall of flats which fly in and out. Why "French"? I have no idea, except perhaps like a "French scene," they indicate some change. Drawing II-52 shows a group of flats. For clarity, the battens across the rails and toggles are not drawn. Note the unit is lifted from the bottom and not pulled from the top. This greatly reduces the stress and strain within the frames and avoids the guillotine effect (do you suppose that's why they're French?). Some of the many pieces of hardware available from any good theatrical supply house are shown in Drawing II-53.

A word of caution regarding the use of piano wire. It can be deadly. It can puncture skin, and if it breaks under tension, it will flail about dangerously. It also requires special hardened cutters. However, it becomes "invisible" because of its thinness and great strength. Never use a piece with a kink in it.

Piano wire has been superseded by $\frac{1}{16}''$ aircraft cable and the Nicopress sleeve. This copper tube slips over the aircraft cable and is permanently crimped at the union. If you have trouble finding Nicopress equipment, call the maintenance department at the phone company or try an aviation company. There are also some thin cables and crimping tools made for fishermen which are wonderful for stage use, but not for the weight encountered in French flats.

DUTCHMEN

A dutchman is the cloth strip which is affixed over a crack or cracks created when two flats or flats and a tumbler are joined (see Drawing II-54). It is as wide as the distance between the outside edges of the two stiles. This is usually 6″, but with a 1 x 3 tumbler would be 9″. The stiles can be useful guides to make sure the dutchman is running straight on the flats.

Dutchmen are usually made by tearing strips from the muslin left over when covering flats, but new muslin can, of course, be used. Always remove the selvage; it shrinks differently and leaves a visible line. Roll each dutchman for storage. It is also easier to remove the stray "strings" when dutchmen are rolled.

It is efficient to use the primer or base coat paint to attach a dutchman. Never glue a dutchman unless it is to be permanent. There is sufficient binder in the paint to hold dutchmen, even for most touring situations.

To apply the dutchman, start at the top of the flat and paint a wide stripe covering the stiles from the top down as far as is easily reached. Let the dutchman unroll, and

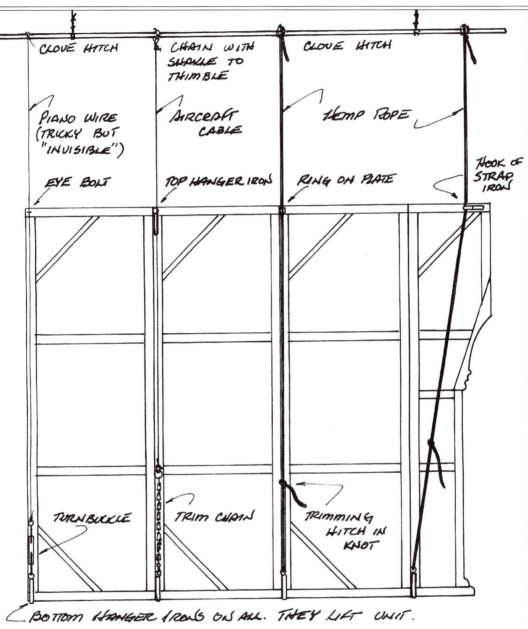

CLOVE HITCH

CHAIN WITH SHACKLE TO THIMBLE

CLOVE HITCH

PIANO WIRE (TRICKY BUT "INVISIBLE")

AIRCRAFT CABLE

HEMP ROPE

HOOK OF STRAP IRON

EYE BOLT

TOP HANGER IRON

RING ON PLATE

TURNBUCKLE

TRIM CHAIN

TRIMMING HITCH IN KNOT

BOTTOM HANGER IRONS ON ALL. THEY LIFT UNIT.

THE WALL OF FRENCH FLATS (BATTENED FLATS DESIGNED TO FLY) DEMONSTRATES ONLY SOME OF THE VARIOUS WAYS TO RIG FLATS FOR FLYING. THE METHODS CAN BE USED IN OTHER COMBINATIONS.

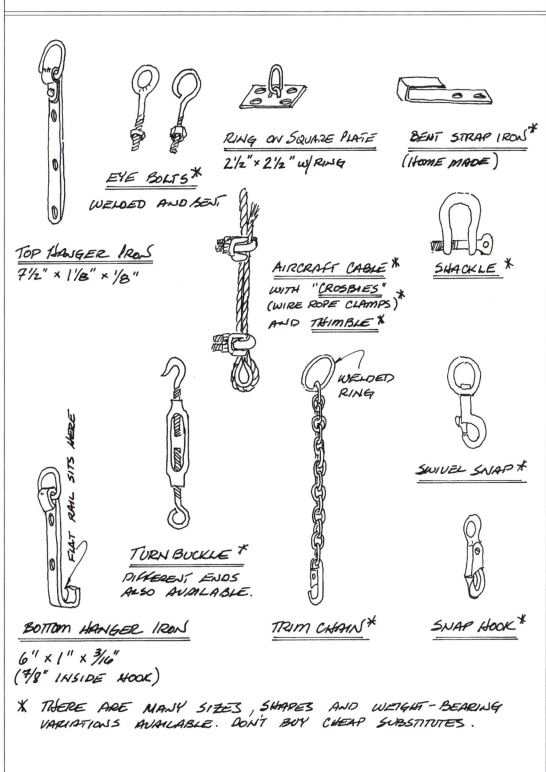

TOP HANGER IRON
7½" × 1⅛" × ⅛"

EYE BOLTS *
WELDED AND BENT

RING ON SQUARE PLATE
2½" × 2½" w/ RING

BENT STRAP IRON *
(HOME MADE)

AIRCRAFT CABLE *
WITH "CROSBIES"
(WIRE ROPE CLAMPS) *
AND THIMBLE *

SHACKLE *

WELDED RING

SWIVEL SNAP *

FLAT RAIL SITS HERE

TURN BUCKLE *
DIFFERENT ENDS
ALSO AVAILABLE.

TRIM CHAIN *

SNAP HOOK *

BOTTOM HANGER IRON
6" × 1" × ³⁄₁₆"
(⅞" INSIDE HOOK)

* THERE ARE MANY SIZES, SHAPES AND WEIGHT-BEARING
VARIATIONS AVAILABLE. DON'T BUY CHEAP SUBSTITUTES.

1. PAINT FLAT AT JOIN.

2. PAINT BACK OF DUTCHMAN

3. PUT PAINTED SURFACES TOGETHER.

4. PAINT DOWN. "FEATHER" OUT.

5. LIFT UNPAINTED DUTCHMAN AND PAINT BACK. PAINT FLAT.

6. REPOSITION AND PAINT DOWN. "FEATHER" OUT.

7. REPEAT #5.

8. REPEAT #6.

1. WALK ON THE FLAT'S FRAME.
   ROLL PAINT ON STILES.
   ROLL PAINT ON DUTCHMAN.

2. FLIP DUTCHMAN OVER AND
   ALIGN PAINTED SURFACES.

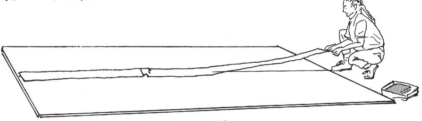

3. SMOOTH OUT DUTCHMAN,
   AND PAINT IT DOWN.
   "FEATHER" EDGES AS NEEDED.

TO REMOVE A DUTCHMAN,
CAREFULLY PULL IT OFF,
KEEPING IT CLOSE TO THE FLAT
TO AVOID LIFTING COVERING.

paint the back of it the same distance. Place the two painted surfaces together. Make sure the dutchman does not extend over the top of the flats or it risks being pulled off if the flats are folded or if it snags on something. Recharge the brush and paint the top of the dutchman. Before continuing be sure to brush away from the center of the dutchman to help blend the "fringes" or frayed edge into the flat.

Now, lift the remaining part of the dutchman up over the painted part and paint the back of it. Paint another stripe on the flat, and put the two painted surfaces together. Again, paint over the top and brush the "fringe" away from the center. Continue down the flat until the dutchman is completed. The dutchman should stop about an inch from the floor. If it is longer, cut it off with a pair of scissors. Do not use a utility knife or the like because the blade might snag in the wet cloth and pull the freshly applied dutchman from the flat. Always trim dutchmen immediately, however, so you don't catch the loose tail with the ladder and unleash the expletives. Do not disturb the flats—don't move them, or even slide them about—until the dutchman is completely dry. If necessary, by using similar methods, dutchmen can be put on flats which are lying on the floor (see Drawing II-55). Simply walk on the stiles or place a board across the flats to support your weight. You can use a roller to cover the stiles and back of the dutchman. With help, lift, turn over the painted dutchman, and lay it over the stiles. Roll over the top to paint it down. A brush in a bamboo (see Drawing VIII-5) can also make quick work of a dutchman on horizontal flats.

New or "raw muslin" flats need a new or "raw" dutchman. Old flats need a well-used dutchman. This is a subtle clue to save dutchmen when striking a show. Dutchmen can be carefully removed and rolled for reuse. The dutchmen should be pried from the flat at one end and pulled from the flats as close to the surface as possible (see Drawing II-55). This lessens the chance of pulling up the muslin covering.

On raw muslin dutchmen, a second coat of paint is usually needed after they have dried. This is a primer which will help it blend into the flat surface when the whole unit receives its base coat. A well-applied and primed dutchman is virtually invisible when the flats are painted.

Where, you may ask, does the word "dutchman" come from? After exhaustive research, I answer, "Beats me." Dutch has had a meaning of being fake or cheap, which certainly could never apply to anything theatrical, and a "Dutchman" is a stick which is placed between the outer logs of a load to keep the inner logs from rolling off. (A tumbler is sometimes called a wooden dutchman.) "Dutchman's Breeches" refers to a streak or patch of blue in a cloudy sky, but that's stretching it a bit. However, I have been told by an old stagehand that the dutchman was named after the patches on the pants of poverty-ridden scene painters, most of whom were Dutch. I find but quaint credence in the story.

Probably an acceptable etymological explanation comes from an older meaning of "dutchman," which was a contrivance to hide or counteract defective work (as an odd piece inserted to fill an opening or a paste mixture to fill cracks in marble). And this is, after all, fake and virtually cheap. But why "dutchman?" Well, it's something to chat about at cocktail parties.

PATCHING FLATS

The goal in patching a flat is to leave the surface with no trace of the wound. The most common damage seems to be a tear which occurs when the flat falls on a sharp object, or a sharp edge runs through the surface. This not only separates the cloth but also stretches it. Have someone behind the flat hold a board to the back or lay the flat face up with a board the correct thickness to keep the surface on the same plane as the face of the frame. Push the damaged muslin back into place. Secure the tear with masking tape, trying to mesh the fringes of the rip. Once taped smooth, move the board to the front and glue the patch on the back. The patch should be about the "same age" as the flat. This "age" refers to the number of coats of paint, etc. on the muslin. Old flats or dutchmen may be a good source for the patch. Cut the patch bigger than the tear and round the edges to prevent curling. Put glue on the patch and press it against the flat. The board in front will prevent undue stretching. Smooth out any wrinkles and excess glue. Let it dry thoroughly. If any stretch or sag is left, spritz the back with hot water. It should re-activate the sizing and shrink tight. Remove the tape when the patch is completely dry.

Holes which need mending can have a "plug" of muslin, roughly the same age as the flat, inserted in the hole and then be repaired as described above. It is always wise to save the cloth removed when the hole is cut. Tape it to the back of the flat until repair time. Emergency repairs can be done by holding a board to the front and taping the back. Make sure, however, this temporary patch is replaced with a properly glued one before the next paint job.

HARDWALL SCENERY

If you are planning a hardwall stock for theatre or television, follow the "rules" discussed for flats. These may help determine some of the limitations. What is seen on television is limited by the "eye" of the camera, not to mention the person who is using it. The camera can control visual height, but beware of the old rule of 8'-0" being enough for television scenery. It really limits the types of shots available; 10'-0" is a better minimum height for most situations.

Construction techniques are variations on standard flat frame methods...the frame is merely "on-edge" and not flat (see Drawings II-56 and II-57). Notice that the toggles can be narrower and allow scenery with mouldings on the face to stack tightly and safely (see Drawing II-60). This is also handy for permanent pictures and dressings, and is especially good in situations where studio space is limited and many shows must be set up and struck.

Many covering materials are available on the market other than the popular ¼" plywood. Some which come to mind are ⅛" veneer, textured hardboard panels (brick, plaster, etc.), hardboard panels or other veneer types with "wood" finishes, Upsom board and thin particle board. It is also good to scrim the hardwall by gluing muslin over the plywood which hides the wood grain. Hardwall is ideal to accept textures, wallpaper and other "realistic" treatments.

When hardwall units are designed wider than covering materials (4'-O"), many

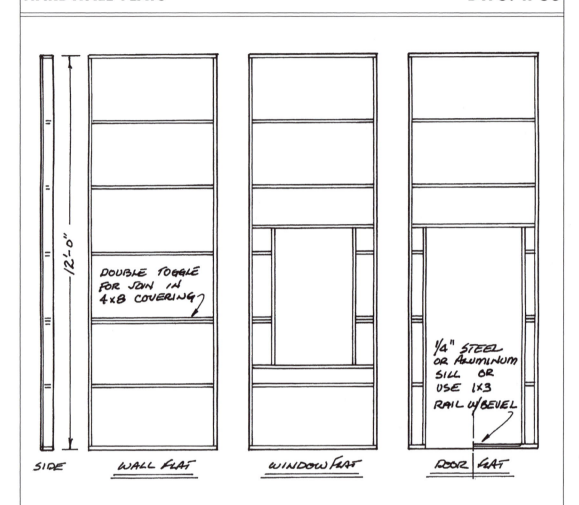

12'-0"

DOUBLE TOGGLE
FOR JOIN IN
4X8 COVERING

¼" STEEL
OR ALUMINUM
SILL   OR
USE 1X3
RAIL W/BEVEL

SIDE   WALL FLAT   WINDOW FLAT   DOOR FLAT

HARDWALL SCENERY, ONCE THE BUTTRESSED BACKING OF FILM AND TELEVISION, IS BECOMING INCREASINGLY POPULAR IN THEATRE. IT IS DURABLE, STABLE AND OFFERS AN EXCELLENT SURFACE FOR HEAVY TEXTURES, WALLPAPER, MOULDINGS, ETC. HARDWALL, HOWEVER, IS MORE EXPENSIVE THAN CONVENTIONAL FLATS, HEAVIER, BULKIER TO STORE AND INSIDIOUSLY MARRIED TO THE 4X8 SHEET OF CONSTRUCTION PANEL.

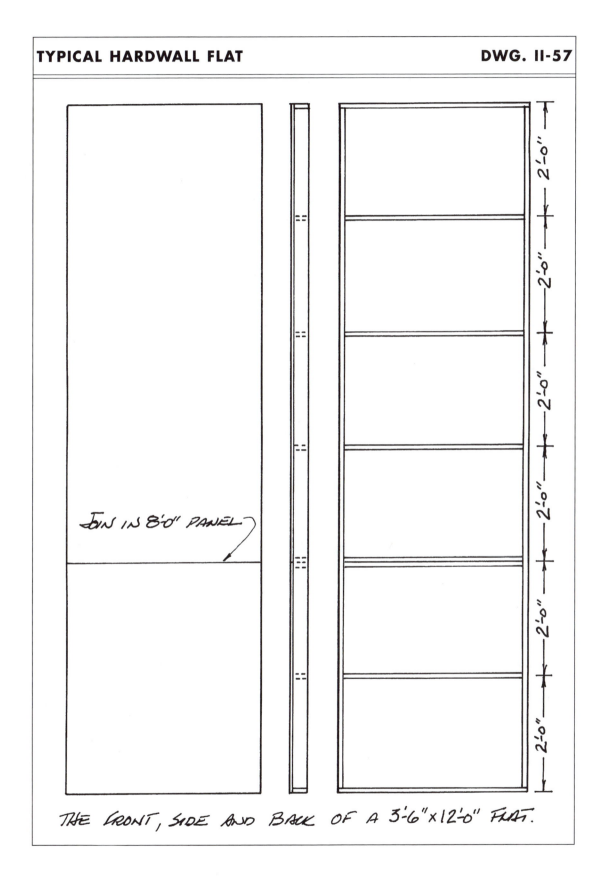

JOIN IN 8'-0" PANEL

2'-0"
2'-0"
2'-0"
2'-0"
2'-0"
2'-0"

THE FRONT, SIDE AND BACK OF A 3'-6"×12'-0" FLAT.

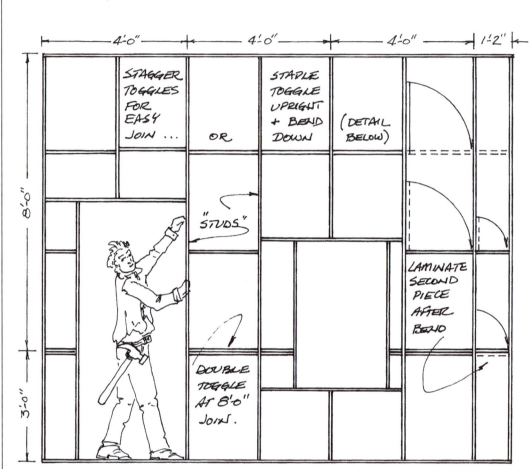

4'-0"   4'-0"   4'-0"   1'-2"

8'-0"

3'-0"

STAGGER TOGGLES FOR EASY JOIN ...

OR

STAPLE TOGGLE UPRIGHT + BEND DOWN

(DETAIL BELOW)

"STUDS"

DOUBLE TOGGLE AT 8'-0" JOIN.

LAMINATE SECOND PIECE AFTER BEND

A 13'-2" × 11'-0" "STUD" WALL WITH FRAMED-IN OPENINGS

Hardwall units wider than 4×8 sheet stock may be constructed as above. Note 2'-8" spacing on upper toggles to lessen top weight. "Studs" are spaced every 2'-0" to align with covering material. Adjust to suit whim of designer or other perversity.

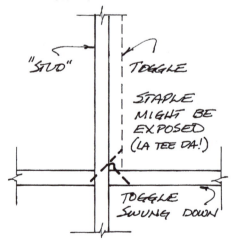

"STUD"

TOGGLE

STAPLE MIGHT BE EXPOSED (LA TEE DA!)

TOGGLE SWUNG DOWN

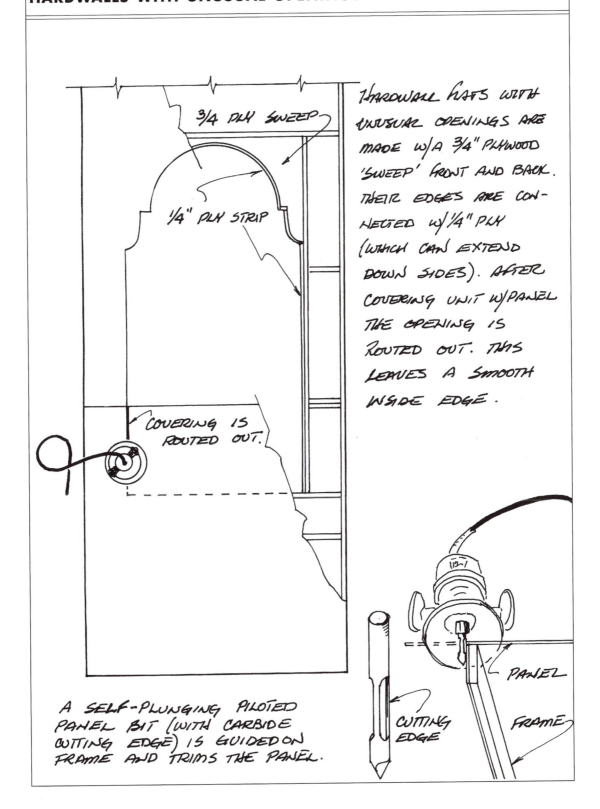

3/4 PLY SWEEP

1/4" PLY STRIP

COVERING IS ROUTED OUT.

HARDWALL FLATS WITH UNUSUAL OPENINGS ARE MADE W/A 3/4" PLYWOOD 'SWEEP' FRONT AND BACK. THEIR EDGES ARE CONNECTED W/ 1/4" PLY (WHICH CAN EXTEND DOWN SIDES). AFTER COVERING UNIT W/PANEL THE OPENING IS ROUTED OUT. THIS LEAVES A SMOOTH INSIDE EDGE.

A SELF-PLUNGING PILOTED PANEL BIT (WITH CARBIDE CUTTING EDGE) IS GUIDED ON FRAME AND TRIMS THE PANEL.

CUTTING EDGE

PANEL

FRAME

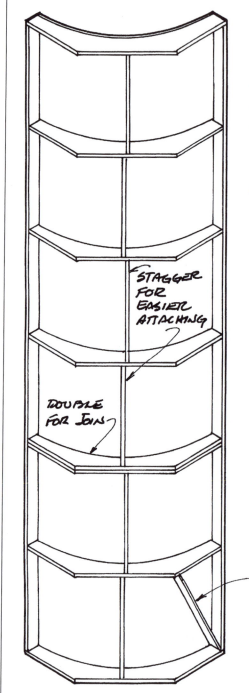

STAGGER FOR EASIER ATTACHING

DOUBLE FOR JOIN

KEEPING IN MIND THAT PANEL STOCK (ESP. ¼" PLYWOOD) BENDS MORE EASILY IN THE 4'-0" DIRECTION, PLAN SWEEPS WHICH DO NOT EXCEED THIS MEASUR-MENT. SEPARATE THE SWEEPS (WHICH HAVE BECOME TOGGLES) WITH STILES AND VERTICAL BATTENS. GLUE AND FORCE THE COVERING PANEL TO THE SWEEPS. THIS IS MORE EASILY DONE IF THE BACK OF THE SWEEPS ARE FLAT. IT IS POSSIBLE TO STAND INSIDE THE CURVE TO FORCE IT TO THE SWEEPS OR PUT SANDBAGS, ETC. INSIDE. FOR TIGHT CURVES, "E-Z" CURVE OR EVEN LINOLEUM MAY BE A USEFUL CHOICE. HOWEVER, NEITHER HAS THE STRENGTH OF ¼" PLY.

A "CORNER BRACE" MAY HELP HOLD FRAME SQUARE UNTIL COVERING IS APPLIED.

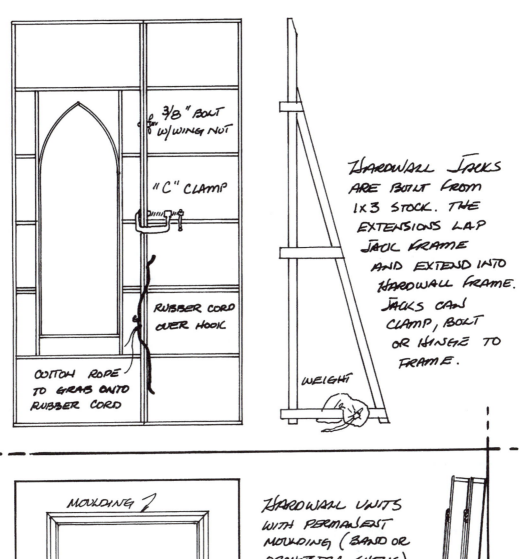

3/8" BOLT
w/ WING NUT

"C" CLAMP

RUBBER CORD
OVER HOOK

COTTON ROPE
TO GRAB ONTO
RUBBER CORD

HARDWALL JACKS
ARE BUILT FROM
1 X 3 STOCK. THE
EXTENSIONS LAP
JACK FRAME
AND EXTEND INTO
HARDWALL FRAME.
JACKS CAN
CLAMP, BOLT
OR HINGE TO
FRAME.

WEIGHT

MOULDING

TOGGLES ARE
ONLY 1½" WIDE

HARDWALL UNITS
WITH PERMANENT
MOULDING (BAND OR
ORCHESTRA SHELLS)
OFTEN HAVE THE
TOGGLES NARROWER
THAN OUTSIDE
FRAME. THIS
PROVIDES A SAFE
'POCKET' FOR THE
MOULDING WHEN
STORED.

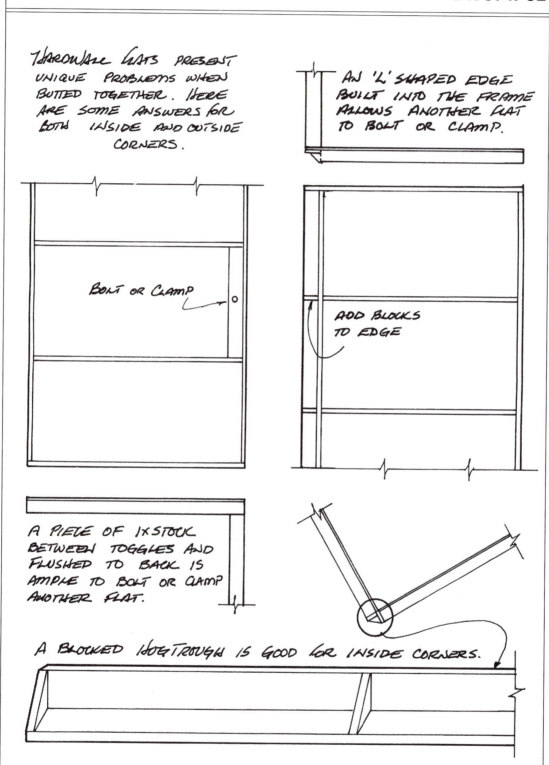

Hardwall flats present unique problems when butted together. Here are some answers for both inside and outside corners.

An 'L' shaped edge built into the frame allows another flat to bolt or clamp.

Bolt or clamp

Add blocks to edge

A piece of 1x stock between toggles and flushed to back is ample to bolt or clamp another flat.

A blocked hogtrough is good for inside corners.

shops build them using methods common to house construction. Of course the 2x4 is replaced by a more svelte 1x3 and sheet rock is banned in favor of much lighter materials. As seen in drawing 11-58, the top and bottom rails are still separated by stiles. The addition of vertical "studs" (it is hoped the gratuitous sex sprinkled about in this section will help sell the film rights) are derived from the construction trades. While uprights are certainly not required on 2'-0" centers, the additional studs do give good support to a wall unit. The horizontal toggles must be staggered to attach easily—again a technique found in house construction. The common use of pneumatic staplers has evolved a method for toggle attachment which allows continuous alignment. The toggle is placed face-to-face against the stud and stapled through into the upright. It is then pulled down and wedged against the next vertical. The flexibility of the wire staple acts as a "hinge." The other end is stapled through the next stud or stile. While this is certainly not structurally the strongest joint, it does do the job, i.e., keeps the verticals the proscribed distance and it gives additional support to the covering material. There is little chance of the bent-staple joint pulling apart because the covering material is applied over the joint. A bit of care and practice can make an acceptable joint with no shiners from the staples.

Hardwall flats which have unusual openings (see Drawing II-58) can be made easily by inserting matched ¾" plywood pieces (or 1 x stock if it works) flush to the front and back of the frame, with the desired shape cut out of them. Connect these pieces with a narrow plywood or veneer strip. Glue and attach the facing material to the frame. Using a router with a self-plunging piloted panel bit, drop through the covering within the opening and the bit will guide the router around the faced edge. It will neatly trim the covering material flush to the facing material.

Hardwall lends itself to curved surfaces (see Drawing I-59) which are either convex or concave. The success of any curved surface depends greatly on the covering material and the number of people available to help bend the flat sheet to the frame.

Hardwall flats are not quite as easy to join as standard flat frames but, as Drawings II-60 and II-61 show, some fairly basic solutions are available, many of which can become stock with the flats.

The hardwall false proscenium (see Drawing I-62) is a slightly heavier version of a simple hardwall flat. These proscenia are often used for "permanent" installations when a season or years of use will subject them to long-term wear and tear. The vertical legs of the false proscenium can attach to the floor with lag screws (Yikes! Not in the stage floor!!!) or by other secure method (mastic, double-faced tape, weight) while the top can bolt into the header piece.

The header in the drawing is hung by cable which is attached to the bottom of the frame so it is lifting the piece, not pulling it from above and thus pulling it apart. The aircraft cable which is passing through the frame can be replaced by chain or any other secure material, but the turnbuckles should remain to allow any subtle trimming required.

The flat hinged to the edge could readily be made of additional pieces of hardwall, but may be a cheaper solution. You may not even need it. The drawing indicates the frame to be 1 x 6, but that, too, is easily adjusted to suit the particular need of the situation. The wider material is really for visual "bulk" and not for strength—the sheet of plywood provides that. The framework is merely holding the plywood together. Indeed, the ⅜" plywood only provides a more solid surface and no real additional structural strength.

False proscenia can be covered with many materials, but are often treated with a slightly textured fabric to help "soften" the surface and absorb any stray light which might hit it. The section on Soft Masking may have some useful hints about materials and Drawing II-36 on covering flats with outrageously expensive fabrics may also be useful. However, false proscenia have been covered with burlap (watch out for unsightly wavy patterns in the weave and when stretching it), others with dark-napped carpet made for automobile floors, and even grass matting which has been painted. Some are originally covered with a textured panel, while others have been covered with muslin to kill the plywood grain and painted to match the interior of the theatre. Need is the mother of necessity; the inventive grandchildren will follow.

Most jacks for hardwalls are a variation on those for normal flats. However, a fairly common variety includes a jack with horizontal members lapped on the frame and extended to slip inside the unit and attach to the stiles or studs (see Drawing II-60).

Two flat frame jacks commonly used with hardwalls are shown in (see Drawing II-63). These attach to the ends of a hardwall wall unit and are both quite stable, especially with the addition of some weight, either a sandbag or stray counterweight. The hinged jack is especially useful in crowded studios but is also handy in shops and paint areas where space and traffic patterns can put those of the studio to shame.

The rolling jack (see Drawing II-64) is a shop-made substitution for a commercially available jack which has pneumatic pumps to lower casters and thus raise the wall unit for easy shifting. Basically a lift jack, the unit requires only the hot air of a stagehand. Note the manner in which the layers are laminated. The 1 x 3 vertical which ultimately attaches to the hardwall unit is laminated to the back of the piece of ¾" plywood. The horizontal 1 x 3 laminated to the front of the ¾" plywood is placed above the hinged board with the casters. Thus, it is lifted by the casters and in turn, because it is laminated to the plywood and the 1 x 3 vertical, will transfer the lift to the hardwall unit and the hinges are not stressed. The diagonal braces rest on the horizontal 1 x 3 and attach to the ¾" plywood and to the vertical through a ¾" spacer which keeps them in the same plane. The folding hinged support also attaches to the ¾" spacer. A standard l x l x 6" tapered foot (see Drawing IV-26) makes an ideal stop. Because the folding support is hinged on the front at the top and on the back at the break, it will lift out of the way for lowering the caster board and set into place against the cleat.

The addition of a tie line on the 1 x 3 vertical will allow the folding support to be tied against unit and hold everything together.

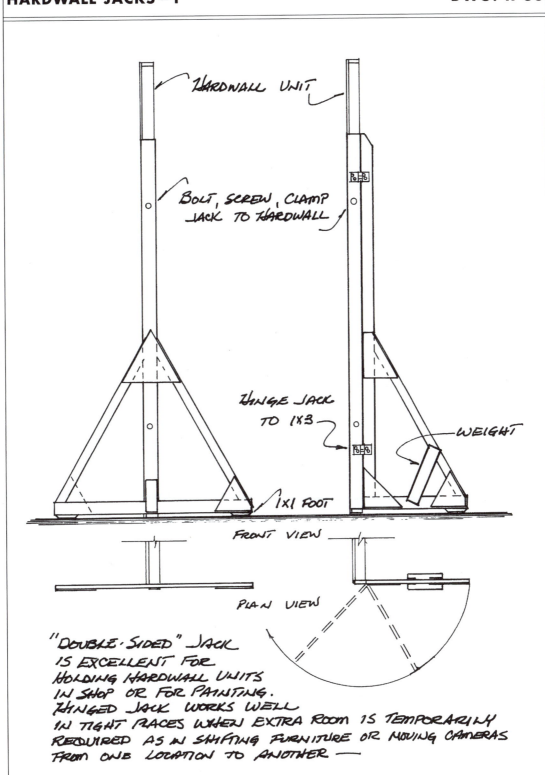

HARDWALL UNIT

BOLT, SCREW, CLAMP
JACK TO HARDWALL

HINGE JACK
TO 1×3

WEIGHT

1×1 FOOT

FRONT VIEW

PLAN VIEW

"DOUBLE-SIDED" JACK
IS EXCELLENT FOR
HOLDING HARDWALL UNITS
IN SHOP OR FOR PAINTING.
HINGED JACK WORKS WELL
IN TIGHT PLACES WHEN EXTRA ROOM IS TEMPORARILY
REQUIRED AS IN SHIFTING FURNITURE OR MOVING CAMERAS
FROM ONE LOCATION TO ANOTHER —

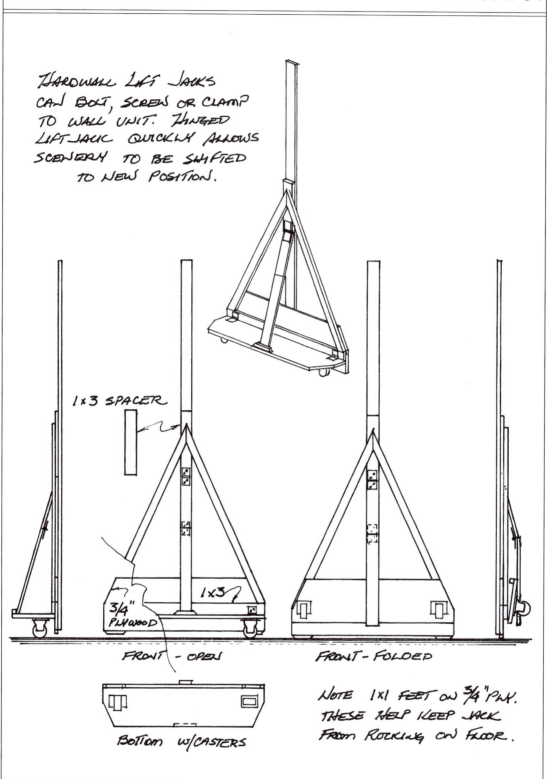

HARDWALL LIFT JACKS
CAN BOLT, SCREW OR CLAMP
TO WALL UNIT. HINGED
LIFT JACK QUICKLY ALLOWS
SCENERY TO BE SHIFTED
TO NEW POSITION.

1x3 SPACER

3/4"
PLYWOOD

1x3

FRONT - OPEN

FRONT - FOLDED

BOTTOM w/CASTERS

NOTE 1x1 FEET ON 3/4" PLY.
THESE HELP KEEP JACK
FROM ROCKING ON FLOOR.

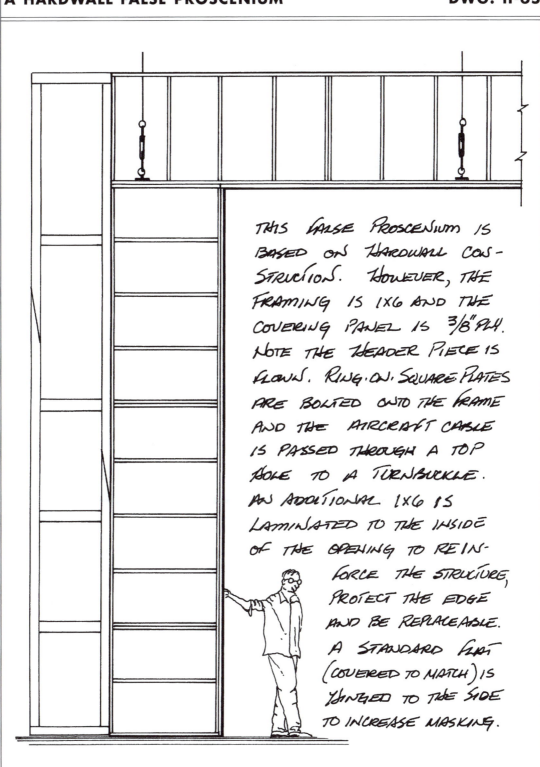

THIS FALSE PROSCENIUM IS
BASED ON HARDWALL CON-
STRUCTION. HOWEVER, THE
FRAMING IS 1X6 AND THE
COVERING PANEL IS 3/8" PLY.
NOTE THE HEADER PIECE IS
FLOWN. RING·ON·SQUARE PLATES
ARE BOLTED ONTO THE FRAME
AND THE AIRCRAFT CABLE
IS PASSED THROUGH A TOP
HOLE TO A TURNBUCKLE.
AN ADDITIONAL 1X6 IS
LAMINATED TO THE INSIDE
OF THE OPENING TO REIN-
FORCE THE STRUCTURE,
PROTECT THE EDGE
AND BE REPLACEABLE.
A STANDARD FLAT
(COVERED TO MATCH) IS
HINGED TO THE SIDE
TO INCREASE MASKING.

PART III • SOFT SCENERY

SOFT MASKING

Many theatres rely on soft masking to support their scenery by providing a neutral surround behind it. The masking is often called "blacks" because the curtains are usually made of black velour, which is noted for its great light absorbing quality and resistance to wrinkling (Drawing III-1)

This masking consists of three groups of pieces. Narrow, vertical panels on each side of the stage are called *legs*, which mask the audience's view of the wings. Overhead and running from the outside edges of the legs is the *border*. This narrow, horizontal curtain masks the audience's view into the fly loft and helps hide the tops of pipes or battens. Usually behind the legs and borders is a curtain as tall as the legs and as long as the border called a *full black*. This curtain is often made of two large panels, and is on a track which allows it to open and close. To add to the confusion, some theatres call legs "tormentors" and borders "teasers." Think of the miniskirt, and it's all clear.

Almost all the blacks and similar masking for professional theatres (and many, many others) are sewn in shops equipped to deal with the special requirements of velour, *i.e.*, its weight and bulk, creeping and puckering characteristics when sewn, and its natural "crush-ability." Heavy-duty sewing machines with a walking foot are used.

However, it is possible to make soft masking which will do many things the professionally made curtains do and save some of the great expense. Never, even for a brief moment, think you can duplicate a good set of professional masking pieces unless you have the correct velour, the proper tools and the skilled workers for fabrication.

The words *velvet* and *velour* derive from the Latin *vellus*, meaning a fleece or tufted hair. *Velours* is the French word (masculine, of course) for velvet. Regardless of the word, the fabric has a tightly woven back with additional thread added as loops into the warp threads when woven. If these loops are cut to make a pile, it is known as cut velvet, which is what we usually see. Many specialized types and variations are available. Regardless of how the real world separates velvets and velour, in theatre parlance velvet is considered a fancy cloth often of silk or rayon, and velour is made of cotton. It is sold in different weights which refer to the thickness and depth of the pile. The longer the pile, the more luxurious the cloth, and luxury ain't cheap.

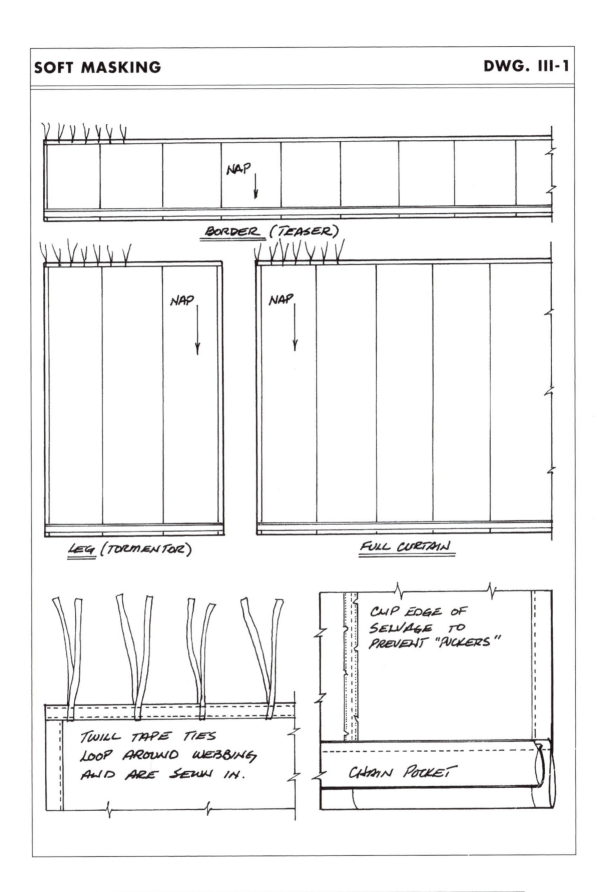

BORDER (TEASER)

NAP

LEG (TORMENTOR)

FULL CURTAIN

NAP

TWILL TAPE TIES
LOOP AROUND WEBBING
AND ARE SEWN IN.

CLIP EDGE OF
SELVAGE TO
PREVENT "PUCKERS"

CHAIN POCKET

Unfortunately, the more luxurious the velour, the better it does its job in the theatre, *i.e.*, absorbs light and backstage noise, prevents bleed-through, hides wrinkles and exudes luxuriance.

Usually a colored velour is used for the main curtain and its coordinated grand valance and grand border (if there is one); and black velour is used for the masking curtains because of its neutrality. However, masking can be any color desired, especially if it is not needed to "fade into the background."

Fabrics which will substitute for velour are many and varied, but they will work better if they have the characteristics of velour, namely the fine appearance, solidity and especially the ability to absorb light.

Duvetyne is a heavy cloth with soft "velvety" surface, created by brushing the top of the fabric. It has a definite nap and direction. It is also available in some colors in addition to black, but is usually a specialty fabric and must be ordered from a supplier.

Corduroy is a fabric with cut-pile ribs. These can be very fine, pinwale, to quite heavy, wide wale. It is a good light absorber and available in many colors.

Robe Velour is an acetate material with a velvet finish. It has great advantages because it is wide and fairly inexpensive. However, it is also shiny and fire marshals don't like it.

Terry Cloth, commonly known as the bath towel, is available by the bolt in many colors. It will also take dye well. It is not fun to sew.

Cotton Flannel is another napped fabric worth considering, though it is rarely very heavy and the little duckies and plaids tend to limit its usefulness.

FULLNESS OR NOT

…that is the question. Some theatres prefer to have fullness in their curtains (see Drawing III-2). This does "soften" the appearance and give them more visual interest with highlights and shadows. Other theatres prefer to leave their curtains flat to gain the advantage of the width of the curtain for masking. However, if fullness is built in (sewn into the webbing), then it is impossible to flatten them out, but flat curtains can be gathered by placing the ties on the webbing closer together on the pipe. Perhaps the flat curtain does have a bit more advantage; and it is certainly easier to sew and fold up.

Even if a fabric does not have a nap or pile, it may have an "up and down" direction, and this should be checked before sewing up the curtains. Be sure to hang the pieces in good light and move away far enough to see. If you discover a direction, be sure to mark it on the back of the fabric, on each piece, so there is no slip-up when sewing.

The webbing at the top of the curtain is important because it not only carries the weight of the entire curtain to the ties, but also helps even out the hang from the tie. A wide, jute webbing is available from any upholsterer's shop or their supplier. It should not be very expensive, and is really needed if you are using grommets. It will also work well with the twill tape ties which can be pre-sewn to it before it is sewn to the curtain (see Drawing III-1).

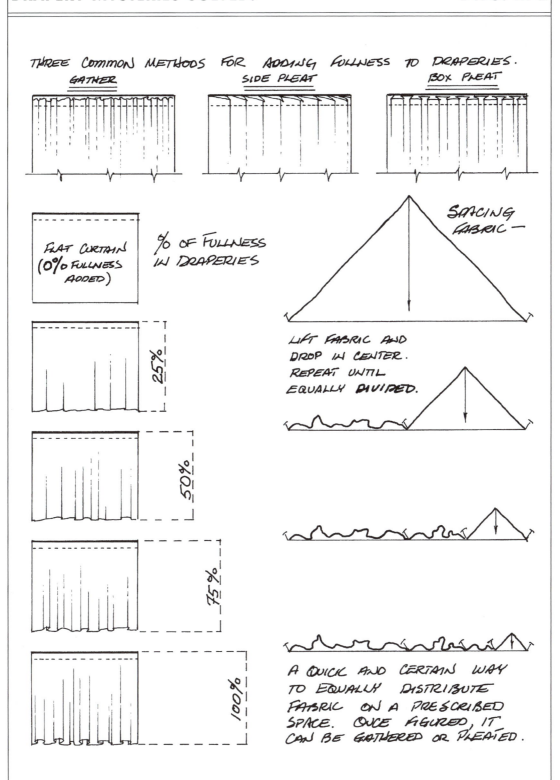

THREE COMMON METHODS FOR ADDING FULLNESS TO DRAPERIES.
GATHER   SIDE PLEAT   BOX PLEAT

FLAT CURTAIN
(0% FULLNESS
ADDED)

% OF FULLNESS
IN DRAPERIES

25%

50%

75%

100%

SPACING
FABRIC —

LIFT FABRIC AND
DROP IN CENTER.
REPEAT UNTIL
EQUALLY DIVIDED.

A QUICK AND CERTAIN WAY
TO EQUALLY DISTRIBUTE
FABRIC ON A PRESCRIBED
SPACE. ONCE FIGURED, IT
CAN BE GATHERED OR PLEATED.

A grommet is a metal ring which is set around a hole in the webbing and curtain through which a cord or line is tied with a simple cow hitch (see Drawing III-6). For each size grommet there must be a hole cutter and a stand to hold one part of the grommet and a setting die to clinch it over a second metal ring. These can be ordered, with the grommets, from any good hardware store or from theatrical supply houses. Always order extra grommets.

When sewing curtains, always sew in the same direction, *i.e.*, from top to bottom; this will help them hang better because the tension is always the same. Make sure there is a 4" to 6" hem along each leading edge; this will give stability, a good surface on which to attach lining if needed, and a solid edge for folding the curtain.

Once the requisite number of panels have been stitched together, lay out the curtain on a clean floor to make sure there are no puckers and the curtain is even at the top and bottom. You may find a slight puckering along the seams caused by the selvage or woven edge of the fabric. Often this is a slightly tighter weave than the fabric, and the tension will pucker the seam. Snipping the edge every few inches will alleviate the problem (see Drawing III-1). If the sewing machine is the cause of the problem (not feeding the fabric correctly) you should open the seam and correct the problem. Vertical puckers will not hang out. If the top and bottom of the curtain are irregular, now is the time to correct the problem and make them parallel. Next, attach the webbing to the top and place a 4" to 6" hem in the bottom.

Weights (pipe, chain, etc.) should never be put directly into the hem of a curtain. It will quickly wear through the fold in the cloth. Therefore, a pocket slightly less deep than the hem should be attached to the back of the curtain. This can be sewn on with the hem or attached on the same seam line (see Drawings III-1 and III-7).

If you must add a lining to opaque the curtains, it can be sewn in at the top with the webbing and tacked along the sides as necessary, but should hang separately from the curtain so as not to pull or warp it. The lining will hang differently. Some theatres make separate panels with ties which they use only behind those curtains which might have a strong light source behind. A flat placed behind the curtain will also block any light which is bleeding through.

FIRE-PROOFING

First of all, there is no such thing as fire-proofing when it comes to curtains. At best, a fabric should be used for the curtain which doesn't "carry flame" and a flame-retardant can then be sprayed to it, from the back. Great care must be used in order to preserve the texture and quality of the fabric and not stain it from over-spraying. The salts in the retardant can easily bleed through and leave a definite stain line. There are many retardants on the market, and each should be tested before being used.

One "homemade" retardant which might work is a mixture of one pound of sal ammoniac, one pound of borax and three quarts of water. This mixture can be brushed or sprayed. It is quite corrosive, so wash up any metal pieces thoroughly. The best flame-retardant is really a good working relationship with the local fire marshal. His knowledge and expertise will be most beneficial and can save untold problems down the road.

FOLDING CURTAINS

A goal when folding a curtain is to have the finished bundle clearly labeled for easy identification and ready to unfold and tie to the batten. To this end, all legs, borders and full curtains should have their size clearly indicated with a large marker on both ends of the webbing. The center of full curtains and borders should also be marked (see Drawings III-3 and III-4).

Sweep the floor and lay the curtains out, face up. Have one worker grab the webbing at the leading edge and another worker grab the hem of the same leading edge. Have them pull toward themselves, creating tension in the vertical hem and lifting it off the floor to about waist height. Each worker quickly walks to the other leading edge, maintaining the tension and trapping enough air inside the leg to float the fold. Place the leading edges together on the ground, and ease out any irregularities. A bit of practice will quickly dictate tension, speed of walking and amount of air to capture. Repeat the fold with tension now being placed on the first fold which is floated to the edge of the leg. Repeat this step until the leg is about three feet wide, or some convenient width to pick up when the rest of the folding is completed. Next, take the bottom and carry it to the top. Repeat until the bundle can be picked up and placed in a bag or rolling cart for storage. The written information on the webbing will be clearly visible so that the bundle may be situated properly beneath the batten before it is retied and re-flown. When retying, one little trick which will make the leg look better is to fold the leading edge back about a foot or so. This will create a smooth, clean edge which is less likely to pick up light from any wrinkles in the seam or any soiled marks.

When folding borders and full drops, which are usually centered on battens, the center line mark is clearly visible when they are folded (see Drawing III-4). Remember to keep the tension between the two" folders" and the air will float the cloth, making the job quite easy.

SOFT SCENERY

Many people forget that soft scenery (curtains, scrims, cycloramas and drops) can be a flexible, relatively inexpensive and easily reusable type of stock scenery. Curtains, scrims and cycs are usually commercially made and purchased through theatrical supply houses. Soft masking can be made in the shop as just discussed.

As can be seen in the Drawing III-5, one of the common characteristics of the drop is the horizontal seam. This is done because the weight of the bottom of the drop (both from the drop itself and any added weight) will help pull out puckers and wrinkles caused by the seam. Vertical seams tend to take the weight and leave "soft" areas between them. However, for some applications, notably translucent drops, vertical seams could be used.

Notice that the sides of the drop are tapered slightly. This will help remove a natural "sag" which occurs on the outer edges. Take great care when hemming the side not to pull and stretch the drop, which is easily done because the cloth is cut on the bias. To achieve the taper, lay the drop face down on a clean floor and smooth it

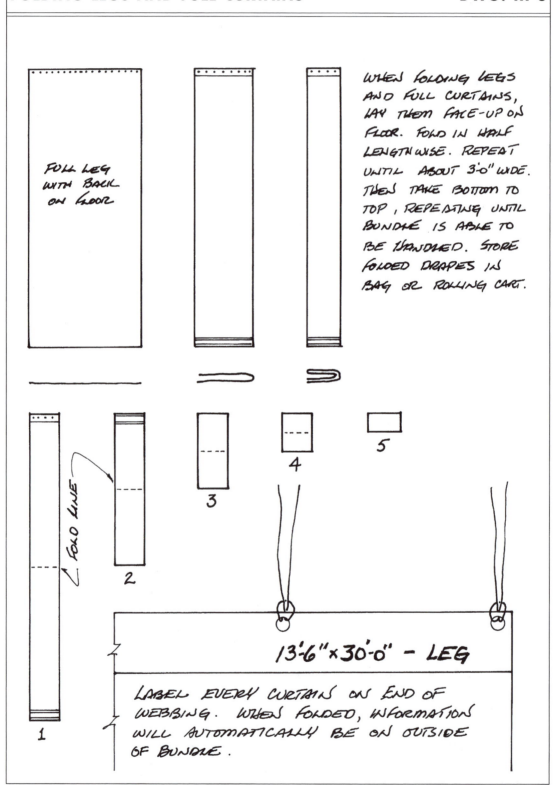

FULL LEG
WITH BACK
ON FLOOR

WHEN FOLDING LEGS
AND FULL CURTAINS,
LAY THEM FACE-UP ON
FLOOR. FOLD IN HALF
LENGTHWISE. REPEAT
UNTIL ABOUT 3'-0" WIDE.
THEN TAKE BOTTOM TO
TOP, REPEATING UNTIL
BUNDLE IS ABLE TO
BE HANDLED. STORE
FOLDED DRAPES IN
BAG OR ROLLING CART.

FOLD LINE

1   2   3   4   5

13'-6" x 30'-0" - LEG

LABEL EVERY CURTAIN ON END OF
WEBBING. WHEN FOLDED, INFORMATION
WILL AUTOMATICALLY BE ON OUTSIDE
OF BUNDLE.

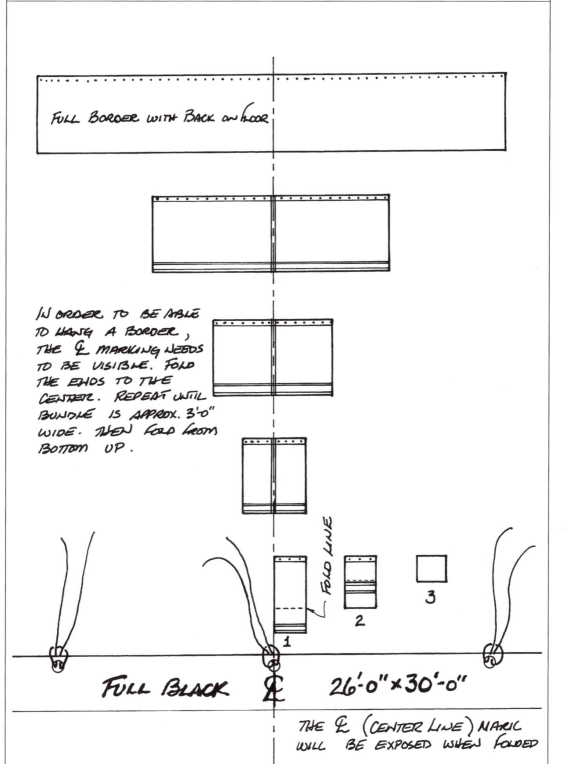

FULL BORDER WITH BACK ON FLOOR

IN ORDER TO BE ABLE
TO HANG A BORDER,
THE ℄ MARKING NEEDS
TO BE VISIBLE. FOLD
THE ENDS TO THE
CENTER. REPEAT UNTIL
BUNDLE IS APPROX. 3'-0"
WIDE. THEN FOLD FROM
BOTTOM UP.

FOLD LINE

1

2

3

FULL BLACK ℄ 26'-0" × 30'-0"

THE ℄ (CENTER LINE) MARK
WILL BE EXPOSED WHEN FOLDED

out. Establish the center and measure out to determine the taper. This is usually no more than one inch for each foot of height. Thus a 30'-0" high drop will taper 2'-6" on each side. Keep the taper in mind when figuring needed width in the finished drop. Once a taper is marked, snap a line on the drop. Before cutting and folding for the hem, a piece of masking tape can be smoothed onto the snapped line. This will help prevent the fabric from stretching when sewn and the tape will end up inside the hem which affects nothing.

TOPS OF DROPS

LAMINATED BATTENS

Once a drop is sewn up, it can be hung from the top by laminating it between a 1 x 3 or 1 x 4 batten (see Drawing III-6). When doing this, snap a line on the floor and lay out the 1 x stock. This line assures a straight top. Staple the drop to the 1 x stock and laminate the second piece over it. Make sure the joints alternate and are well attached. It is possible to drill holes through the laminated batten for the hanging ropes or to tie the batten onto another batten or pipe for flying it. Some shops cut a curved slit beneath the drop about 6" to 8" long, shaping it away from the batten to allow the rope to pass through it and tie around the batten. If you do this, make sure the drop is reinforced with some flexible glue (electric glue gun) where the edge of the cut meets the batten, to prevent it from tearing. Theatrical supply houses sell batten clamps or drop hooks (see Drawing III-6) which are metal jaws that can lock around the batten and offer a ring for hanging the drop. Do not put battens on a drop until it has been painted, because a battened drop is awkward to stretch. This is not a major problem when repainting, because the initial sizing and priming of the drop have already taken place. However, it must be stretched smooth and square and tacked down. It will still shrink some.

WEBBING

A far more efficient method for hanging drops is to use a 3" jute webbing (like the kind upholsterers use to support springs in furniture). Sew this to the top of the drop (see Drawing III-6). Using a grommet kit, which consists of a cutting die, a setting tool and holder, plus the male and female grommets, place a grommet about every 12" across the top of the drop, approximately ½" from the top of the webbing. Make sure there is a grommet at each end. A No. 2 brass grommet is usually sufficient. The hole in this is ⅜", which is adequate to anchor the tie-line (light sash cord—#4 or venetian blind cord). Make sure the tie-lines are long enough to loop and knot (a cow hitch) into the grommet and still go around the pipe or wood batten and then tie in a bow. The bow is for easy striking of the drop. Knots are not fun to untie. A 36" tie when fixed to the drop has about 16" on each end for the bow knot.

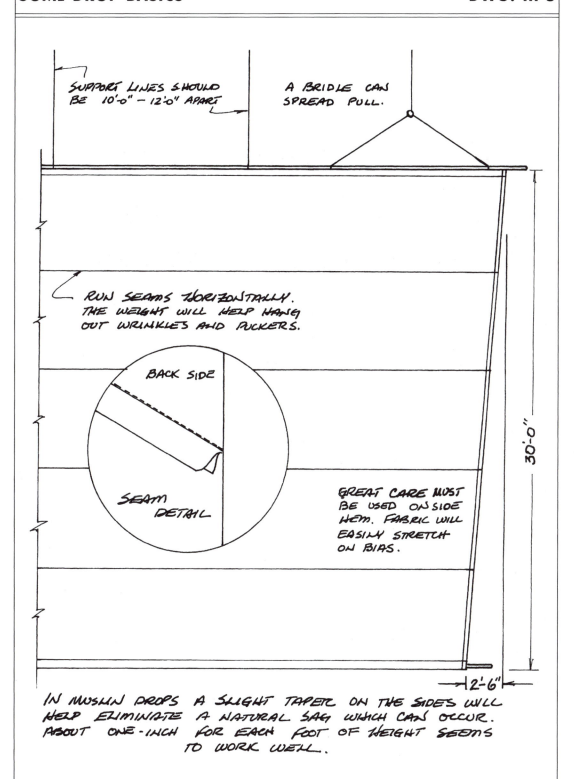

SUPPORT LINES SHOULD BE 10'-0" – 12'-0" APART

A BRIDLE CAN SPREAD PULL.

RUN SEAMS HORIZONTALLY. THE WEIGHT WILL HELP HANG OUT WRINKLES AND PUCKERS.

BACK SIDE

SEAM DETAIL

GREAT CARE MUST BE USED ON SIDE HEM. FABRIC WILL EASILY STRETCH ON BIAS.

30'-0"

2'-6"

IN MUSLIN DROPS A SLIGHT TAPER ON THE SIDES WILL HELP ELIMINATE A NATURAL SAG WHICH CAN OCCUR. ABOUT ONE-INCH FOR EACH FOOT OF HEIGHT SEEMS TO WORK WELL.

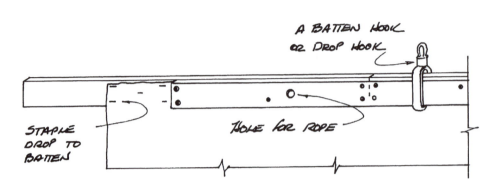

A BATTEN HOOK
OR DROP HOOK

STAPLE
DROP TO
BATTEN

HOLE FOR ROPE

1x3 STOCK CAN BE LAMINATED WITH THE DROP SAND-
WICHED BETWEEN. THIS MAKES A USEFUL (THOUGH RATHER
PERMANENT AND CUMBERSOME) METHOD OF HANGING A
DROP. BE SURE TO ALTERNATE JOINS IN BATTENS. ALSO
ROUND OVER THE OUTSIDE EDGES WITH A ROUTER AND
THE DROP WILL ROLL-UP WITH FEWER CREASES. THE
METHOD DRAWN BELOW ALLOWS FOR BETTER STORAGE.

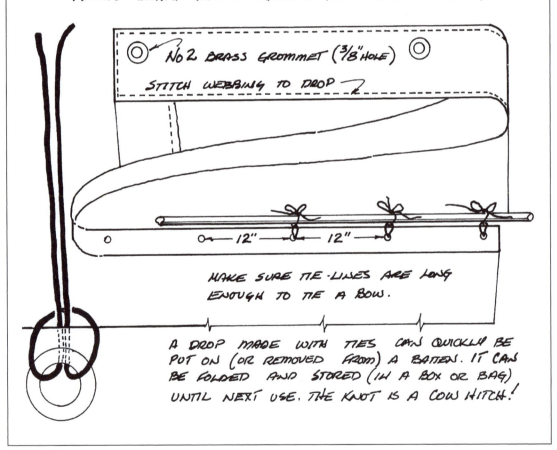

No 2 BRASS GROMMET (3/8" HOLE)

STITCH WEBBING TO DROP

12" — 12"

MAKE SURE TIE-LINES ARE LONG
ENOUGH TO TIE A BOW.

A DROP MADE WITH TIES CAN QUICKLY BE
PUT ON (OR REMOVED FROM) A BATTEN. IT CAN
BE FOLDED AND STORED (IN A BOX OR BAG)
UNTIL NEXT USE. THE KNOT IS A COW HITCH!

DROP BOTTOMS

The above title is not to be misconstrued with a certain flaccid and dragging quality common to the gluteal areas of exhausted stagehands.

LAMINATED BATTEN

This method is usually used on a drop which has a laminated batten on top. The attaching method is similar, but the finished batten should have its edges rounded (see Drawing III-7). A router is the fastest tool for this step, and it can be used before lamination or afterwards if all nails and screws are held back from the edge of the batten. Rounding the bottom batten lessens the wrinkles and creases when the drop is rolled. Battened drops which are for stock must be stored, and their length can be a problem. Many theatres "dead-tie" them to the grid or store them on racks mounted to the back wall or orchestra pit.

POCKETS

Sewing a simple hem in the bottom of a drop is the easiest way to make a pocket (see Drawing III-7). Allow the extra cloth for this hem when figuring the total height of the drop. The pocket can be wide enough to slip in a piece of 1 x 3 stock or pipe. Pipe has the advantage of being heavier than wood, and additional pieces can be coupled on from standard fittings for a continuous length. There are also special foot irons for pipe battens to hold the drop to the floor. These are available from theatrical supply houses, but the design is so basic that any shop can mock up a suitable substitute from strap iron or a wood block.

CHAIN POCKETS

The chain pocket (see Drawing III-7) is exactly like the other hem pockets, but chain is used in place of pipe or wood. This is needed for drops which must conform to irregular shapes, hang in pleats or folds, and for touring situations where it is expedient to leave the weight with the drop to lessen set-up/strike time and avoid carrying pipe. Be sure to pick a heavy but smooth chain. The chain can be "caught" with a needle and thread at several places along the pocket to keep it in place. Many shops encase the chain in a cloth tube and sew the tube into the hem, which suspends the chain in the pocket. This acts very much in the same way as the added pocket. Most chain is coated with oil when bought and must be cleaned before being used. Solvents will work, as will the jet hoses in a car wash. Don't tell your mother, but the dishwasher does a dandy job, too.

ADDED POCKET

As can be seen in the Drawing III-7, the advantage of an added pocket is more than cosmetic. It will allow a drop to "sit" on an irregular or uneven floor and will stop backlight from pouring under the bottom edge. The pocket can be made for any type of batten—wood, pipe or chain. Because this pocket is not dragged against the floor, it will last much longer than one which wears through from the friction.

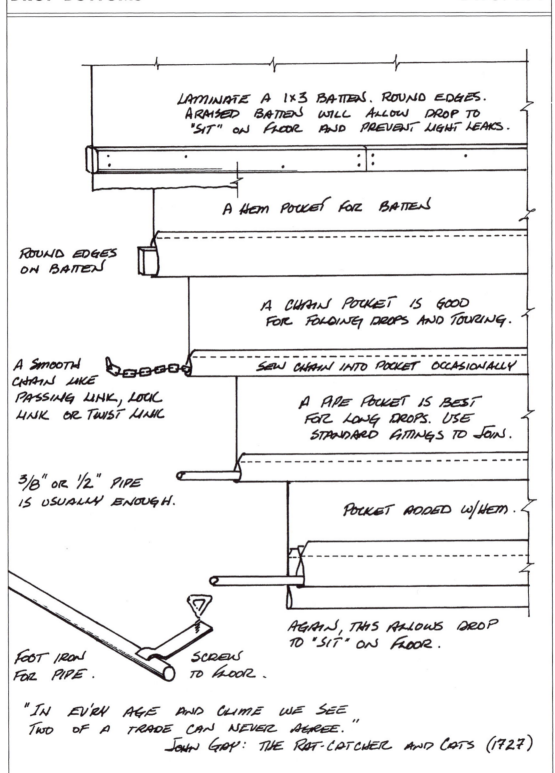

LAMINATE A 1x3 BATTEN. ROUND EDGES. A RAISED BATTEN WILL ALLOW DROP TO "SIT" ON FLOOR AND PREVENT LIGHT LEAKS.

A HEM POCKET FOR BATTEN

ROUND EDGES ON BATTEN

A CHAIN POCKET IS GOOD FOR FOLDING DROPS AND TOURING.

A SMOOTH CHAIN LIKE PASSING LINK, LOCK LINK OR TWIST LINK

SEW CHAIN INTO POCKET OCCASIONALLY

A PIPE POCKET IS BEST FOR LONG DROPS. USE STANDARD FITTINGS TO JOIN.

3/8" OR 1/2" PIPE IS USUALLY ENOUGH.

POCKET ADDED W/HEM.

AGAIN, THIS ALLOWS DROP TO "SIT" ON FLOOR.

FOOT IRON FOR PIPE.

SCREWS TO FLOOR.

"IN EV'RY AGE AND CLIME WE SEE
TWO OF A TRADE CAN NEVER AGREE."
JOHN GAY: THE RAT-CATCHER AND CATS (1727)

TRIP DROPS

Because "form follows function" is a concept which escapes most architects who design theater spaces, is anathema to producers who find "ideal" spaces to convert into theaters and seems unknown to many designers, technical personnel are often faced with drops which are larger than the fly space allows. "Fly space" can usually be defined as the space cut from the building plans to save money.

Two common solutions for inadequate height above the stage are trip drops and roll drops. Drawing III-8 shows a combination of solutions which can be used to trip a drop. Example A shows a drop with just enough height to be flown. When this height is less than needed, the drop can be tripped. A trip line can be attached to the bottom of a drop (Example B) and in combination with raising the batten at the top, lift the drop above sight lines. It is also possible to dead-hang the drop (Example D) and place a trip line in the middle of the drop. This will also pull the drop above sight lines.

If the fly space is less than half the drop height (Example E), a combination of methods B and D could give enough travel. Example F begins to carry the sublime to the ridiculous. In addition to requiring three stagehands to raise and lower the drop, the cost of rigging could begin to suggest the desirability of a roll drop. Example C has rolled his own and is tripping until he drops.

ROLL DROPS

Roll drops are one of the most delightful methods of shifting scenery ever invented (Drawings III-9, 10, 11). There is nothing quite so magical as a scene which can appear or vanish almost instantly. In its theatrical tradition, the roll drop is one of the oldest living relics. De rigueur for melodramas, operettas and many musical comedies, the honesty of its theatricality puts kitchen-sink dramas into their proper ring in the netherworld.

The roll drop is neither difficult nor outrageously expensive to build, rig and operate. It does require a certain amount of time to set up. The three basic components are the drop, the roller and the rigging.

The drop can incorporate many of the methods discussed earlier. The fabric, usually muslin, can be sewn up from narrower pieces. If seams are required, they should be lapped and double stitched to prevent any "bump" when the drop is rolled. The fabric should lap on the front of the drop so the lower piece of cloth is on top (Drawing III-10). This keeps the seam from puckering and does not cast a shadow which "reads" more than the highlight on the top-lapped edge. The top of the drop can have webbing and tie-lines which allow it to be easily recycled back to the paint shop for the next show. The tie-lines also give some adjustability for removing possible sag and pucker in the drop. Always allow enough extra fabric at the bottom of the drop to wrap and attach to the roller.

The roller or drum must be strong, light and rigid. Traditionally made of wood, the roller can still be constructed with circular discs about 6″ in diameter threaded onto a T-shaped batten which helps stabilize them. The discs are fixed to the batten approximately every couple of feet and connected on the circumference with thin

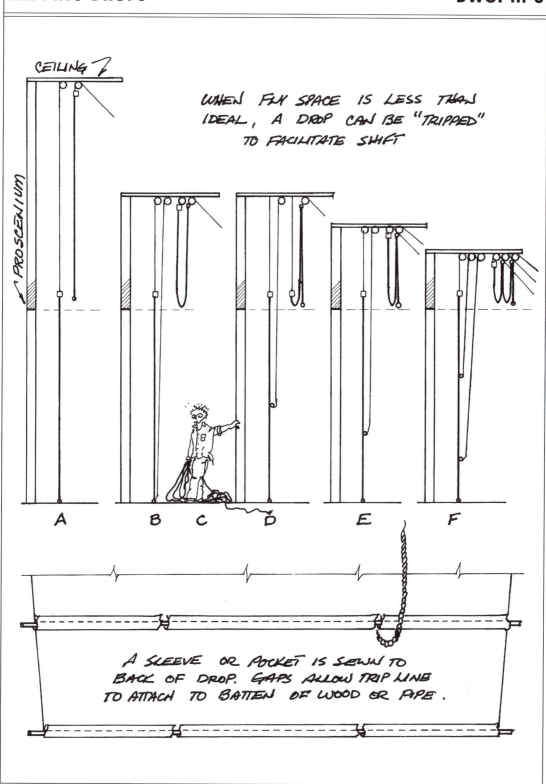

CEILING

PROSCENIUM

WHEN FLY SPACE IS LESS THAN IDEAL, A DROP CAN BE "TRIPPED" TO FACILITATE SHIFT

A   B   C   D   E   F

A SLEEVE OR POCKET IS SEWN TO BACK OF DROP. GAPS ALLOW TRIP LINE TO ATTACH TO BATTEN OF WOOD OR PIPE.

strips of lath. The joints are staggered on the discs. Care must be taken to build the roller straight and free of any deviations in diameter as well as along its length. Once the lath has been attached and the glue dried, the entire unit should be scrimmed with several layers of muslin glued onto the lath and to itself. When this has dried the unit is quite strong and rigid.

There are several tubular products available which can substitute for the shop constructed roller. Sonotube, a trademark of Sonoco, is one of many fiber tubes manufactured. The tubes are made from layers of a paper-like fiber, spirally wound and laminated with special adhesives. When not appearing on stage, these become cement forms, often coated with a wax-like material designed to help the tubing be peeled away once the pour has set. Unfortunately, this coating also resists glue and paint, making it less than compatible for some jobs. Sonotubing can be cut easily with saws and drilled or nailed into. The most common length available is 12'-0" which can be joined with shop-made wood inserts. The six-inch diameter weighs 1.3 lbs per foot and the 8" weights 1.7 lbs. Different brands of fiber forms will, of course, vary and individual dealers will no doubt have several choices available. The adverse conditions of the release coating can be somewhat mitigated by scrimming the tube with muslin which will glue to itself and give a workable surface.

In agricultural areas, a most useful tubing can be found—irrigation pipe. Made of aluminum and available in 40'-0" lengths, it is only slightly heavier than sonotube but its length and lack of waxy finish give it advantage. While not designed to nail or staple into, the surface seems designed for duct-tape. The six-inch tube is amazingly rigid and the four- and five-inch diameter tubing is also viable through the lesser weight and cost. Because of the smaller diameter, thinner tubing requires more rotations to raise or lower the drop.

To figure up and down travel, one rotation of the tube is pi (3.14 etc., etc., etc.) times the diameter. For chatting purposes, use three—thus a 6-inch tube will travel 18 feet for each rotation.

Regardless of the tube selected for a roll drop, the length must be longer than the drop is wide by the space required on each end for the rope to coil and uncoil as the drop moves. This actually requires little space, but it is easier to cut a roller shorter than to add-on. As a general rule of thumb on each end, figure one inch of extra tube length for each wrap of rope. The height of travel divided by three will give you the number of wraps. Add a couple of extra wraps for good luck and you'll be close. The ends of the tube will need a cap. This could be a circle of plywood inserted into the end of the tube with a concentric circle laminated to it which is no wider than the outside diameter of the tube and two thicknesses of the rope being used for the rigging. This will prevent the rope from slipping off the tube. This end cap will need a hole drilled into it for the rope to pass through before it has a figure-8 knot tied into the end (Drawing III-11). Note also that the rope passes through a hole in the side of the tube. When the figure-8 knot is tied and the rope pulled tight, the cap will be held snugly to the roller.

To rig the roll drop start with the longer rope and thread the rope through the hole in the tube and the hole in the end cap. Tie the figure-8 knot and pull it tight. Take a couple of wraps around the roller. Make sure the rope is feeding from the back of the

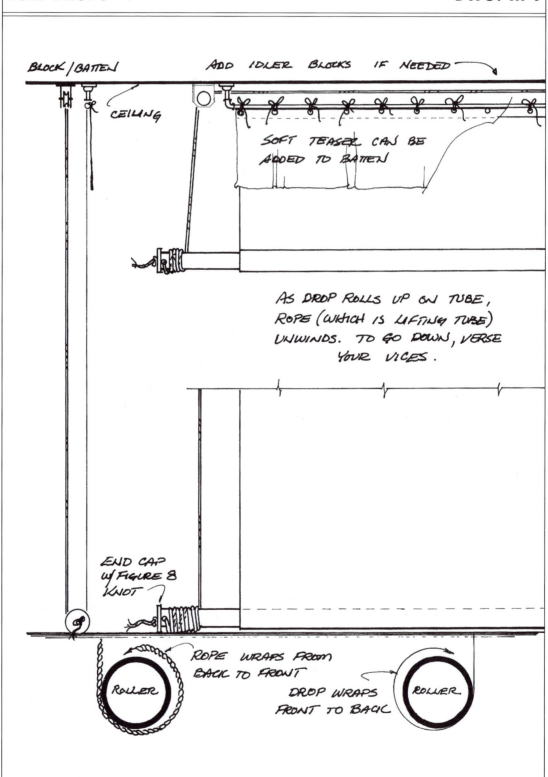

BLOCK/BATTEN

ADD IDLER BLOCKS IF NEEDED

CEILING

SOFT TEASER CAN BE ADDED TO BATTEN

AS DROP ROLLS UP ON TUBE, ROPE (WHICH IS LIFTING TUBE) UNWINDS. TO GO DOWN, VERSE YOUR VICES.

END CAP w/ FIGURE 8 KNOT

ROPE WRAPS FROM BACK TO FRONT

ROLLER

DROP WRAPS FRONT TO BACK

ROLLER

CEILING WITH FLANGE FOR PIPE BATTEN

WEBBING WITH GROMMETS AND TIE LINES HOLD DROP TO BATTEN

SINGLE OR DOUBLE SHEAVE MOUNTS TO CEILING

DOUBLE SHEAVE UNITES BOTH LINES

N.B. — IN DOWN POSITION, LINE IS PARALLEL TO DROP

CHECK PAUL CARTER'S BACKSTAGE HANDBOOK FOR DETAILS ON ROPE SIZES, LOADS AND VARIETIES.

TO SEAM DROP OVER LAP AND DOUBLE STITCH

TIE OFF RAIL W/PINS OR WALL MOUNTED CLEAT

LIFT LINES CAN BE GANGED TOGETHER W/RING OR KNOT

EXTEND DROP FABRIC ENOUGH TO WRAP AROUND ROLLER. TACK, STAPLE OR TAPE TO TUBE.

FOR GRIDLESS THEATRES, UNEVEN CEILINGS, OR ....
2x8 LAGGED INTO CEILING HOLDS DROP (AND BORDERS)
PLUS BLOCKS, PULLEYS AND OTHER REQUIRED HARDWARE.

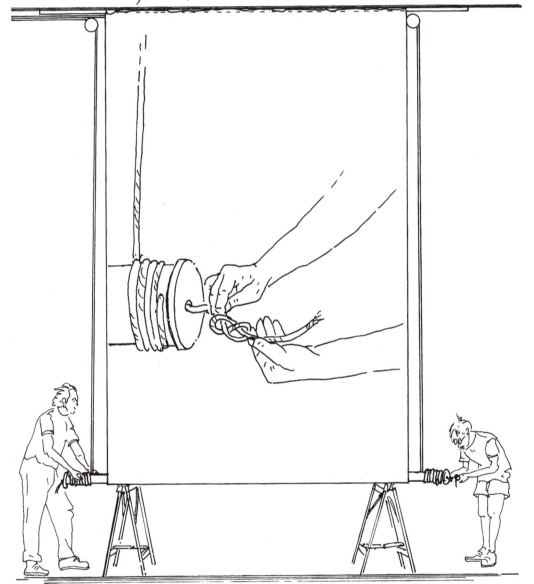

TO ADJUST ROPE TENSION ON ROLLER, REST DROP ON
HORSES AND CORRECT DIFFERENCE IN LINE WITH THE
FIGURE-EIGHT KNOT.

roller—wrapping in the opposite direction of the drop. Now wrap one time for each needed rotation of travel. Pass the line through the pulley at the top and then to the double pulley at the other end. Include any idler pulleys needed. Repeat for the short rope end. After passing through the double pulley, gang the two pull lines together into a ring and attach a single line for moving the drop. You are able to adjust the lines at the ring and at the figure-8 knot on the end-cap. When all rope tension is correct—it may take a few trial rolls to get this—you have one of the most delightfully engineered pieces of scenery ever invented.

PAINTING DROPS

Raw muslin drops must be *stretched square* and *securely tacked* down to a paint frame or the floor before they are painted. Make sure the top and bottom are parallel or the drop will hang askew. Put a staple or tack about every 6″ all around the edge. If working on a floor, make sure it is clean and free of sharp objects. Lay out paper or plastic before painting unless you don't care about the floor. Take care to smooth the plastic so that it is free of wrinkles. The pattern of the wrinkles can transfer to the drop by creating a surface that attracts extra dirt or spray dust. It can also force the paint to dry in puddles.

WEBBING

It will greatly aid in removing drops (and other soft goods) from the floor if there is a length of nylon seat-belt webbing placed between the drop and the floor. Pulling the webbing will "pop" the staples. If you try to pull the muslin drop, it will rip and tear. The nylon webbing can be reused, especially if left in long pieces, and it is a tremendous time (not to mention back) saver. The webbing should be available from any shop which does canvas work.

SIZING

Size the drop with the same wall size solution used for flats, previously discussed, which has been put into a Hudson sprayer. Working with someone else, spray the size on the drop while the other person, using a clean, soft bristle push-broom, spreads the size and forces it into the muslin. It is also propitious to have a third person around who keeps a careful eye on the staples or tacks, making sure that the shrinking drop does not pull them from the floor, and who can quickly remedy the situation should it arise. After the size has dried, proceed with laying out the design and painting. For a semi-transparent or translucent drop, use a starch (Argo) primer instead of size. On transparent drops which need to be partially opaqued or on drops which will later be cut, lay out the design with aniline dye or a bleedable marker so it will bleed through to the back of the drop and facilitate locating the areas which will require the additional work. This opaquing is done after the front is painted and dried.

Drops which have been painted previously do not need to be restretched with the staples as close together for the second painting. However, the drop will still shrink some.

Drops (especially sharkstooth scrims) which are for touring are usually painted with aniline dyes and must be bleached before they can be repainted or the first design will bleed through. Bleaching of drops usually requires a commercial laundry's washing machine and dryer.

CUT DROPS

Cut drops (see Drawing III-8), commonly used for foliage but equally applicable for any open work, are giant, time-consuming pains. However, nothing does the job as effectively or "theatrically." The netting is 100% cotton with a 1″ mesh. It is available, at considerable expense, from theatrical supply houses (see p. 268 for dealer information). The netting must be dyed to match whatever is behind the netted opening in order to "disappear" and allow the applied pieces to "float."

After the drop has been painted, the openings are cut and the drop is carefully stretched flat, with the face to the floor. The cutout areas, if any, are set in place. The dyed netting is stretched over the back of the drop so the stretched strings in the net run in a grid which is perpendicular and parallel to the top of the drop. It is very important that the netting be taut or the cut areas will sag when the drop is flown, for the net is taking the weight and stress once held by the removed muslin. Bricks or stage weights are excellent "hands" to hold the net in place until glued.

GLUING THE NET

Make sure the net is glued to the drop at each knot closest to the cut edge. It is good to periodically glue the net in the middle of large, uncut areas also, to keep it held to the drop. The electric glue gun provides an excellent, quick but expensive glue to attach the net. A flexible glue in a squeeze bottle will also work, but it will take much longer to dry. Do not use a glue which, when dry, makes a sharp, razor-like edge, or you chance cutting the net and drop when folding it for storage.

There are two fairly common materials which can pinch hit for cotton mesh. One is plastic, called birdnetting. This is found in garden supply centers and is designed for covering trees and the like. It is large, cheap and shiny. A second product which can be glued to the cut area is charcoal-colored fiber-glass window screen. Available in 6′–0″ widths, it will fold up with the drop; not happily, but it will fold.

CUTTING EXCESS NET

When cutting away excess netting, make sure you leave sufficient vertical strands of net to carry pieces lower on the drop. If in doubt, leave more than you think necessary and trim after the drop is flown.

Netted drops tend to crease and curl on the cut edges, exposing the back of the drop. It is, therefore, advisable to backpaint the drop before painting the front if time permits. This involves several flippings of surfaces (sizing/flip/back painting/flip/front painting, etc.) and is often more work than getting up on a ladder and bending back the offending edges with one's dainty little digits.

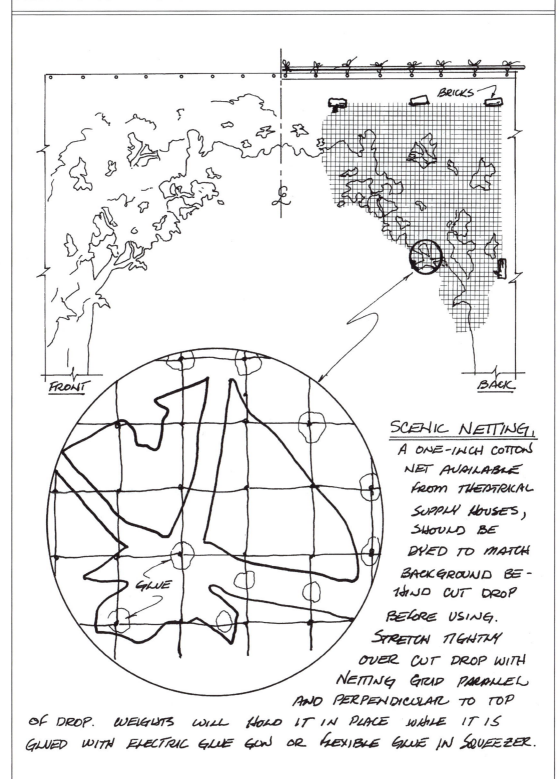

FRONT

BACK

BRICKS

GLUE

SCENIC NETTING, A ONE-INCH COTTON NET AVAILABLE FROM THEATRICAL SUPPLY HOUSES, SHOULD BE DYED TO MATCH BACKGROUND BEHIND CUT DROP BEFORE USING. STRETCH TIGHTLY OVER CUT DROP WITH NETTING GRID PARALLEL AND PERPENDICULAR TO TOP OF DROP. WEIGHTS WILL HOLD IT IN PLACE WHILE IT IS GLUED WITH ELECTRIC GLUE GUN OR FLEXIBLE GLUE IN SQUEEZER.

PART IV • PLATFORMS

There are two basic types of platforms: the rigid platform and the parallel or folding platform. Both types serve the same goals—to elevate actors and scenery. Both types, to be efficient in a stock situation, must conform to certain rules and regulations. Major among these are a consideration of the platform's surface dimensions, which must be compatible with the physical space of the theatre, the stock scenery of that theatre (flats, stair units, curtains, etc.), and the ever-popular team of time, money, and personnel. Many theatres base their stock platform standard on the 4'-0" x 8'-0" sheet of plywood. And why not, inasmuch as the plywood sheet is probably the most limiting of all elements, though the most constant and available.

SIZE LIMITATIONS

Probably the most restrictive limitations which can be placed on the sizes of stock platforms, reducing their number to a minimum, yet still giving good flexibility to the designer, are shown on Drawing IV-1. This allows 8'-0" as the maximum length (logical, isn't it?) and decreases it in two-foot increments. 4'-0" is the maximum width (again, isn't practicality the mother of logic?) with a decreasing increment of 1'-0". Thus, platforms can be 2'-0", 4'-0", 6'-0" and 8'-0" long and 1'-0", 2'-0", 3'-0" and 4'-0" wide. These sizes, with the addition of certain diagonally-cut platforms, give a very flexible stock. Of course "unusual shapes" will be needed on occasion, and these can be kept or discarded at the end of production, depending upon storage space. Often unusual platforms become stock. Examples which immediately come to mind are curved pieces which combine with stock platforms to make large circles or revolves (see Drawing IV-7 and IV-9), and possibly a set of platforms which mocks the curves of the stage apron or the audience seats to use at the end of a thrust stage or as an apron extension. Remember that anything which is built for many re-usings is a good example of stock.

The Drawing IV-2 shows how the previous drawing of platforms was derived using a 1'-0" module. Also shown are two other modules, one creating larger platforms utilizing an entire 4' x 8' sheet of plywood and the other, using the same methods, creating odd-sized platforms which can still group into useful combinations. This last method would certainly affect the size of stock flats and stairs.

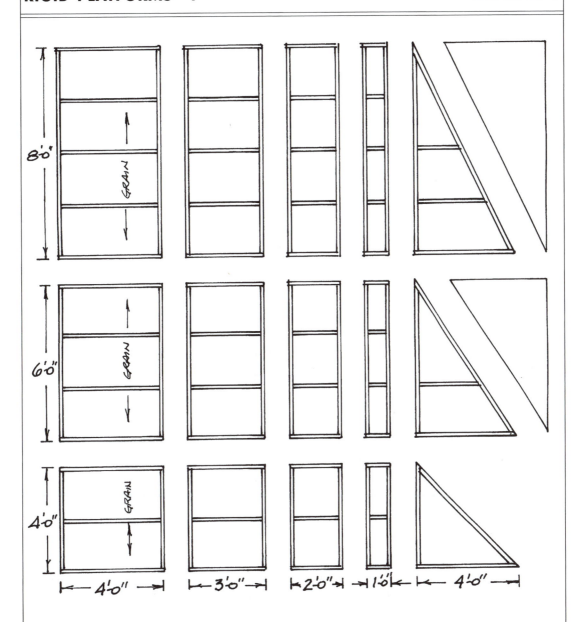

THE 17 RIGID PLATFORMS ABOVE ARE BASED ON THE 4×8
SHEET OF PLYWOOD. THEY WERE PLANNED ON A 1-FOOT
MODULE. ADDITIONAL PIECES COULD EASILY BE ADDED:
3×3, 2×3, 1×3 — 2×2, 1×2 — DIAGONALS OF OTHER
SIZES. PRODUCTION DEMANDS WILL DICTATE HOW MANY
OF EACH WILL BE BUILT. HOWEVER A "MASTER PLAN"
IS HELPFUL FOR THE DESIGNER AND TECHNICAL STAFF.

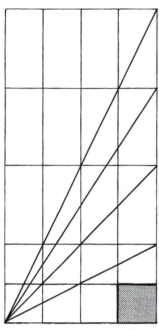

4 x 8 SHEET

A 1'-0" MODULE
WILL GIVE GOOD
FLEXIBILITY AND
ALLOWS INTERES-
TING COMBINATIONS.
THIS MODULE IS
UTILIZED FOR
DRAWING IV-1.

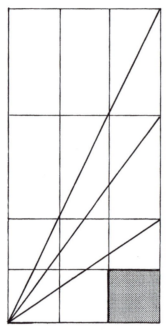

4 x 8 SHEET

A 1'-4" MODULE
CREATES FEWER
PIECES TO HAVE IN
STOCK. HOWEVER,
EACH UNIT IS A
USEFUL SHAPE.

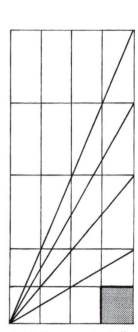

3'-9" x 7'-6"
(½ + ¼ OF 30' x 30')
AN 11¼" MODULE
(DERIVED FROM
A 30' x 30' STAGE)
CREATES SHAPES
WHICH WILL RE-
LATE BACK TO
STAGE AREA.

NOTE THAT ALL THE BREAKDOWNS ARE BASED ON A
SHAPE WHICH IS TWICE AS LONG AS IT IS WIDE. THIS WILL
CREATE A STOCK OF PLATFORMS WHICH WILL RE-COMBINE
IN USEFUL AND EFFICIENT SHAPES.

REMEMBER STOCK PLATFORMS SHOULD RELATE IN SIZE TO
STOCK FLATS AND STEP UNITS. BECAUSE THE 4x8 SHEET OF
PLYWOOD IS SO COMMON AND USEFUL, IT HAS BE-
COME THE MAJOR DETERMINING FACTOR. HOWEVER,
DON'T ACCEPT THIS IF CIRCUMSTANCES DICTATE OTHERWISE.

RIGID PLATFORMS

Rigid platforms are boxes with solid sides, inner supports, and a nonremovable top (see Drawing IV-3). The most common ones are constructed with a frame of on-edge lumber and a plywood top. Usually these are made with either 2 x 4, 1 x stock, or for professional and some touring situations, 1⅛″ or ⁵⁄₄ stock. A sheet of ¾″ plywood is the most common top material, but many people prefer ⅝″ plywood for the slight loss of weight. Actually, ½″ plywood will work, but it does have an unsettling "give" in it which needs to be reinforced with additional supports, thus perhaps defeating its savings of weight and cost. I have seen platforms with ⅜″ plywood tops in a grade school. Particle board is usable… cost vs. weight…

The advantages of 2 x 4 construction lie in the availability of the wood, the "thinness" of the finished platform (for storage) and little else. These platforms are unnecessarily heavy, awkward to build without large pneumatic nailers, and always look like rejected concrete forms which ambled in from a construction site. However, they do the job. 1 x stock offers certain advantages (and disadvantages) over the 2 x 4 method. The major advantage is its lighter weight. A platform of 1 x stock, 5¼″ wide (with a ¾″ top it becomes 6″ high) is considerably lighter than a 2 x 4 unit (a 1 x 7″ frame is closer to a 2 x 4 in weight). There is an additional advantage to being 6″ high when finished. This height is the most common rise for stock steps in theatre, making it a compatible partner. It is certainly easier to work the 1 x stock for construction, but the platforms do occupy more storage space per unit. The major drawback is the necessity of a fairly good grade of carefully chosen lumber. The framing in a 1 x stock platform must be free of all knots except for the tightest and smallest ones.

The remaining diatribe on Rigid Platforms uses the 1 x 5¼″ method for all examples, primarily because of the weight advantage over 2 x 4, but also out of a stubborn desire to leave construction materials at the building site where they properly belong. Besides, it is the only time 2 x 4 lumber would need to be in the shop except for special designer requirements. Framing of ⁵⁄₄ stock, ideally pine, is so expensive that it is practically dreaming to even discuss it. But, for permanent scenery and in situations where units take a great deal of abuse (touring) or are expected to last for many, many years (which is almost the same), ⁵⁄₄ stock is an ideal building material. It is stronger proportionately to its weight than almost anything else. It can be used in the same ways as 1 x stock by shifting dimensions to take into account its increased thickness.

CONSTRUCTION TECHNIQUES

Regardless of the lumber stock being used for the framing (even, cough, 2 x 4), it is necessary to standardize construction for rigid platforms if they are to be effectively used in a stock situation. Settle on a set "toggle" or cross-member placement. One at least every 2′-0″ is quite good. Those closer are usually unnecessary with a ¾″ plywood top, and farther apart (2′-8″) tend to encourage some "spring." The 2′-0″ measurement is compatible with the length changes suggested earlier, and also prevents most problems with legging and matching castered units to the platforms, which can be seen in a later section of this handbook. A construction method to follow is shown and explained in some detail (see Drawing IV-5). This method will work for all rigid platforms. Drawing IV-4 offers some alternatives to the standard butt joint in platform construction. Though each is stronger, the additional labor, materials and time must be considered.

THE ALL PLYWOOD PLATFORM

If a platform does not need to be higher than 48″, and storage is no problem, perhaps a rigid platform with ¾″ plywood frames is a good solution. As shown (see Drawing IV-6), the ends and sides are made with plywood which has had much of its weight removed by cutting in lightening holes. This creates a frame which has a top "rail" and center support about 6″ wide and the remaining framework about 4″ wide. The cross members under the top are 1 x 6, much stronger (and lighter) than the same size piece of plywood, and the 1 x stock has a better edge onto which to attach the top. Note the glue block in the corners. An excellent strip can be cut from 2 x stock. It should run from the bottom of the foot to slightly below the top. This assures it does not push the lid away from the frame.

Because the frames are always being attached to the edge of the plywood, which has little holding power, pneumatic staplers are ideal for fastening; however, screws or nails will also work.

Once the frame is together and the lid is secured, the glue blocks can be mounted into the corners. Make sure they are well glued and attached. Some shops screw them from the outside at the corner, utilizing the drawing ability of the screw to snugly pull in the block. Once the glue has set, the corner is quite strong.

Notice also the raised notch at the bottom of Drawing IV-6; this removes the bulk of the unit from the floor, which will prevent any rocking due to unevenness, and adds a handy grip if the unit is faced. This notch, which is time consuming to cut (and, for some, difficult to do accurately), can be eliminated by attaching a foot of 1 x stock to the bottom. This is a slightly faster method, but remember to deduct the thickness of the foot from the height of the unit when laying out the frames.

If weight is a real concern, the framework and lid can both be made from ½″ plywood. Extreme care must be used when attaching the pieces to prevent the plywood from separating between the veneers. Additional cross-members will probably be needed to help support the weight of the top. Some compare these platforms with eating artichokes; when finished, indeed, there does appear to be more material left over from the lightening holes than in the product itself.

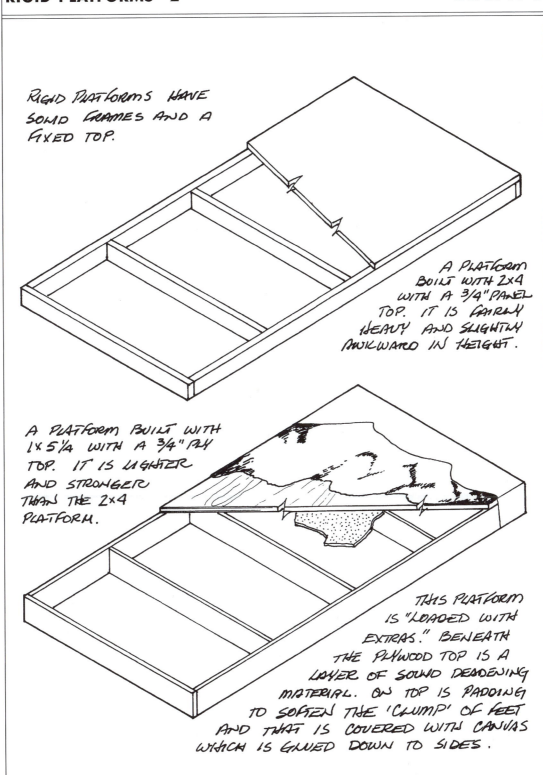

RIGID PLATFORMS HAVE SOLID FRAMES AND A FIXED TOP.

A PLATFORM BUILT WITH 2x4 WITH A 3/4" PANEL TOP. IT IS FAIRLY HEAVY AND SLIGHTLY AWKWARD IN HEIGHT.

A PLATFORM BUILT WITH 1 x 5 1/4 WITH A 3/4" PLY TOP. IT IS LIGHTER AND STRONGER THAN THE 2x4 PLATFORM.

THIS PLATFORM IS "LOADED WITH EXTRAS." BENEATH THE PLYWOOD TOP IS A LAYER OF SOUND DEADENING MATERIAL. ON TOP IS PADDING TO SOFTEN THE 'CLUMP' OF FEET AND THAT IS COVERED WITH CANVAS WHICH IS GLUED DOWN TO SIDES.

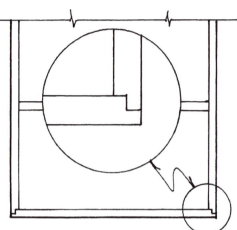

ON PLATFORMS MADE OF
2×4 STOCK A RABBETED
JOINT WILL ADD CON-
SIDERABLE STRENGTH TO
THE FRAMES.

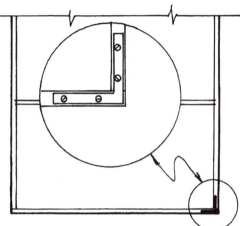

ON 1× STOCK A FLAT ANGLE
IRON SCREWED INTO THE
EDGE WILL HOLD JOINT.
THIS MUST BE "LET-IN"
TO FRAME OR IT WILL
AFFECT HEIGHT.

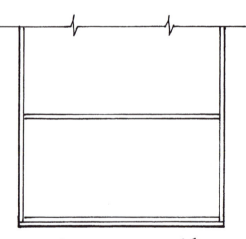

A 'FALSE RABBET' (NOT
THE PHONY CONY) MADE
BY LAMINATING AN
ADDITIONAL PIECE OF
1× STOCK WILL CERTAINLY
'BEEF-UP' FRAME. IT WILL
AFFECT LEG PLACEMENT.

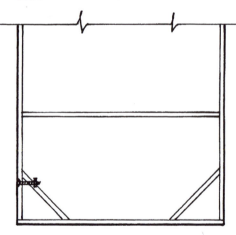

A "CORNER BRACE" MADE
OF 1× STOCK CAN BE
BOLTED INTO PLACE FOR
AN EXTREMELY STRONG
CORNER. ALLOW ENOUGH
SPACE IN CORNER TO
BE ABLE TO ATTACH LEGS.

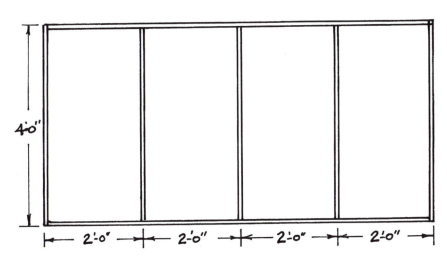

4'-0"

|← 2'-0" →|← 2'-0" →|← 2'-0" →|← 2'-0" →|

TO ATTACH PLYWOOD (OR OTHER PANEL BOARD)
FOLLOW THE FOUR STEPS BELOW. YOU ONLY
NEED A FASTENER (NAIL, STAPLE, SCREW) ABOUT
EVERY 12 -18 INCHES.

1. GLUE THE FRAME. LAY
THE PLY ON AND FLUSH ONE
CORNER. ATTACH A LONG SIDE.

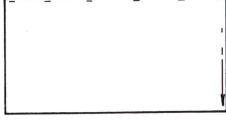

2. RACK FRAME TO FIT PLY.
FROM ORIGINAL CORNER,
ATTACH SHORT SIDE.

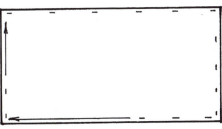

3. PROCEED AROUND FRAME
ATTACHING TOP.

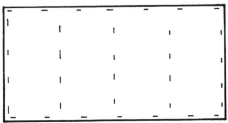

4. MARK AND ATTACH INSIDE
MEMBERS.

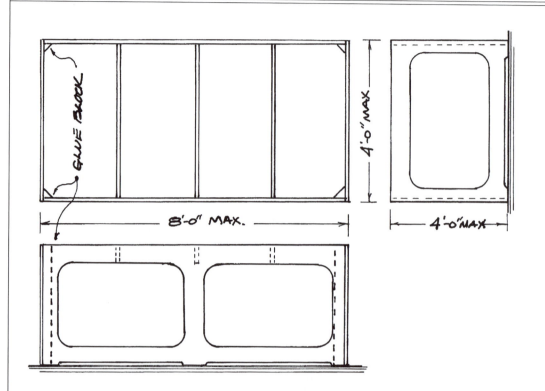

THE NAME IS A BIT DECEPTIVE BECAUSE THE INSIDE
SUPPORTS FOR THE TOP ARE 1x6 BUT THE FRAME-
WORK IS ALL PLYWOOD. IT IS FAIRLY LIGHT, STRONG
AND NOT COMPLICATED TO BUILD. BUT, IT IS BULKY
TO STORE. 3/4" PLY IS GOOD. HOWEVER, WITH CARE,
1/2" PLY CAN BE USED.

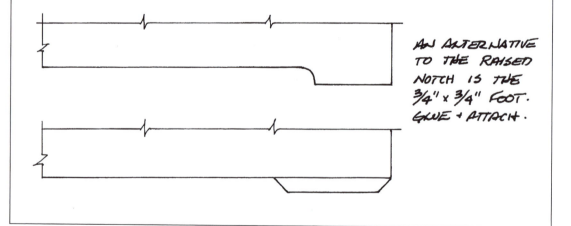

AN ALTERNATIVE
TO THE RAISED
NOTCH IS THE
3/4" x 3/4" FOOT.
GLUE + ATTACH.

IRREGULAR PLATFORMS

One of the easiest ways to ensure an accurately built platform with unusual angles is to loft up the desired shape on the piece of ¾" plywood which will become the lid. Cut out the piece as drawn. With a marking pen, chalk, heavy pencil or blood, label in large, unmistakable letters TOP. Flip the plywood over and write BOTTOM. This is not subtle, but safe. Next, lay out the necessary framing members on the plywood (BOTTOM side) and cut the 1 x stock to fit. Angles can be cut on the table saw, large band saw, circular saw or, God help us, with a hand saw. As the framing members are cut, glue and attach them. When the frame is completed, flip it over and glue and attach the ¾" plywood top. Use coated nails, ring nails or staples for the best hold. The finished platform had better have TOP on top or…

CURVED PLATFORMS

Curved platforms (see Drawings IV-7, IV-8 and IV-9) present another variation on the never-ending battle of trying to ignore the 4 x 8 sheet of plywood. Again (see Drawing IV-8), loft up the desired shape on ¾" plywood and mark the TOP and BOTTOM. With the BOTTOM side up, scribe a line ¾" inside the curved edge. Lay out the framing for the straight sides and the inner members and make sure they stay behind the ¾" line. Where possible, conform to standard platforming rules. Attach the straight members of the frame to the plywood lid.

TRIANGULAR GLUE BLOCKS

Next, cut triangles of 1 x stock which are 5¼" high and long (this assumes you are building with 1 x 5¼" stock in your stock platforms). A 5¼" by 5¼" block cut on the diagonal works quite well. Attach these blocks (see Drawing IV-7) to the plywood, with the grain of the 1 x block running perpendicular to the lid and the vertical side on the ¾" line which was scribed on the plywood. Make sure the blocks are tangent or as close to 90° as possible to the curved line. These blocks are usually 8" to 12" apart, depending upon the severity of the curve.

Next, take ¼" plywood and cut strips across the grain (the 4'-0" direction on the full sheet) which are 5¼" wide. Cut sufficient strips to travel the curve three times plus some extra for matching joints and breakage.

LAMINATING PLYWOOD CURVES

Take the first piece of ¼" plywood and center it on a triangular block or on the end of an inner frame member inside the platform. The other end should extend past the end of the platform (see Drawing IV-8). Put glue on the blocks and on the edge of the plywood which will touch the ¾" plywood lid. Force the plywood to follow the prescribed line and attach it to the triangular glue blocks. A pneumatic or electric stapler is a wonderful tool for this job, but small nails or screws will work. Take a second piece of plywood and start it at the center of the block, butting against the end of the first piece. Continue bending it around, following the curved line which is ¾" in from the edge. If it does not pass the end of the platform, cut it off so it "breaks" on the center of a triangular block or inner frame member. Attach it like the first piece. Continue until one strip of ¼″ plywood is on the entire curve of the platform.

The second layer of plywood is attached in a similar manner, except that the entire surface of the first piece of plywood and the surface of this one are glued together. A tight fit against the first piece is the goal. Use standard wood glue (Elmer's, Wilhold, etc.) to which just a bit of water is added. Apply liberally with a brush or small roller to both faces to be glued. Be sure the joints start and stop on the center of the triangular block or center on the end of the frame member, and be especially sure to stagger these breaks on different layers. The third and final layer is applied in the same way. If there are slight gaps in between the plywood layers, be sure to clamp them or somehow get them together while the glue is still wet.

Once the plywood lamination has dried (overnight is best), remove all clamps, etc., and trim away the overhanging edges to flush with the contour of the platform. You may, if you wish (though there is absolutely no reason to do so), remove the triangular glue blocks and the curved edge would not change its shape. It is, indeed, probably stronger and more stable than the 1 x stock framing to which it is attached. Once the platform is finished, it can be padded, covered and back-painted. It is also able to utilize stock legs and stock-castered pieces in the same way as any straight-sided platform.

COVERING PLATFORMS

As Drawing IV-3 indicates, there are several finishes available for platforms. They should be consistent in your stock.

CARPET

Some theatres automatically cover their platforms with a neutral, and usually fairly dark, felt-type indoor/outdoor carpet. This is glued to the top of the platform with carpet mastic and helps deaden the "clump" of actors. (This term is not to be confused with a "thud" of dancers or even a "draft" of designers.) While carpeting creates an attractive, uniform and quiet stage floor, it is not paintable. A ground cloth is required if the surface must be painted and coordinated into the design scheme.

CANVAS

Other theatres cover their platform tops with a commercial carpet pad (hair mat, not foam rubber) and then cover that with canvas or duck. This not only deadens the sound, but gives a paintable surface. It is also quite expensive. It is possible to glue carpet to the platform with the back side up. This gives a solid surface and the pile of the carpet is the major deadening agent. The entire platform is again covered with duck to give a paintable surface. This requires tremendous "quality control" over the carpet used, because it is usually secondhand carpet and thus free. Check carefully that all thicknesses are constant or the stage will take on overtones of a cobblestoned street.

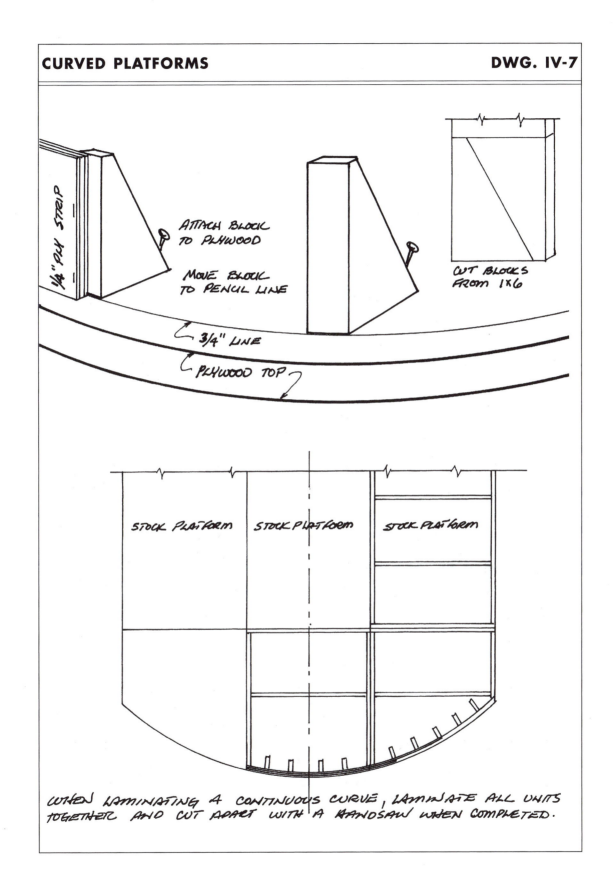

¼" PLY STRIP

ATTACH BLOCK
TO PLYWOOD

MOVE BLOCK
TO PENCIL LINE

CUT BLOCKS
FROM 1X6

3/4" LINE

PLYWOOD TOP

STOCK PLATFORM   STOCK PLATFORM   STOCK PLATFORM

WHEN LAMINATING A CONTINUOUS CURVE, LAMINATE ALL UNITS
TOGETHER AND CUT APART WITH A BANDSAW WHEN COMPLETED.

THE STEPS BELOW WORK WELL FOR ALL CURVED
PLATFORMS. ALWAYS ALLOW 24 HOURS FOR GLUE
TO SET WHEN LAMINATING. YOU CAN'T HURRY THIS JOB.

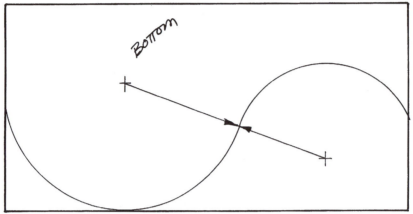

WHEN DOING LAY OUT WORK ON A PLATFORM,
MAKE SURE TO MARK THE "BOTTOM" OF THE
SHEET... YOU THEN HAVE NO EXCUSE FOR BUILDING
ON THE WRONG SIDE. CUT OUT THE PLATFORM TOP.

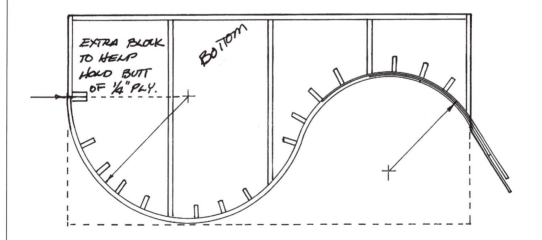

DRAW A LINE 3/4" FROM THE CUT EDGE. THIS
WILL HELP SET ALL OTHER PIECES. LAYOUT
FRAMING (WHICH CONFORMS TO STANDARDS SET
FOR STOCK PLATFORMS). SHAPE ENDS TO FIT 3/4"
LINE. SET BLOCKS TO LINE. ATTACH FRAME +
BLOCKS. NEXT GLUE AND ATTACH 1/4" PLY STRIPS.

THE CIRCULAR PLATFORM BELOW IS MADE UP OF STOCK PLATFORMS AND 8 SHALLOW ARCS. IF THE CIRCLE IS TO BE USED MORE THAN ONCE, THE ARCS COULD BECOME STOCK. IF NOT... DUMPSTER FOOD!

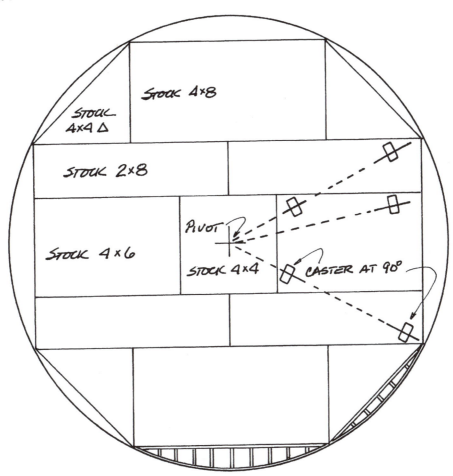

STOCK 4×8

STOCK 4×4 △

STOCK 2×8

STOCK 4×6

PIVOT

STOCK 4×4

CASTER AT 90°

BECAUSE THE ARCS ARE SO NARROW IT IS EASIER TO USE 1×STOCK FOR ALL THE INTERNAL PIECES. SHAPE THE ENDS TO THE 3/4" LINE AND LAMINATE 1/4" PLY. ON SHALLOW CURVES LIKE THESE IT IS POSSIBLE TO USE STRIPS CUT 8'-0" LONG. TRY ONE TO SEE.

IF THIS UNIT IS CASTERED AND HAS A PIVOT POINT, NON SWIVEL CASTERS MUST BE SET AT A RIGHT ANGLE (90°) TO A RADIUS LINE.

SOUND-DEADENING MATERIALS

It is possible to put the sound-deadening materials beneath the platform. Commercial materials designed for walls and ceilings are available at many lumberyards. These materials can be cut to fit and glued with the proper mastic to the bottom of the lid between the platform's framework. Some insulating foam sheets can be effectively used here also. One advantage of laminating these products beneath the lid is the ability to use thinner panel products for creating the platform top. The drop from ¾″ plywood to ½″ is a considerable weight difference, rarely equalled by the additional sound-deadening materials, especially foam. It is worth building a prototype to see just how much weight loss can be gained for the sound deadening achieved. If a totally silent platform is required, give up. Such a thing existed only in movies made before *The Jazz Singer*.

WEAKNESSES IN PLATFORMS

Never stand inside an inverted platform. This is contrary to the use for which they were designed, and the plywood can easily be separated from the frame. If you must walk on the back of a platform, do so on the frame. People who stand in platforms go to the same lower regions as those who leave ratchet screwdrivers open on the floor.

STEP LEGS

Of all the methods devised for legging stock platforms (and other units), the step leg is undoubtedly the most efficient and satisfactory (see Drawing IV-10). The step is a two (or more) part animal. The step is the piece of 1 x 3 which sits under the frame of the platform and runs to the floor. A second piece of 1 x 3 laminates to the back of the step piece and travels from the floor to inside the frame of the platform and is bolted to the frame. Additional "steps" can be applied to the sides (see Drawing IV-11). The major advantage the step leg has over its ugly stepsisters is that it supports the platform from the bottom of the frame and not from within the frame itself. It is also capable of supporting the ends and inner members of the frame at the same time (side steps). It is firmly held to the platform, easily standardized for stock situations, and does not push against the platform lid. How can you argue?

CONSTRUCTION

The length of the step is the desired height of the platform minus the thickness of the platform. The length of the laminated extension piece is the step length plus the width of the platform frame stock minus ¼″. This ¼″ difference assures a gap between the leg and the top of the platform. Thus the frame will sit on the step and the top cannot be pushed from the frame. For example, assume the platform is made of 1 x 5¼″ stock with a ¾″ plywood top. If you want to elevate the platform 36″ you would have a 30″ step (36″ minus the 6″ total platform thickness) and the laminated extension piece would be 35″ (30″ step plus 5¼″ frame minus ¼″ gap at the top). If additional steps are desired on the side of the leg (see Drawing IV-11), and they are certainly recommended, make them of 1 x 1½″ stock the length of the other step. Glue and attach these to the basic step leg.

On long legs, you can conserve material if you shorten the side steps to about 16″. These shorter pieces can be made ahead from scrap and stored until needed. This is another excellent way to use scrap materials and fill those rare lagging hours.

HEIGHTS OF LEGS

Step legs can be any height—well, any reasonable height. However, after 7′-0″ they can become awkward to attach, because it is easiest to do this with the platform inverted. However, they can be put on, properly crossbraced, and the unit carefully inverted. A 12′-0″ leg offers the same support as a 2″ one (see Drawing IV-13). Note that on very tall legs a horizontal batten is run around the legs for additional support.

STANDARD BOLT HOLES

To make the step leg and platforms as flexible as possible, it is best to standardize the holes used for bolting them on. Two jigs or templates (see Drawing IV-12) will aid in this. They can be made in any metal shop from ¼″ steel. One slips over the extension on the leg and the other slips over the frame of the platform. Both have ⁵⁄₁₆″ holes which must correspond. By drilling a ⁵⁄₁₆″ hole and using a ¼″ flat head stove bolt to hold the leg to the frame, there is enough "slop" to assure the inter-changing of legs and still have the frame seat itself solidly on the step. Make sure the head of the bolt is sucked into the frame so the platforms can butt tightly. The bolt can be pulled in with the nut and a little friendly persuasion from a hammer.

LEGGING TALL PLATFORMS

A platform is legged while it is resting upside down on its lid. With shorter legs it is easy to lift the legged unit and flip it over. NEVER roll over a platform on its unbraced legs, because the legs, or the frame, or both, will surely split apart. Always lift and flip without putting pressure on the legs. Excessively tall platforms (see Drawing IV-14) need to have their legs partially cross-braced before turning them upright. This allows the legs (which become the pivot for raising the unit) enough rigidity not to bend or give. Note the horizontal piece which transfers the support of the bracing to the opposite leg. Other bracing, if needed, can be added after the uprighted platform has been moved into place. The platforms at the bottom of Drawing IV-13 indicate another way of bracing to pivot the unit.

STORING STEP LEGS

A stock of legs will accumulate quickly. Mark the length of the step in inches on the bottom of the leg. When the legs are stored on their sides, it is easy to inventory them. It is also a sure way to know if the leg has been shortened, because the old size has been cut off.

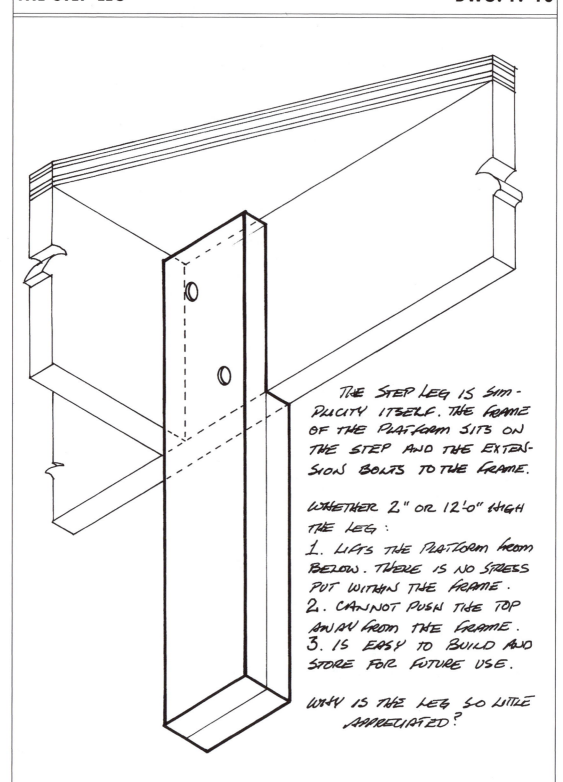

THE STEP LEG IS SIM-
PLICITY ITSELF. THE FRAME
OF THE PLATFORM SITS ON
THE STEP AND THE EXTEN-
SION BOLTS TO THE FRAME.

WHETHER 2" OR 12'-0" HIGH
THE LEG:
1. LIFTS THE PLATFORM FROM
BELOW. THERE IS NO STRESS
PUT WITHIN THE FRAME.
2. CANNOT PUSH THE TOP
AWAY FROM THE FRAME.
3. IS EASY TO BUILD AND
STORE FOR FUTURE USE.

WHY IS THE LEG SO LITTLE
APPRECIATED?

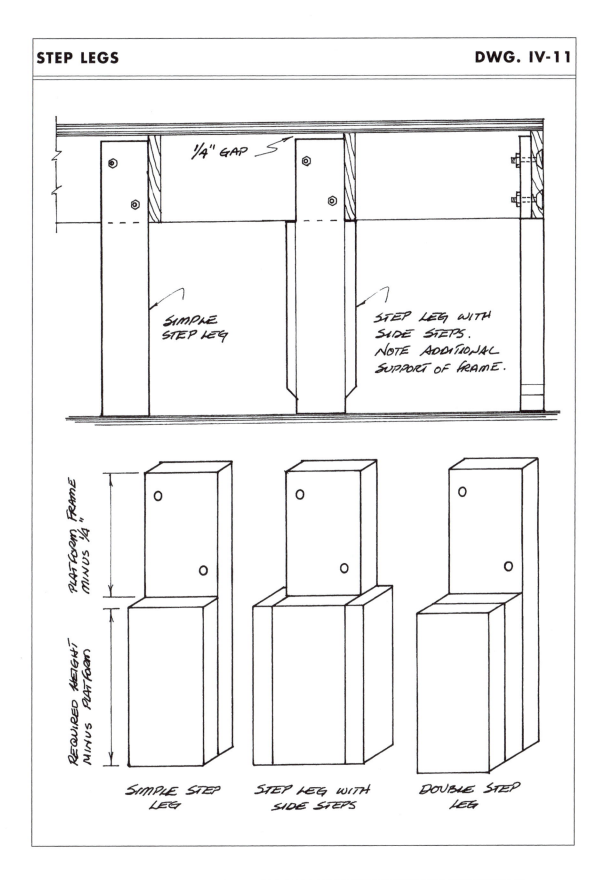

¼" GAP

SIMPLE
STEP LEG

STEP LEG WITH
SIDE STEPS.
NOTE ADDITIONAL
SUPPORT OF FRAME.

PLATFORM FRAME
MINUS ¼"

REQUIRED HEIGHT
MINUS PLATFORM

SIMPLE STEP
LEG

STEP LEG WITH
SIDE STEPS

DOUBLE STEP
LEG

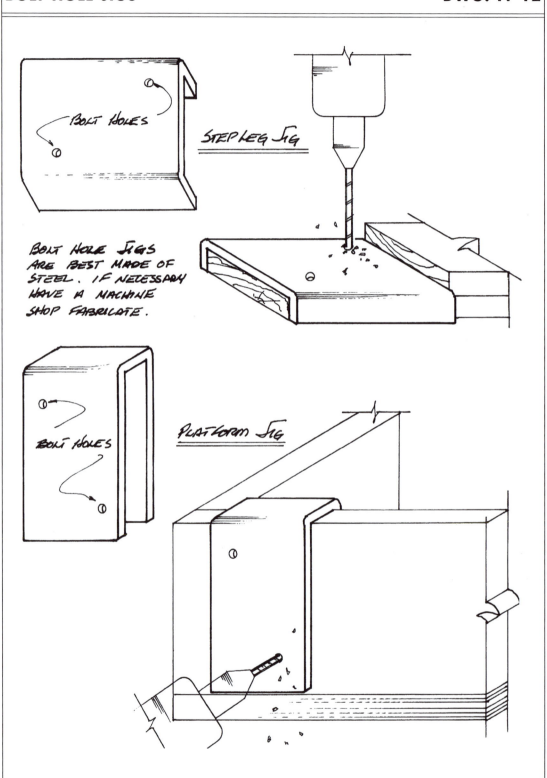

BOLT HOLES

STEP LEG JIG

BOLT HOLE JIGS
ARE BEST MADE OF
STEEL. IF NECESSARY
HAVE A MACHINE
SHOP FABRICATE.

BOLT HOLES

PLATFORM JIG

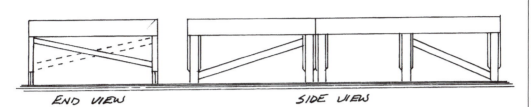

 END VIEW   SIDE VIEW

THIS DRAWING SHOWS A 4x10 PLATFORM (MADE OF A 4x4
AND 4x6 STOCK PLATFORM) LEGGED AT 2'-0" AND 12'-0".
NOTICE HOW THE "X" BRACING CAN BE ON OPPOSITE
ENDS (DASHED LINES) OR FORM A 'TRIANGLE' AS ABOVE.

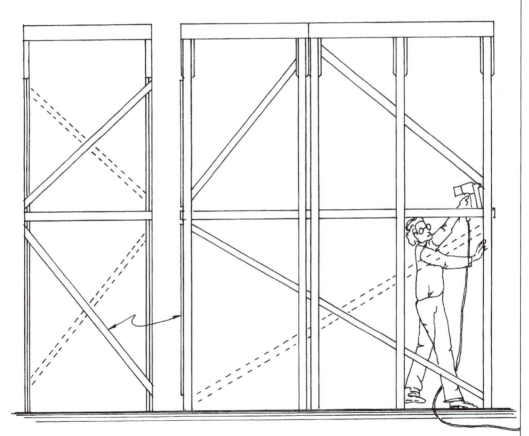

IN TALL PLATFORMS A "TOGGLE" OR HORIZONTAL MEMBER
WILL STABILIZE LEGS AND HELP DISTRIBUTE THE SWAY
BRACING'S EFFECTS. IT IS ALWAYS BEST TO SCREW
OR STAPLE BRACING. NAILING TENDS TO 'BANG-APART' UNIT.

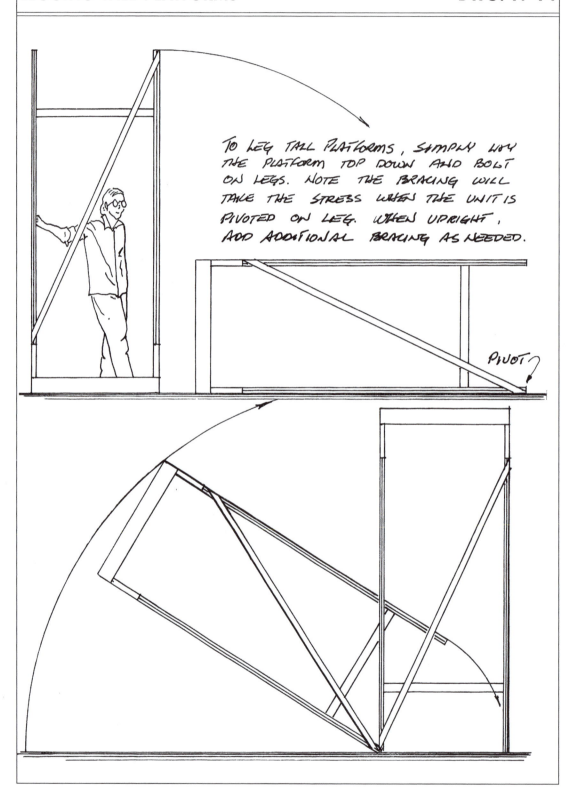

TO LEG TALL PLATFORMS, SIMPLY LAY THE PLATFORM TOP DOWN AND BOLT ON LEGS. NOTE THE BRACING WILL TAKE THE STRESS WHEN THE UNIT IS PIVOTED ON LEG. WHEN UPRIGHT, ADD ADDITIONAL BRACING AS NEEDED.

PIVOT

CASTER BOARDS AND DOLLIES

Both the caster board (or plank) and castered dollies are a great aid in shifting stock scenery. They and their component pieces can be utilized in many different ways.

CASTER BOARDS

The board is made of laminated 1 x stock, plywood, particle board (or any combination of these) or 2 x stock. It should be 1½" thick. The casters mount to these boards or planks, which have metal brackets bolted to each end. With the platform inverted on its lid, the caster board is placed inside with the brackets resting on the frame. A bolt through the frame and bracket holds it in place. Note that when the platform is flipped over, the frame is resting on the bracket and is being carried by it. Note also that the board is under the bracket and is carrying it (see Drawing IV-15). This minimizes the stress on the wood and bolts. It should be mentioned that a commercial bracket is available from some theatrical supply houses. It is designed to set into a 90° corner with the caster mounted to the bottom surface of it. It is a well designed unit, but the mounting position must be a right angle and it is expensive. Most metal shops, including sheet metal shops, can manufacture the brackets to your specifications. Remember that it will take six brackets (three caster boards) for a 4'-0" x 8'-0" platform.

PLACEMENT OF CASTER PLATES

The caster board should be as wide as the longest dimension of the caster's top plate. A template is also made to ensure identical placement of all caster top plates. This is not too critical for swivel or "crazy" casters, but becomes terribly important for non-swivel or stationary (straight) casters, because it is possible to track a castered platform by putting a guide on either side of the wheel of the caster. If the casters line up, this is easier to do. Also, if the same height and brand of caster is used, the top plates should fit the bolt holes . One of the best casters available is made by the Darnell Corporation, Ltd. Their address is listed in the back of this handbook.

A medium duty industrial caster with a 3" wheel is usually sufficient for stage use, and the caster fits well into a 1 x 5¼" framed platform and onto dollies (making them a total height of 6"). Please try to avoid buying cheap casters. They are usually loose at the joints, NOISY, have fairly low weight tolerances, and don't hold up for years of hard wear. Make sure for stage purposes that you get casters with a rubber-tired wheel. Drawings IV-15, IV-16, and IV-18 show caster boards being used on rigid platforms.

LIFT JACK

The lift jack shown in Drawing (IV-17) illustrates a type of outrigger created by utilizing several stock component pieces. The platform (minus a complete top) is standard construction and the caster boards are inserted with stock brackets. The casterboard at the back of the unit has a caster mounted to it. The front board has a handle of the same thickness as the casterboard hinged to it. On the underside of the handle is a piece of ¾" material which will slip under the caster board and lift it. A caster is mounted beneath this ¾" material and bolted through the handle. When the

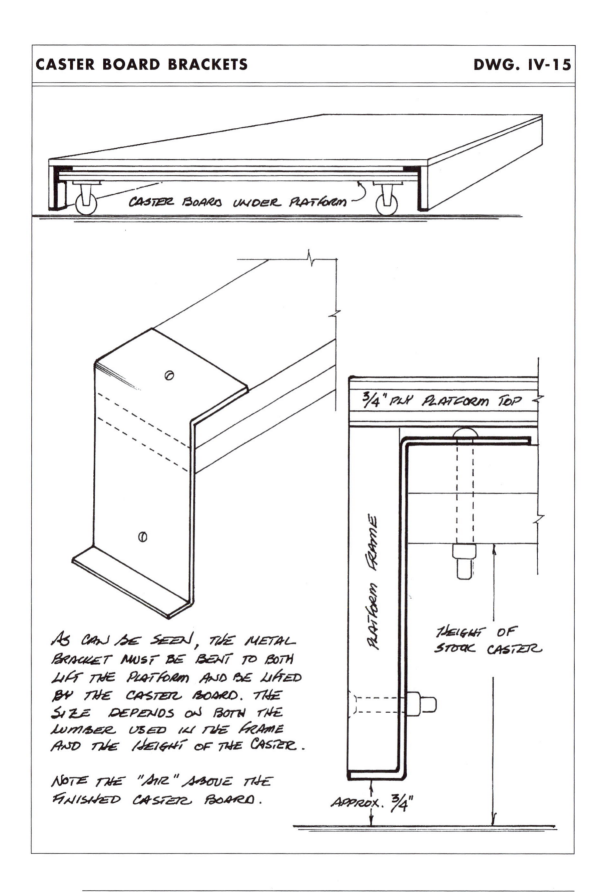

CASTER BOARD UNDER PLATFORM

3/4" PLY PLATFORM TOP

PLATFORM FRAME

HEIGHT OF STOCK CASTER

APPROX. 3/4"

AS CAN BE SEEN, THE METAL BRACKET MUST BE BENT TO BOTH LIFT THE PLATFORM AND BE LIFTED BY THE CASTER BOARD. THE SIZE DEPENDS ON BOTH THE LUMBER USED IN THE FRAME AND THE HEIGHT OF THE CASTER.

NOTE THE "AIR" ABOVE THE FINISHED CASTER BOARD.

THE UNIT AT RIGHT IS MADE UP OF STOCK PLAT- FORMS AND CASTERED WITH STRAIGHT CASTERS. THE CASTERS IN THE CIRCLES COULD POSSIBLY NOT BE MOUNTED BECAUSE ANOTHER CASTER IS CLOSE ENOUGH TO CARRY THE LOAD. THIS ASSUMES THE PROPER BOLTING TOGETHER OF PLATFORMS.

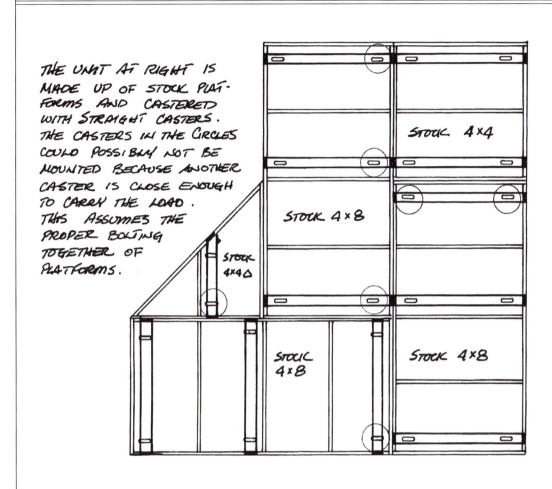

STOCK 4×4

STOCK 4×8

STOCK 4×4 △

STOCK 4×8

STOCK 4×8

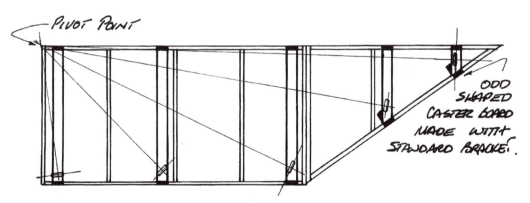

PIVOT POINT

ODD SHAPED CASTER BOARD MADE WITH STANDARD BRACKET.

WITH A PIVOT, STRAIGHT CASTERS MUST MOUNT AT A RIGHT ANGLE TO A RADIUS LINE.

handle is pushed own, the caster is forced to the floor and pushes up the unit. A simple S.H. door button is bolted to the opposite caster board. A 90-degree turn of this primitive holding device will keep the handle in place while the unit is rolled away. Swivel casters are usually placed on lift jacks and outriggers, but straight or rigid casters would be used if the unit tracked.

CASTER DOLLIES

The caster dolly is a lightweight frame made in the same dimensions as the top of the platform it is designed to carry (see Drawing IV-17). The frame's wood is 1 x stock, as wide as the longest side of the caster's top plate (minimum), and the joints are glued, lapped and attached. Some shops standardize the frame material at 5¼". This is convenient to cut from a 1 x 10 (leaving a tailing piece wide enough for flat construction) or to cut from two widths from a 1 x 12. It is also the width of the stock cut for platform construction, but may be structurally unsuited for this due to excessive knots, etc., thus allowing "waste" to be used up. The dolly frame could also be made from a piece of scrap from platform work, or it could be the whim of some crazy person trying to make busy work. Regardless of the source of the dolly frame stock pieces, lap them so the long pieces run beneath the shorter pieces and try to make this a constant. It facilitates tying them together when connecting several units castered in this manner.

Notice in Drawing IV-17 that the casters mount beneath the legs of the platform, or very nearly beneath them. This is necessary to put the weight on the platform through the leg, the dolly and through the caster to the floor in as direct a line as possible. It should be pointed out that caster dollies are excellent for parallel platforms also, and are interchangeable with rigid platforms of the same lid measurements (see Drawing IV-31). Both legged platforms and parallels can be held to the dolly with 2" backflap hinges.

When moving castered units on dollies it is mandatory to push/pull the dolly and not the scenery mounted to it, or you chance pushing or pulling the scenery off the dolly. A bent hanging iron (see Drawing II-53) hooked to the dolly frame and bolted into place gives an excellent ring to attach pull ropes.

TRACKING PLATFORMS

Many professional theatres track platforms by building a false floor above the stage deck. The rigging for the tracking mechanisms runs in the hollow between these floors. While it is ideal to have only a narrow slit in the floor, it is beyond most theatres' means to do this. The Drawing IV-18 shows three ways to track stock platforms utilizing a piece of bull-nosing, a moulding available at any lumber yard (or easily replicated in the shop).

If all casters are aligned, the moulding fits to both sides of the wheel and is a useful guide. Otherwise, a knife blade made of steel, polypropylene or even sheet nylon can be mounted to the platform and tracked. A special outrigger can be made to bolt or clamp onto a castered dolly with a knife blade attached to it. All these methods of tracking create a slight rise off the floor, but it is not enough to bother most actors

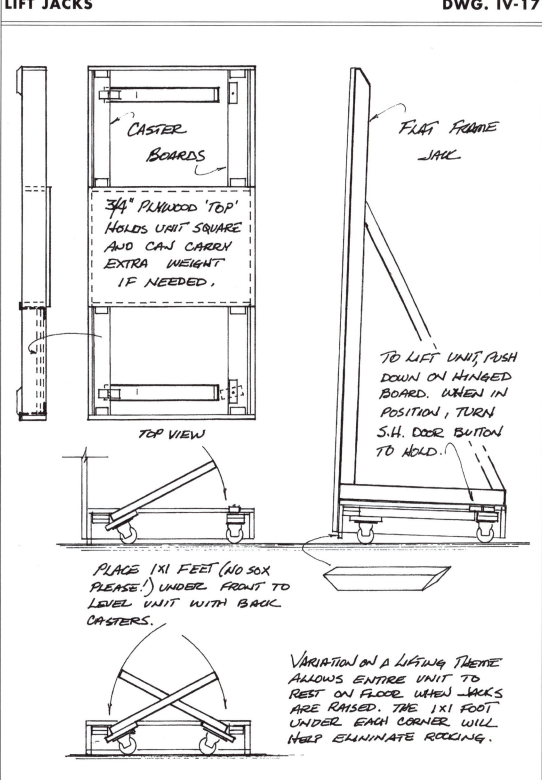

CASTER BOARDS

3/4" PLYWOOD 'TOP' HOLDS UNIT SQUARE AND CAN CARRY EXTRA WEIGHT IF NEEDED.

TOP VIEW

FLAT FRAME JACK

TO LIFT UNIT, PUSH DOWN ON HINGED BOARD. WHEN IN POSITION, TURN S.H. DOOR BUTTON TO HOLD.

PLACE 1X1 FEET (NO SOX PLEASE!) UNDER FRONT TO LEVEL UNIT WITH BACK CASTERS.

VARIATION ON A LIFTING THEME ALLOWS ENTIRE UNIT TO REST ON FLOOR WHEN JACKS ARE RAISED. THE 1X1 FOOT UNDER EACH CORNER WILL HELP ELIMINATE ROCKING.

THE CASTER DOLLY IS A FACE-LAPPED FRAME
OF 1X6 STOCK THE SAME DIMENSION AS THE
PLATFORM IT CARRIES.

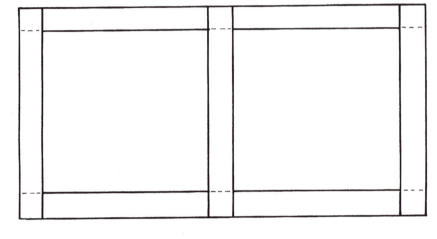

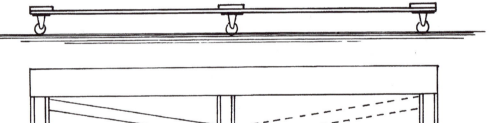

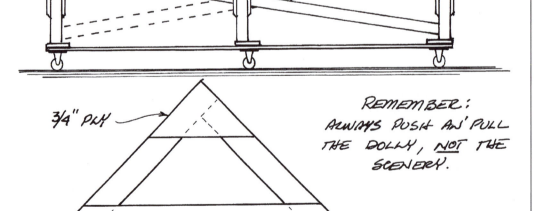

3/4" PLY

REMEMBER:
ALWAYS PUSH AN' PULL
THE DOLLY, NOT THE
SCENERY.

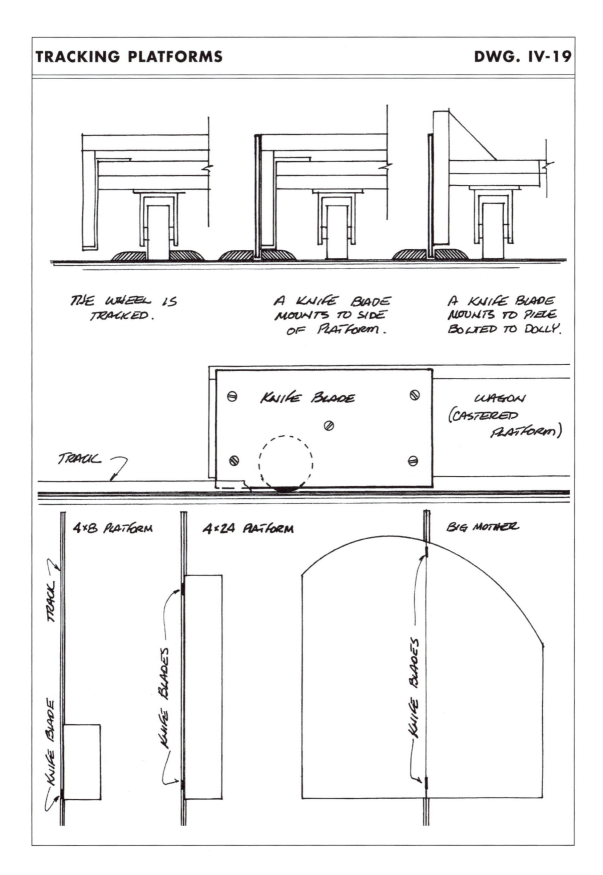

THE WHEEL IS
TRACKED.

A KNIFE BLADE
MOUNTS TO SIDE
OF PLATFORM.

A KNIFE BLADE
MOUNTS TO PIECE
BOLTED TO DOLLY.

KNIFE BLADE

WAGON
(CASTERED
PLATFORM)

TRACK

4×8 PLATFORM

4×24 PLATFORM

BIG MOTHER

TRACK

KNIFE BLADE

KNIFE BLADES

KNIFE BLADES

or dancers, once they become aware of it. However, it does prohibit rolling units to move across them. However, if the knife blade is long (12"-18") and the casters are aligned in the crossing unit, it is possible to cut away short sections of the track for the wheels to pass through. The longer knife blade will move through the cuts and rejoin the track without working out of the path. A slight widening of the track opening (with a chisel) often assures a smooth reentry.

Notice in Drawing IV-18 that the large wagon on the lower right has two knife blades "centered" in the unit. These will help control any wayward pull exerted by the casters or uneven floor. On this unit, as on all other wagons, you should push/pull the rolling unit, and not the scenery on it. You should also exert this pressure as close to the knife blades as possible (that was so basic it probably didn't need to be said).

RAMPS AND RAKES

A ramp is an inclined or sloping platform (see Drawing IV-20). "Rake" is the word for the amount of angle on the ramp, but the term has taken on a broader meaning, as in a "raked stage," which refers to the stage platforms and not just the angle.

In stock situations ramps (and rakes) usually conform to a predetermined height which corresponds to stock platforms and stock stairs. This relationship, combined with the sheet of plywood, usually makes a stock ramp 6" or 8" high with an 8'-0" length (or modules of this proportion). The 6" height would, in an 8'-0" run, have a rake of ¾" to the foot, and the 8" ramp would be 1" to the foot. This incline is also referred to as the rise of the ramp. In actuality, unless you are tapering the plywood at the "zero" end, the ramp platform starts at +¾" and rises to 6" or 8" in the 8'-0" distance, which slightly changes the degree of the rake.

TAPER JIG

Once the rise of the ramp (rake) has been settled, one should build a taper jig (see Drawing IV-19). This jig is dandy for easily making the many tapers required to build ramps and related pieces.

CONSTRUCTION

On a standard ramp, say 4'-0" wide and 8'-0" long, the tapers become the outside members. A "rail" butts at the high end, and can have a hand hole notched into the bottom of it to help lift the ramp. The "toggles" or the inner frame members run parallel to the "rail" and should be spaced like the inner members in stock platforms (usually 2'-0" apart). Both the "rail" and the "toggles" require an angle cut on the top edge to match the side tapers, thus assuring a good, constant glue surface for the plywood top. Glue and attach the framing, and glue and attach the plywood as in formal rigid platforms. Use coated staples, coated nails or ring nails for the top. The ramp can now be padded if desired (see Covering Platforms, pages 139 and 144). Glue the padding to the plywood top to prevent its scrunching up. All raked surfaces take an inordinate amount of stress from actors and scenery moving on them. Mostly from actors. Cover and backpaint the ramps like any other platform.

TO MAKE A JIG TO CUT TAPERS FOR THE SIDES
OF A RAMP, DO THE FOLLOWING:

1. CUT A PIECE OF 3/4" PLYWOOD 1'-0" x 8'-0"

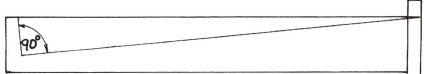

2. EXTEND THE END (TEMPORARILY) AND LAY OUT
THE RAKED PATTERN.

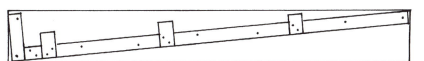

3. ATTACH 1x STOCK FOLLOWING LAYOUT. ADD
CLEATS TO TOP OF 1x STOCK TO HOLD WOOD. DONE.

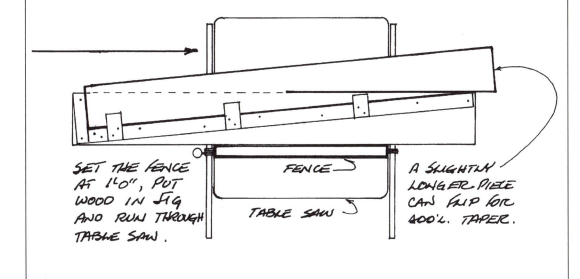

SET THE FENCE
AT 1'-0", PUT
WOOD IN JIG
AND RUN THROUGH
TABLE SAW.

FENCE

TABLE SAW

A SLIGHTLY
LONGER PIECE
CAN FLIP FOR
400'L. TAPER.

USING STOCK RIGID PLATFORMS FOR RAKES

Stock platforms can be legged (see Drawing IV-21) with specially built carriages to support them, which allow them to work in conjunction with ramps to create a raked stage. Step legs (see Drawing IV-11) can also be adapted with an angled step to support the platform. Make sure the leg is perpendicular to the floor. Be sure to use the standardized leg holes in the platform for mounting special "rake" legs. Ramp units cannot be legged, but they can be put on top of stock platforms which are.

2 X 6 SUPPORT

Drawing IV-21 shows a variation on a raked support system which will carry stock platforms. A piece of 2 x 6 is legged to follow the desired rake. It is best to lay out the rake, full scale, on the floor. Use a chalk line. You can even work "backwards" and lay out the platforms and then snap lines for the 2 x 6 to figure any taper, if utilized. It is also useful to work full scale, because you can easily measure onto the 2 x 6 where the legs need to go, being sure to miss the platform structure. When the unit is complete, notice how the legs also cleat around the platforms and lock them together.

A simple triangle of plywood holds each unit upright. This could be screwed on and removed if the rake supports are to be saved for future use. The outside support can be 1 x 6 or a variation on the leg unit shown in Drawing IV-20.

WARPED RAMPS

If you require a ramp that travels different distances in more than one direction, you will probably create a warp in the top plane. To construct this warped top, loft up the desired shape on a piece of ¼" plywood. Cut this and two other ¼" pieces to match. Build the tapering frame on top of the ¼" plywood, as with any irregular platform, to be sure the frame will conform to the top. Then screw the frame from the outside to cleats on the work table or the floor. Glue and bend the ¼" plywood to the frame. Repeat this step with the two additional sheets of ¼" plywood with glue between each layer. If the plywood tries to return to its flat shape and pull the frame off the table, place weights on it until the glue dries. Let the plywood-laminated top dry thoroughly (usually overnight). Unscrew the frame. The warp will now hold its shape and not try to twist the frame. Pad, cover and backpaint as with any other stock platform.

ADJUSTING STOCK FLATS TO THE RAKE

With care, practice and ingenuity, stock flats can be used on rakes. The Drawing IV-22 shows four of the many ways to build or adapt flats to fit a raked stage. Remember that the only flat frame which will have a tapered bottom with the same degree of incline as the rake's is one which travels or sits in the same direction as the true rake. Those which sit perpendicularly to the travel of the rake (Flat C on Drawing IV-22) have no taper. However, flats which sit perpendicularly to the rake at different heights must be built to different heights if they are to match at the top.

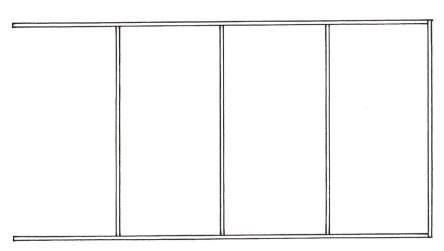

FOLLOW STANDARD PLATFORM TECHNIQUES.

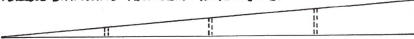

WHEN CUTTING OUT PIECES FOR THE RAMP REMEMBER THE
BACK AND INSIDE MEMBERS HAVE A TAPER ON THE TOP.

A RAKED STAGE FROM RAMPS
AND STOCK PLATFORMS

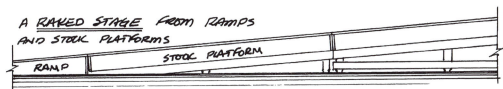

EASY TO BUILD 1X3 CARRIAGES CAN BE BUILT TO CARRY
STOCK PLATFORMS. LAY OUT TOTAL RAKE ON FLOOR AND
PLACE PLATFORMS ON SIDE TO BUILD IN PLACE.

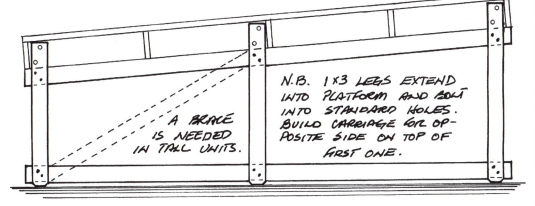

A BRACE
IS NEEDED
IN TALL UNITS.

N.B. 1X3 LEGS EXTEND
INTO PLATFORM AND BOLT
INTO STANDARD HOLES.
BUILD CARRIAGE FOR OP-
POSITE SIDE ON TOP OF
FIRST ONE.

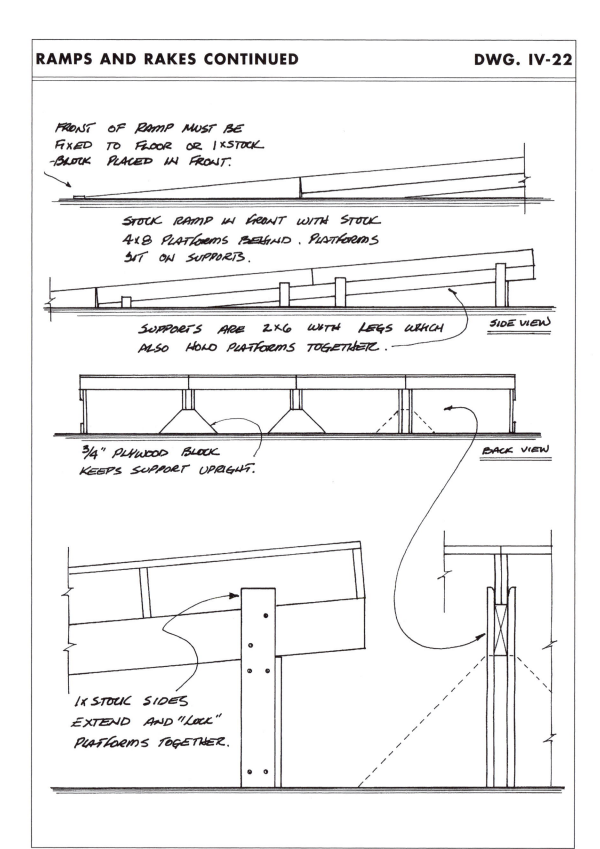

FRONT OF RAMP MUST BE
FIXED TO FLOOR OR 1×STOCK
BLOCK PLACED IN FRONT.

STOCK RAMP IN FRONT WITH STOCK
4×8 PLATFORMS BEHIND. PLATFORMS
SIT ON SUPPORTS.

SIDE VIEW

SUPPORTS ARE 2×6 WITH LEGS WHICH
ALSO HOLD PLATFORMS TOGETHER.

3/4" PLYWOOD BLOCK
KEEPS SUPPORT UPRIGHT.

BACK VIEW

1× STOCK SIDES
EXTEND AND "LOCK"
PLATFORMS TOGETHER.

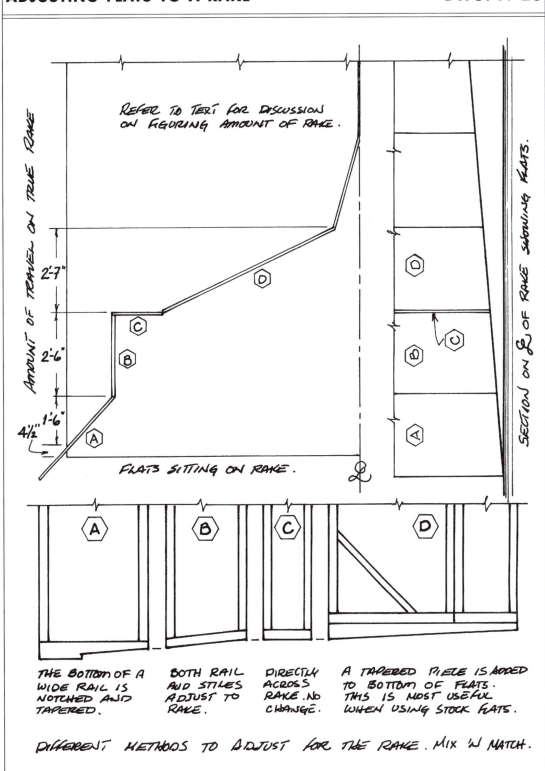

REFER TO TEXT FOR DISCUSSION ON FIGURING AMOUNT OF RAKE.

AMOUNT OF TRAVEL ON TRUE RAKE

2'-7"

2'-6"

1'-6"

4½"

FLATS SITTING ON RAKE.

SECTION ON ₵ OF RAKE SHOWING FLATS.

Ⓐ Ⓑ Ⓒ Ⓓ

THE BOTTOM OF A WIDE RAIL IS NOTCHED AND TAPERED.

BOTH RAIL AND STILES ADJUST TO RAKE.

DIRECTLY ACROSS RAKE. NO CHANGE.

A TAPERED PIECE IS ADDED TO BOTTOM OF FLATS. THIS IS MOST USEFUL WHEN USING STOCK FLATS.

DIFFERENT METHODS TO ADJUST FOR THE RAKE. MIX 'N MATCH.

REVERSE RAKES

An excellent way to alleviate some of the rake problems is to put the flats on a reverse rake. A reverse rake is a ramp or raked platform which is the same rake as the stage but running in the opposite direction. It creates a level base for the flats, but it automatically creates a step back to the raked stage. Quite often these reverse rakes can serve as landings, entry ways, foyers, etc., which can be incorporated into the design. Flats on these landings, etc., will often stick up higher than the ones in front of them. *C'est la guerre.*

FIGURING REVERSE RAKE FOR SCENERY

To figure how much taper is needed on the bottom of a flat sitting on a rake to make it vertical, measure the beginning and ending points of the flat. This can be done on a floor plan. Construct parallel lines off these points perpendicular to the true rise of the rake. The distance between these lines is the amount of travel on the rake; you can then compute the number of inches which rise with that much travel. That rise amount must then be spread across the bottom of the flat. As can be seen, a flat must always sit on the rake the same way to be vertical (see Drawing IV-22). Changing its relationship to the rake will make it lean—and that's not fat city. The figuring method can also be used on three-dimensional scenery.

PARALLEL PLATFORMS

There are two types of folding parallel platforms (see Drawing IV-23). They are the continental parallel (folds within itself) and the standard parallel (folds along itself). These platforms are called parallels because they are made by hinging flat frames together, usually keeping all frames opposite each other parallel and perpendicular to those adjacent.

There are several advantages to parallels. They are quick and easy to set up for a show. They are strong and well-braced against sway. They store as a unit and are fairly light to move. Of the many disadvantages, time expended on construction and cost are paramount. Also noteworthy is the fact that parallels do not adapt easily, though the tops can be interchangeable with frames of the same length and width. Therefore, storage can be a problem if many sizes and heights are planned and used. Unfortunately, the storage problem alone probably stops many people from building parallels and more's the pity, because the parallel is an ideal solution to an elevated playing area. It is the best solution for touring shows and situations which call for a few platforms which are in constant use.

THE CONTINENTAL PARALLEL

There are three reasons why the particular construction methods for parallel platforms advocated in this handbook are used. They are: 1) to minimize the number of different-sized frames necessary to build the parallel; 2) to give an outside surface which can be covered with muslin or some facing material and therefore be "self-

CONTINENTAL PARALLEL

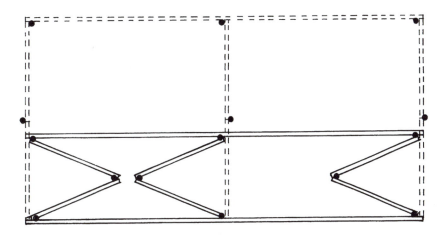

THE PLAN VIEWS OF THESE PARALLELS (DASHED LINE IS OPEN POSITION, SOLID IS PARTIALLY CLOSED) SHOW THE MAJOR DIFFERENCE BETWEEN THEM.

IN ITS PURE FORM, A CONTINENTAL PARALLEL MUST BE AT LEAST TWICE AS LONG AS WIDE TO FOLD WITHIN ITSELF.

THE STANDARD PARALLEL CAN BE ANY SIZE AND IT FOLDS (RATHER AWKWARDLY) TO A LENGTH EQUAL TO ONE LONG AND ONE SHORT SIDE.

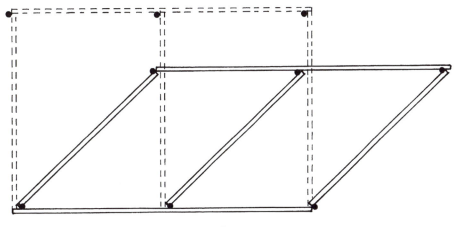

STANDARD PARALLEL

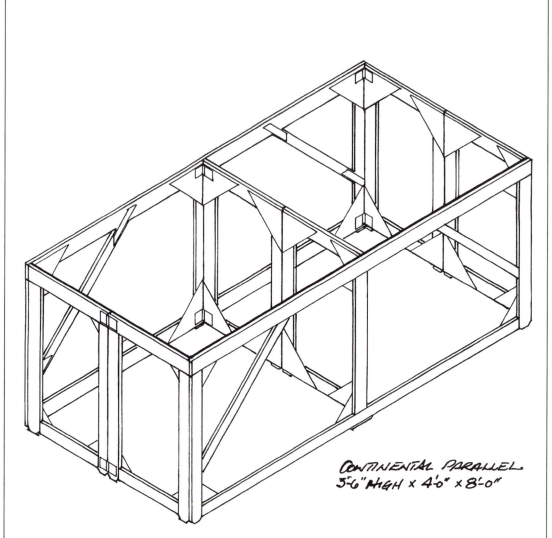

CONTINENTAL PARALLEL
3'-6" HIGH x 4'-0" x 8'-0"

THE FLAT FRAME CONSTRUCTION LEAVES THE OUTSIDE SURFACES ABLE TO BE COVERED WITH MUSLIN AND PAINTED IF DESIRED. THE CORNERS ARE TIGHT AND THE 3/4" RISE OFF THE FLOOR IS HARDLY NOTICEABLE.

THE CORNER BRACES WILL TAKE WEIGHT FROM THE TOP AND DISTRIBUTE IT THROUGH THE LEG TO THE FLOOR. THIS ELIMINATES THE NEED FOR ADDITIONAL LEGS OR A WIDER TOP RAIL.

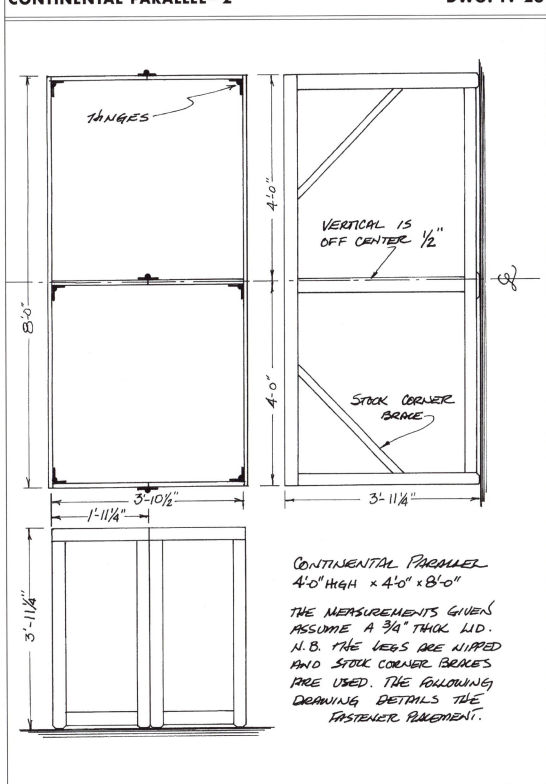

HINGES

4'-0"

VERTICAL IS
OFF CENTER ½"

STOCK CORNER
BRACE

8'-0"

4'-0"

3'-10½"

1'-11¼"

3'-11¼"

3'-11¼"

CONTINENTAL PARALLEL
4'-0" HIGH × 4'-0" × 8'-0"

THE MEASUREMENTS GIVEN
ASSUME A ¾" THICK LID.
N.B. THE LEGS ARE NIPPED
AND STOCK CORNER BRACES
ARE USED. THE FOLLOWING
DRAWING DETAILS THE
FASTENER PLACEMENT.

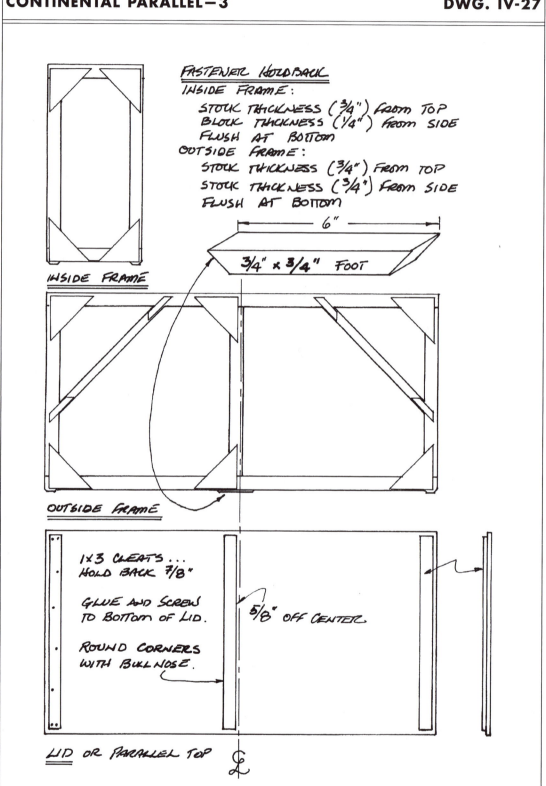

FASTENER HOLDBACK
INSIDE FRAME:
    STOCK THICKNESS (3/4") FROM TOP
    BLOCK THICKNESS (1/4") FROM SIDE
    FLUSH AT BOTTOM
OUTSIDE FRAME:
    STOCK THICKNESS (3/4") FROM TOP
    STOCK THICKNESS (3/4") FROM SIDE
    FLUSH AT BOTTOM

← 6" →

3/4" x 3/4" FOOT

INSIDE FRAME

OUTSIDE FRAME

1X3 CLEATS...
HOLD BACK 7/8"

GLUE AND SCREW
TO BOTTOM OF LID.

ROUND CORNERS
WITH BULLNOSE.

5/8" OFF CENTER

LID OR PARALLEL TOP

facing"; and 3) to use as many stock pieces and techniques of flat frame construction as possible, thus shortening the building period.

Drawing IV-24 shows a typical 4'-0" x 8'-0" continental parallel platform. There are two outside frames separated by three inside frames hinged together. Careful interrelationship and accuracy of all frames is imperative if the platform is to fold.

Drawing IV-25 shows a top view of a typical continental parallel frame with an outside frame and inside frame relating to it. Note that the three inside frames all fit within the outside frames and that the middle inside frame is centered in the unit. This is necessary because the lid (see Drawing IV-26) must sit on top of the frames and be able to interchange with other frames of the same length and width. When building any parallel, be sure that you have an accurate measured drawing of the outside and inside frames in their proper positions.

Note that the stiles for all the frames rest on the floor. Because this is structurally unsound, the ends are nipped off with a 45° cut ¾" up (see Drawing II-34) like the folding sawhorses (see Drawing II-32) and stairs (see Drawing V-17). This ¾" nip also acts as a guide in construction, being the point where the bottom of the toggle is placed. The extended stile with the nip also elevates the majority of the frame to eliminate rocking from uneven or cluttered floors, but it is not so high that the front of the frames cannot be covered with muslin if desired. Note the special block or foot of 1 x 1 (¾" x ¾") stock 6" long with 45° cuts on each end, glued and attached to the toggle under the vertical in the outside frame. Make sure the grain runs with the length of this 1 x 1. This block or foot takes the weight down through the frame to the floor (see Drawing IV-26).

OUTSIDE FRAMES

To build an outside frame, place the top rail on the work table. Place the stiles (desired finished height minus the 3" rail and the thickness of the top, which is usually ¾" plywood) against the rail. Hold these pieces in place with ⅜" corrugated fasteners if desired. Then insert the bottom toggle, flushing it to the top of the ¾" nip on the stile. Hold it with corrugators if desired. It is always best to run this bottom toggle from one end of the frame to the other and use the 1 x 1 foot beneath it. Breaking it around a center leg seriously weakens the frame and "screws up" the center inside frame.

Next, insert the vertical batten of 1 x 3 between the rail and toggle. Hold it with corrugators if desired. Make sure that this vertical batten is ½" off center, as shown in the Drawing IV-25. This allows the center inside frame to rest against the vertical and still have a place for hinges. In frames over 6'-0" high, additional toggles may be needed, and can be inserted between the stile and the inside vertical batten (see Drawing IV-31).

When this is done, check the frame for square and insert two stock 1 x 2" corner braces if they will fit, making them contiguous to the top rail. This not only holds the frame square, but gives additional support to the rail and helps distribute any weight back into the legs and to the floor. If stock 1 x 2" corner braces will not fit, cut them down until they do, or make special ones.

The next step is to apply plywood fasteners to all the joints (see Drawing IV-26). Note that they are held back ¾" or stock thickness from the top rail to allow the cleats

on the lid to rest against the frame (details following). The sides are also held back ¾"
or stock thickness to allow the inside frames to butt against the 1 x 3 of the outside
frame. Note that stock corner blocks are also used on the center vertical. This allows
¾" clearance to the 1 x 3 for the center frame to butt against. The fasteners are
flushed at the bottom; no clearance is needed and extra strength can be gained.
When the plywood fasteners are glued and nailed (or stapled) down, attach the 1 x 1
cleat to the toggle directly under the center vertical.

Now, take the completed frame off the work table and turn it over so the fasteners
rest on the table. Build a second frame directly on top of the first and the center
vertical will automatically align for proper hinging and folding when the unit is
assembled. A great deal of time is also saved by not having to square up the second
frame, because it will match the first.

INSIDE FRAMES

The inside frames are comprised of two smaller frames hinged in pairs. Because
there are many small frames to construct, building is speeded up if you put a jig on
the workbench to hold pieces for assembling. Note that the stiles continue to the floor
and are nipped, as were those for the outside frames. Because the stiles are all the
same length, you can jig them out together for both the inside and outside frames.
The major construction difference in the small frames is in the plywood fasteners.
They are held back ¾" at the top, flushed at the bottom, but are held back only ¼" on
the sides. This ¼" is for two reasons: it allows the fastener to just clear the corner
blocks on the outside frame, and there can still be a flush surface upon which to
mount the hinge. The small frames should be hinged into pairs with 2" backflap
hinges. The hinges are placed on the front of the frames, not on the side with the
plywood blocks. The hinge placement should match that used for attaching the
outside and inside frames together. Screw down the hinges with 1" #8 or #9 wood
screws. If the platform is to take an excessively hard beating, place a ³⁄₁₆" stove bolt in
each flap, sink the nut into the wood and remove the excess bolt.

ASSEMBLY

When all the frames are built and the inside frames paired up, you are ready to
hinge the platform together. Assemble the pieces as shown in the top view (see
Drawing IV-25). Hold the frames in place using clamps (if available) or a few 6d duplex
nails. This will assure that the pieces butt properly and lessens any chance of
slippage while the hinging is being done.

Make sure the three inside frames are flush to the stiles and verticals in the
outside frames and that the center inside frame is centered in the unit. (The center
frame's thickness should include the thickness of its plywood fasteners. This is usually
1".) If not, stop and rebuild until correct. When all pieces fit, start hinging. The hinges
must rest on the plywood fasteners or the framework will bind when it is folded. Place
hinges so the bottom of the top hinge is level with the bottom of the rail and the top of
the bottom hinge is level with the top of the toggle. This allows the hinge to be on the
plywood fasteners and attach into the 1 x 3 frame.

It is easiest to drill and set a ³⁄₁₆" flat head stove bolt in each flap of the hinges first.

Remember to pull the nut well into the wood and cut or break off the remaining bolt. File off any sharp remains. This will hold the hinge in place and make setting the screws a far less tedious job; but 1″ drywall screws are also a good starter and finisher. When all the hinges are on, both bolted and screwed, remove the clamps or pull the nails. The unit should easily fold up within itself, with no binding on the hinges or undue stress and warpage in the wood . If this is not the case, you may get very frustrated and even use no-no words.

THE LID

The top for the parallel platform is quite simple to build and is often constructed before the frame is folded for the first time (see Drawing IV-26). Cut a piece of ¾″ plywood (or whatever is being used for the top) to the required dimensions. Check this on the actual frame to make sure it fits. Flip the top over and on the back scribe a line ⅞″ in from the edge around the entire top. This is the allowance for the ¾″ thickness of the 1 x 3 frame and a ⅛″ slop. The slop clearance is for the 1 x 3 cleats which will be attached to the lid and will slip within the frame, resting just above the corner blocks and next to the 1 x 3 rails. Cut three cleats the necessary length and glue and screw them down, aligning the end ones against the ⅞″ lines. The center cleat should be ⅝″ off center in addition to the ⅞″ from the edge. The ⅝″ is for one-half the thickness of the center frame (½″) plus ⅛″ slop. The placement of the center cleat allows the plywood top to rest on the parallel frame and the cleats to slip into the frame and snug up to it, thereby locking the top in place and holding the frame open and square. If properly constructed, the lid can turn 180° degrees and still fit, which speeds the set-up time considerably.

Glue and screw the cleats to the top with 1½″ #8 or #9 flat-head wood screws. When completed, a slight bullnosing around the cleats will help them slip and lock into the frame, so try to hold the screws back slightly or budget a lot of money for router bits. The bullnosing can be done with a router, a cornering tool or a plane. The same slight bullnosing can be put on the top surface of the lid also, to help eliminate excessive splintering of the plywood. The lids can be padded easily and covered with cotton duck if desired (see Drawing IV-33).

STANDARD PARALLEL PLATFORMS

Do not try to build a standard parallel from the following information alone. Review the preceding section on the continental parallel because the two types share many principles which are more fully discussed there.

The standard parallel is not structurally as satisfactory a unit as the continental parallel. When the standard parallel folds, it exposes its joints to wear and takes more storage space. However, it is the only style of parallel which can be built if the length is less than double the width. It is also faster and cheaper to construct; not points to pass over lightly. Standard parallels can be built with the length more than double the width, also, like their continental cousins. Some scene shops do this.

As can be seen in Drawings IV-27 and IV-28, the inside frames rest against the corner block of the outside frames, not on the 1 x 3 stiles. This is necessary because

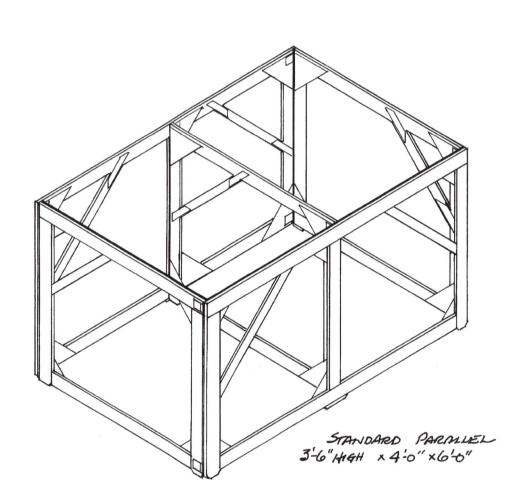

STANDARD PARALLEL
3'-6" HIGH x 4'-0" x 6'-0"

THE FLAT FRAME CONSTRUCTION LEAVES THE OUTSIDE ABLE
TO BE COVERED WITH MUSLIN AND PAINTED IF DESIRED.
NOTE THE ¼" GAP AT POINTS WHERE THE INSIDE FRAME
BUTTS AGAINST THE CORNER BLOCKS OF THE OUTSIDE
FRAME. THIS CAN BE FILLED AND HIDDEN WITH THE
COVERING MATERIAL. THE ¾" RISE OFF THE FLOOR IS
HARDLY NOTICEABLE.

AGAIN NOTE HOW CORNER BRACES HELP SUPPORT 1X3
RAIL AND DISTRIBUTE WEIGHT BACK TO THE FLOOR.

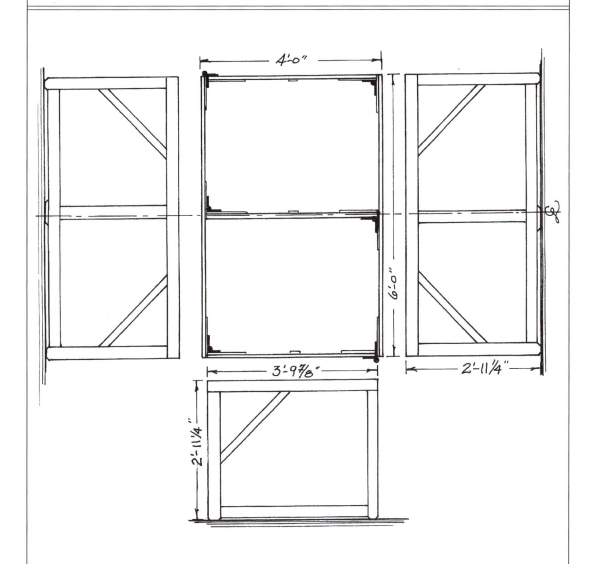

STANDARD PARALLEL
3'-0" HIGH x 4'-0" x 6'-0"
(SIMILAR TO PREVIOUS DRAWING)

THE MEASUREMENTS ASSUME A ¾" THICK LID. N.B. THE
LEGS ARE NIPPED AND STANDARD CORNER BRACES ARE
USED. NOTE TOO, THE UNUSUAL HINGE PLACEMENT. THE
PIN AND ONE FLAP ARE OUTSIDE THE FRAMEWORK. THE
REST ARE INSIDE. THIS ALLOWS THE SIDEWARD FOLD TO
HAPPEN.

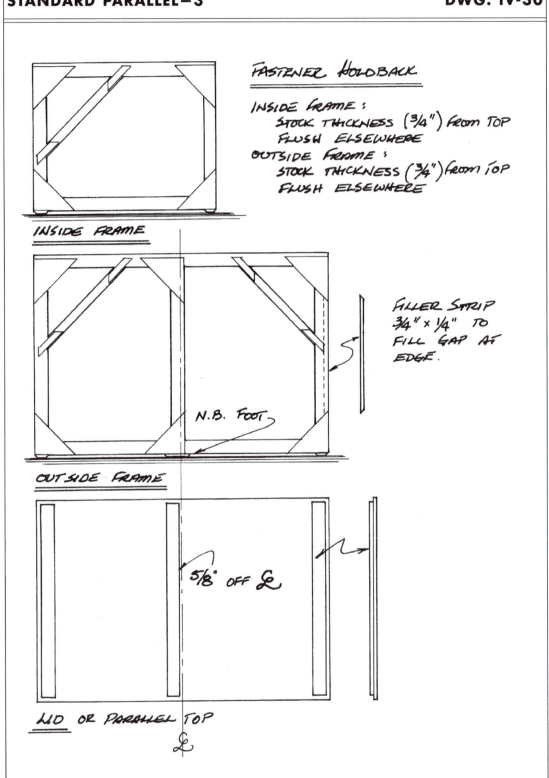

FASTENER HOLDBACK

INSIDE FRAME:
STOCK THICKNESS (3/4") FROM TOP
FLUSH ELSEWHERE
OUTSIDE FRAME:
STOCK THICKNESS (3/4") FROM TOP
FLUSH ELSEWHERE

INSIDE FRAME

FILLER STRIP
3/4" × 1/4" TO
FILL GAP AT
EDGE.

N.B. FOOT

OUTSIDE FRAME

5/8" OFF ℄

LID OR PARALLEL TOP

one flap of the hinges on two opposite ends extends to the outside of the frame and would bind if on the same plane as the internal ones. Note that the basic construction details (stiles, rails, etc.) are similar and follow the same requirements as the continental parallels.

THE OUTSIDE FRAME

To build the outside frames (see Drawing IV-28) cut a top rail the necessary length. The two stiles with nipped ends fit below this and are separated at the bottom by a toggle. Note that the vertical in the center of the frame is ½″ off center. Hold the plywood fasteners back ¾″ at the top but (unlike the continental parallel) flush them elsewhere (see Drawing IV-29). When the frame is squared, add corner braces, either stock or cut down. Hold the half-strap back ¾″ everywhere for a possible filler strip, discussed later. Glue and nail the fasteners down. Then, glue and nail a 1 x 1 (¾″ x ¾″) cleat under the center vertical as in the continental parallel (see Drawing IV-26). To build the opposite side do not turn the frame over as with the continental parallel, but build the second frame directly over it. This will produce two identical frames which, when placed opposite each other in the finished parallel, will properly and automatically offset the center vertical.

INSIDE FRAME

The inside frames are all identical and simple to build. To measure the rail, subtract the following from the required width: two stock thicknesses (¾″ and ¾″), two plywood fastener thicknesses (¼″ and ¼″), and the thickness of the one flap of the 2″ backflap hinge (⅛″) attached to the outside of the frame. Place the stiles under the rail, fit a toggle at the base, and fasten with corner blocks which are held back ¾″ at the top and flushed elsewhere. Insert a corner brace (stock or cut down) in each frame. If these are built identically, the brace will automatically reverse for necessary cross bracing when the frames are assembled.

ASSEMBLY

When the frames are finished, place them in the proper position (see Drawing IV-28). Hold them with clamps or temporarily nail the pieces together with a few 6d duplex nails. Make sure the frame is square and the center frame is centered in the unit. Place 2″ backflap hinges so the bottom of the top hinge is flushed to the bottom of the rail and the top of the bottom hinge is flushed to the top of the toggle. Attach the internal hinges (those which are completely inside the frames) with one-inch #8 or #9 flat head wood screws. Now loosen the clamps or nails on the unhinged corners enough to slip the external hinges (those which have one flap extended to the outside of the frame) between the frames. The pin of the hinge will be snug against the crack in the joint. The hinge flap outside the parallel frames will not have holes which are countersunk on the necessary side. The holes should, therefore, be countersunk to accept the head of the screws used (use care or the hole will get too big). Attach each flap with screws. As with the continental parallel, one ³⁄₁₆″ stove bolt can be put in each flap of the hinges if heavy wear and tear is expected. Remove the clamps or pull the nails and the standard parallel frame should fold to a closed position which will equal the combined lengths of one outside frame and one inside frame.

Make the top or lid following the same procedures discussed for the continental parallel.

THE FILLER STRIP

Inasmuch as the standard parallel does not have a tight butt along all its stiles (see Drawings IV-27 and IV-28), a filler strip of 1 x ¼" stock can be glued and tacked in between the corner blocks, flush to the outside frame. This strip will fill the gap and allow the frames to be covered with muslin or some facing material which will give a finished front yet still allow the parallel to fold. Tight butts are, however, terribly continental.

THE "NON-FRAME" PARALLEL PLATFORM

As with the all-plywood platform discussed earlier (see Drawing IV-6), the ever faithful 4 x 8 sheet is adaptable for the parallel platform. One great advantage is the speed with which it can be constructed because no flat frames need to be built. However, there are some definite height limitations due to the size of the panel. Drawing IV-30 shows a parallel made of ¾" plywood. There are lightening holes cut into each piece to reduce the weight. This leaves a frame with a 6" top "rail" and 6" center support, allowing enough room for the hinges. All other frame dimensions are 4". Of course, lightening holes are not necessary if a solid surface is desired. Weight reduction could still be accomplished however, by covering the surface with muslin. To decrease construction time eliminate the notch at the bottom for the feet, and instead, attach 1 x stock feet directly to the edge of the plywood. Be sure to deduct the added height of the feet from the frame. These parallels hinge together in the same manner as do their flat frame cousins. Simply place one hinge near the top and another near the bottom and screw them into place. You will quickly see if wear and tear will require one screw in each flap of the hinges to be replaced with a ³⁄₁₆" stove bolt. Fortunately, this can always be done later.

For parallels less than 12" high, 1 x stock is an excellent choice. Again, Drawing IV-30 shows the 1 x stock feet applied to the bottom of the frame.

Even though it seems like "overkill," each folding joint should have two hinges, to prevent any twisting in the frame when it is moved. Okay, maybe something smaller than 2" backflaps will do here.

Of course, lids for flat frame parallels will be interchangeable with ones made from ¾" plywood or 1 x stock.

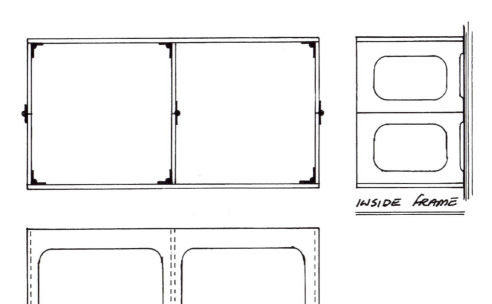

INSIDE FRAME

OUTSIDE FRAME

THE CONTINENTAL PARALLEL ABOVE IS MADE FROM 3/4" PLY-
WOOD. SOME WEIGHT IS REDUCED BY CUTTING LIGHTENING HOLES
IN EACH PANEL. BELOW IS A CONTINENTAL PARALLEL MADE OF
1X STOCK WITH FEET ATTACHED... AN EXCELLENT SOLUTION
FOR FRAMES LESS THAN ONE FOOT HIGH.

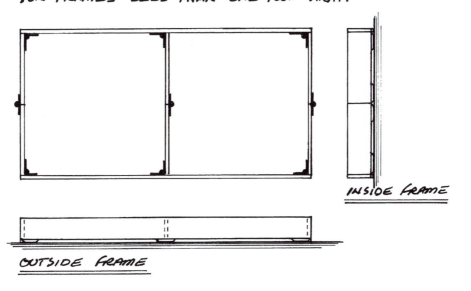

INSIDE FRAME

OUTSIDE FRAME

TALL PARALLEL PLATFORMS

Parallel platforms much taller than 6'-0" should probably have a horizontal toggle. Some of the thinking which dictates toggle placement in flats (see Drawing II-1) could also apply here. The Drawing IV-31 shows a 12'-0" unit mounted to a castered dolly. The centered toggle distributes not only the stress but the support throughout the unit. Two toggles could be incorporated using the "four-to-six" rule.

PARALLEL PLATFORMS WITHOUT CENTER FRAMES

It is possible to eliminate the center frame in a parallel platform. The Drawing IV-32 shows how the lid can incorporate much of the support, albeit in a manner close to cheating.

A piece of ¾" plywood, tapered on the ends to assure no binding, is hinged to the 1 x 3 cleat mounted to the bottom of the lid . Plywood is used because 1 x stock is likely to split from the pressure. This hinged piece is attached with three (or better, four) 2" backflap hinges. This allows it to fold flush for storage and therefore be easily incorporated into existing lids for other parallels. Note the variations drawn. If the lid has a bit of sag, two (or more) "flippers" can be used.

Because the long sides of the parallel frame are no longer held constant by a center frame, they could spread apart enough for the lid to fall through. A rubber rope with hooks which hook into eye bolts in the frame will eliminate this possibility.

A DIATRIBE ON DUCK

"Duck" has become a generic term for many firm, heavy, plain-weave fabrics. To be almost simplistic, duck is divided into four groups: Flat Ducks, Army Ducks, Numbered Ducks and Special Ducks. Before the middle of the nineteenth century, America (and much of the world) imported its sail canvas from England. This cloth was made from Russian flax and was marked with a stencil of a raven. Heavier weights of this cloth were stenciled with a picture of a duck. Soon the word "duck" was synonymous for "heavy fabric," and when Americans began producing cotton canvas, the name duck shifted to it.

FLAT DUCK includes Wagon Cover duck, called "single fill duck" by jobbers. Single fill ducks are imported and generally woven in 48", 50" and 72" widths. Each width, depending upon the thread, can weigh 10, 12 or 14.9 oz. per square yard. The 60" Wagon Cover, in either 10 or 12 oz., is an ideal material for covering padded platforms and parallel lids. There is very little waste; the surface is strong and takes paint quite well. Wagon Cover Duck is sometimes called Wagon Top.

ARMY DUCKS. These are more firmly woven and of a finer quality than Flat Ducks; they are also more expensive. Army duck was designed for the military and is lighter than numbered ducks but as strong.

NUMBERED DUCKS are firmly woven from plied yarns and are free from sizing (starch-like filler). They are available in many widths, from 22" to 120". Numbered

TALL PARALLELS REQUIRE SOME OF THE SAME THOUGHTS AND SOLUTIONS GIVEN TALL FLATS. THEY REQUIRE TOGGLES TO FOLLOW THE "4 TO 6 RULE" AND CORNER BRACES TO HOLD THE FRAME SQUARE. ON THE EXAMPLE BELOW (12'-0" H. × 4 × 6) THE TOGGLE RECEIVES A CORNER BRACE WHICH HELPS KEEP "WOBBLE" OUT OF THE LEGS. THE BRACES AT TOP TAKE WEIGHT TO THE LEGS, THUS ELIMINATING A CENTER SUPPORT. HOWEVER, THEY HELP WITH THE BRACING ALSO.

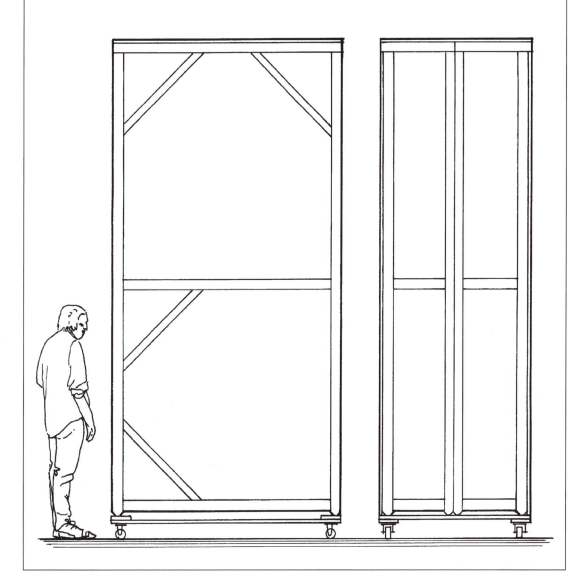

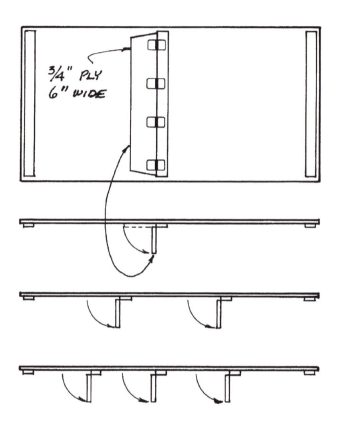

3/4" PLY
6" WIDE

IT IS POSSIBLE TO ELIMINATE THE CENTER FRAME IN A PARALLEL AND HAVE THE LID UTILIZE THE SUPPORT. AS SEEN, THE HINGED FLIPPER WILL SUPPORT WEIGHT WHEN LID IS ON FRAME. A RUBBER ROPE TO EYE BOLTS IN TOP RAILS WILL KEEP FRAME TOGETHER.

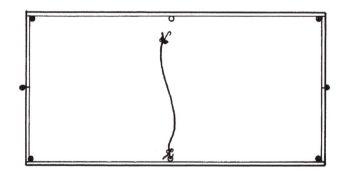

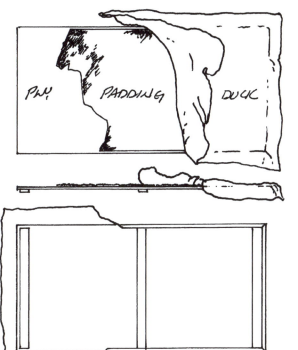

CUT THE PADDING SO IT IS HELD BACK ABOUT 1/4" FROM EDGE. GLUE TO TOP.

COVER THE PADDING (IF NOT THE FINISHED SURFACE) WITH A GOOD QUALITY CANVAS DUCK (10 OZ IS GOOD).

WRAP DUCK AROUND EDGES AND GLUE AND STAPLE TO BACK. TRIM AWAY EXCESS. MITRE CORNERS TO PREVENT BUILD UP.

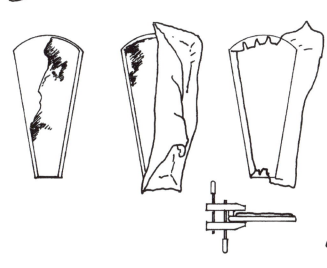

STAIR TREADS FOR FLAT FRAME UNITS MAY BE PADDED AND COVERED LIKE PLATFORM LIDS. BUT HOLD PADDING BACK 3/4" FROM EDGES WHICH SCREW TO CARRIAGES. A 3/4" SQUARE STRIP AND CLAMPS WILL FORCE CANVAS TO GLUE DOWN.

WHEN TRIMMING MUSLIN OR DUCK TO FOLLOW CLEATS, ETC, A PIECE OF 3/4" STRAP IRON IS AN EXCELLENT GUIDE.

Ducks are numbered on a scale inverse to their weight. Number 1 Duck is the heaviest, weighing 18 oz. (per yard of a 22″ width). The lightest is Number 12, which weighs 7 oz. (per yard of a 22″ width). The formula is easy to remember; if you subtract the number of the Duck from 19, you have the weight. To add to the confusion, most jobbers base their standards on a square yard measure. Numbered Duck is excellent for ground cloths. The tight weave and good strength give a solid surface for moving scenery and actors. Probably a Number 8 Duck will be adequate, but do a test first.

SPECIAL DUCKS include a Gear Duck, Filter Duck, Boot Duck and probably a Ruptured Duck.

PADDING AND COVERING PLATFORM LIDS AND TREADS

Many of the padding methods discussed earlier for rigid platforms (see Drawing IV-3 and text following) can also be used for parallel lids and stair treads (see Drawing V-19).

Make sure the padding does not "ooze" over the edge of the piece, because this makes it difficult to achieve tight and accurate fits when putting units together. Always adhere the padding to the surface with glue or mastic. Once the padding is in place, follow the procedures indicated in Drawing IV-33.

PART V • STEPS AND STAIRS

Step units and stairs are probably the most complicated pieces of scenery to build. They have structural problems and people-related demands peculiar to them alone. Fortunately they are not hard to build.

STAIR TALK

A step is a narrow landing either above or below another landing. A stair is a series (or a flight) of steps, and steps and stairs now have an almost interchangeable meaning (see Drawing V-1).

Stairs are created from a series of risers (or rises) and treads. The riser is the vertical part or height of the step, and also refers to the materials which are used to build the front of the step. The tread is the horizontal part of the landing which is walked upon. It too is the name for the piece which is used in constructing that part of the step. The rise and tread have an interrelationship which will be discussed shortly.

The carriage or stringer is the structural member which holds the risers and treads in place. It is usually notched for them to rest on . A step unit usually has two or more carriages, depending upon how wide the treads are and the materials from which the treads are made (see Drawing V-2).

The Drawing V-3 shows six of the most common configurations of stairs. They are combined in every imaginable way.

RISE/TREAD RELATIONSHIP

The human body has an uncanny ability to make natural patterns and relationships which are constant and comfortable; different people make variations on these patterns. Then some nit tries to make sense out of it all and we get charts, graphs, and tables of formulae creating total chaos out of the simple fact that, when walking up or down stairs, the height needed to make the step will affect how far one can move forward. To be scientific about all this, the Drawing V-4 shows three of the common methods of compiling the relationship between the rise and the tread. Keep in mind that the results of these formulae are approximate, and that you will achieve satisfactory results if you are "in the ballpark." Formula A adds the height of the riser and the depth of the tread for a result of approximately 17". Formula B takes the height of two risers plus the depth of a tread for approximately 25". The last multiplies the height of the riser times the depth of the tread for a product of approximately 75". A 6" rise and a 12" tread is close to all three formulae. What luck; this combination is also easy for actors to navigate.

One thing which cannot be stressed strongly enough is the importance of a constant rise/tread relationship. The body automatically adapts to one, and if you change it, the body stumbles, very much like taking the last step on a set of stairs and finding you are already on the landing. This rule of never changing the rise/tread relationship within a run of stairs can be broken, of course, when you are trying to force actors to move in an awkward manner. Such a use of the uneven rise can then be very effective.

In the theatre, reality is tossed to the wings, and directors use stairs for more than getting actors on and off stage. They become important playing areas. This hints that the width of the tread needs to be increased so an actor can pause, turn and pose with some ease. The posing part is often a natural instinct and can be done on any step, or even without one. Be that as it may, stair treads are usually deeper in the theatre than in the real world.

For stock situations a desirable width is one which is a workable module with stock platforms and flats (and that damn sheet of plywood). The easiest is probably 1'-0". The rise must be comfortable and natural to be practical for stock stairs. As Drawing V-4 shows, most rise/tread relationships fall in an area between the 6" and 8" rise and the 8" and 12" tread. Indeed, most theatres limit their standard rises to 6" or 8". These amounts work well, appear quite natural, and seem a good compromise of the plus/minus 7" height which is common outside the theatre. OSHA has set 7½" as the maximum rise for any public access step.

One thing to consider in choosing a stock rise height is how tall the scenery is. A 6" rise gets people slowly up and off-stage, while an 8" rise does the job of getting them up faster but not necessarily getting them off any sooner.

When figuring the run (see Drawing V-5) or distance covered from the first to the last step, you must take into account the nosing (which technically does not affect the run, but does affect the actual step) and whether or not the steps have a raked riser or are a variation on a ship's ladder (see Drawing V-7).

Winders (angled treads, and not regular treads or fliers) provide another means to cram in more steps than the normal rise/tread relationship allows (see Drawing V-3 and V-15).

COMMON TYPES OF STAIRS

Stairs can be independent or dependent—a distinction based upon whether they can stand without additional support. There are many different designs for stairs, but the most common for theatre use are the cut (or notched) carriage, solid carriage, and flat-frame carriage. Some of these can be both independent or dependent.

The step unit at the top of Drawing V-6 shows a cut-carriage with solid sides. This method is excellent for short runs of steps. They are easy to set up and strike, but they are bulky for storage. The outside carriages are made of ¾" plywood, and the

THE RUN OF STAIRS BELOW IS CREATED WITH STOCK PLATFORMS (WHICH ADD TO THE TOTAL RISE) AND TWO STOCK STEP UNITS. NOTICE THE HEADROOM IS ALWAYS MEASURED FROM THE FRONT EDGE OF THE TREAD.

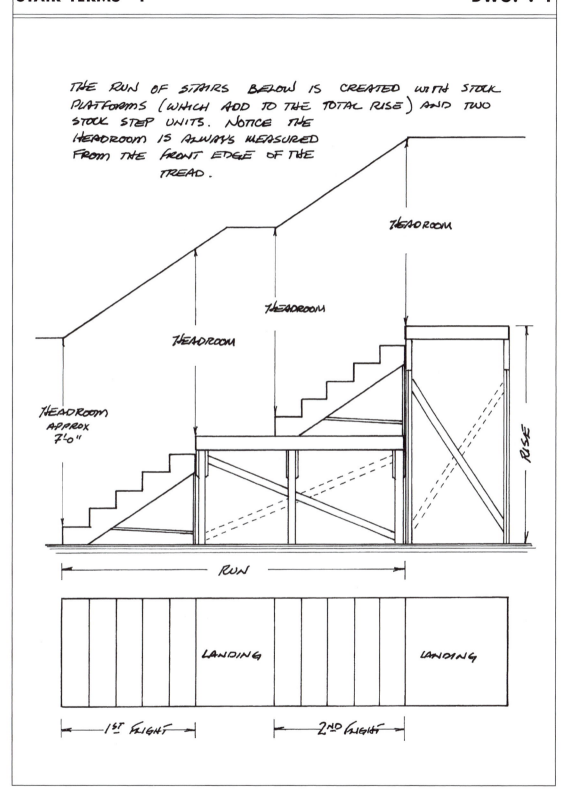

HEADROOM

HEADROOM

HEADROOM

HEADROOM APPROX 7'-0"

RISE

RUN

LANDING

LANDING

1ST FLIGHT

2ND FLIGHT

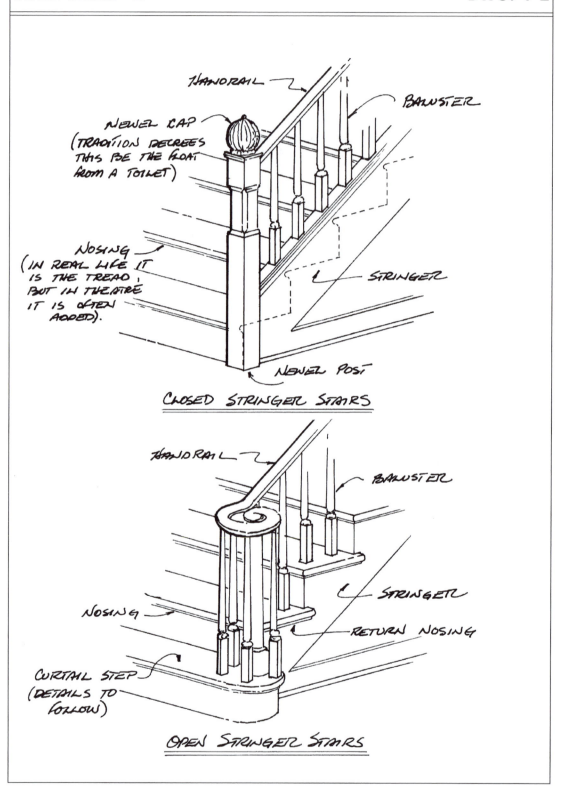

HANDRAIL

NEWEL CAP
(TRADITION DECREES
THIS BE THE FLOAT
FROM A TOILET)

BALUSTER

NOSING
(IN REAL LIFE IT
IS THE TREAD,
BUT IN THEATRE
IT IS OFTEN
ADDED).

STRINGER

NEWEL POST

CLOSED STRINGER STAIRS

HANDRAIL

BALUSTER

NOSING

STRINGER

RETURN NOSING

CURTAIL STEP
(DETAILS TO
FOLLOW)

OPEN STRINGER STAIRS

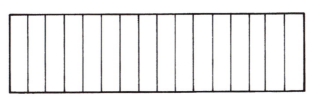

CONTINUOUS FLIGHT

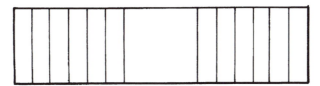

TWO FLIGHTS WITH LANDING

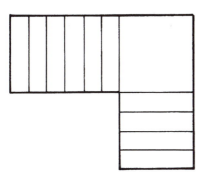

TWO FLIGHTS WITH
¼ LANDING

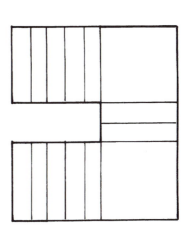

THREE FLIGHTS WITH
TWO ¼ LANDINGS

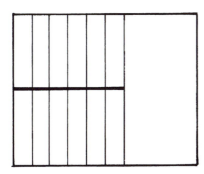

TWO FLIGHTS WITH
½ LANDING

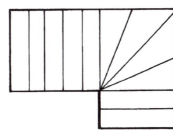

TWO FLIGHTS WITH
90° WINDERS

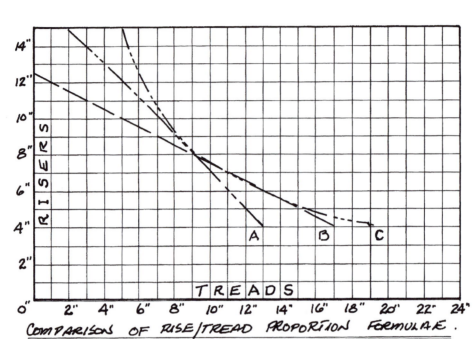

COMPARISON OF RISE/TREAD PROPORTION FORMULAE.

$$A: R + T = 17"$$
$$B = 2R + T = 25"$$
$$C: R \times T = 75$$

RECOMMENDED ANGLES FOR RAMPS, STAIRS AND LADDERS.

BETWEEN 30° - 35° IS THE PREFERRED ANGLE FOR STAIRS.

ALL THREE STEP UNITS HAVE THE SAME RISE/TREAD RELATIONSHIP.

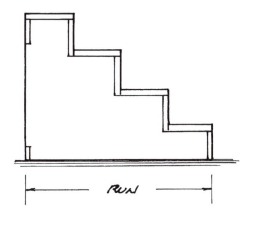

STEP WITHOUT NOSING

THE RUN IS THE TOTAL LENGTH OF THE FOUR TREADS.

RUN

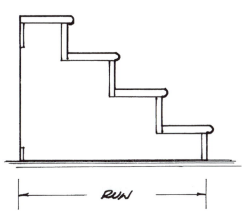

STEP WITH NOSING

THE NOSING IS NOT FIGURED INTO THE TOTAL RUN.

RUN

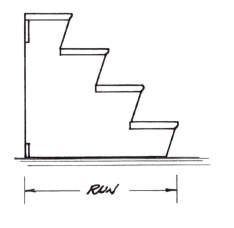

RAKED OR INCLINED RISER

THE INCLINED DEPTH IS NOT FIGURED INTO THE RUN.

RUN

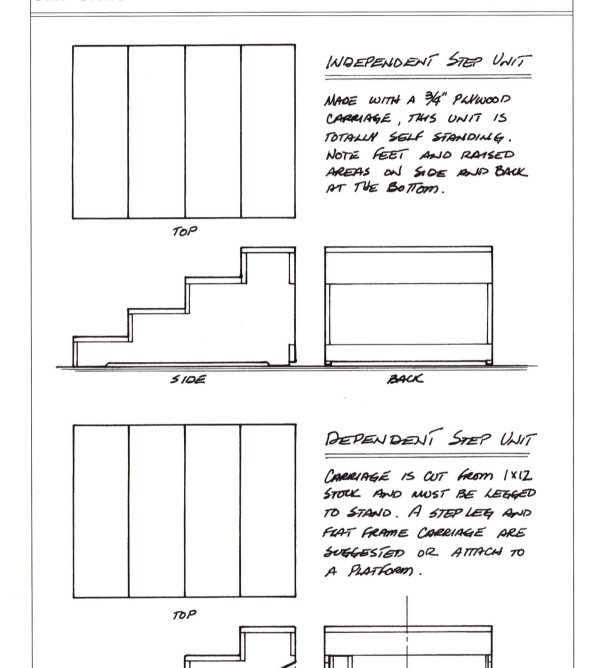

INDEPENDENT STEP UNIT

MADE WITH A 3/4" PLYWOOD CARRIAGE, THIS UNIT IS TOTALLY SELF STANDING. NOTE FEET AND RAISED AREAS ON SIDE AND BACK AT THE BOTTOM.

TOP

SIDE

BACK

DEPENDENT STEP UNIT

CARRIAGE IS CUT FROM 1×12 STOCK AND MUST BE LEGGED TO STAND. A STEP LEG AND FLAT FRAME CARRIAGE ARE SUGGESTED OR ATTACH TO A PLATFORM.

TOP

SIDE

BACK

inside carriage(s) usually of 1 x stock, instead of plywood (to cut down on extra weight).

The second step unit in the Drawing V-6 is a cut-carriage which is made of 1 x stock. The addition of a hinged leg at the back makes it independent. This leg will fold to the back of the carriage, making storage less of a problem (discussed in more detail in Drawing V-12). It could also have step legs as indicated.

The step unit (see Drawing V-7) is a solid carriage unit. This type has the advantage of being easy to build, "thin" for storage and light-weight. However, the width is limited without beefing up the tread and the unit is not aesthetically pleasing for most situations. It does work well for offstage escape units (see Drawings V-11 and V-14).

LAYING OUT CARRIAGES

It is often easiest to understand the details of stair construction and the relationship of parts if you draw the finished unit on a piece of paper (see Drawing V-8). By working "backward" and drawing in the treads and risers and the other extra support pieces, the finished unit is "built" on the paper. By cutting away the riser, treads and extra pieces, an accurate pattern is created. This can be used for a plywood carriage which will hold the pieces to build the step unit.

Note that the rise/tread relationship on the layout is constant throughout the carriage. However, the cut into the carriage (the pattern piece) is also the same as the rise/tread relationship desired on the finished unit, except for the first and last step. On the bottom step, the thickness of the tread material (usually ¾″ plywood) must be deducted from the rise. Make sure it is taken off the bottom. Do not notch the carriage deeper. The Drawing V-8 shows how the relationship remains constant from the first step on.

At the back of the top step, the thickness of the riser material (in the drawing, it is ¾″ material) must be deducted. Again, make sure it is cut from the back, and not removed from the front of the carriage.

A framing square is a valuable tool for laying out the proper relationship of the risers and treads (see Drawing V-9). Special clips can be bought which lock onto the square at the desired position and make it easier to slide it along the mark at each cut. A piece of tape on the square at the desired points can also do the job.

CUTTING THE CARRIAGE

Once the carriage is laid out, it is ideal to be able to cut at one time all carriages needed for the unit. This assures that the pieces will accept the risers and treads in the same manner. Tie the pieces of stock together with a few duplex nails and cut away. A band saw with a wide blade works very well for this job, but a circular saw can cut much of it, with a hand saw finishing the job. Sabre saws should not be used because in a piece this thick, their flexible blade tends to cut a crooked kerf.

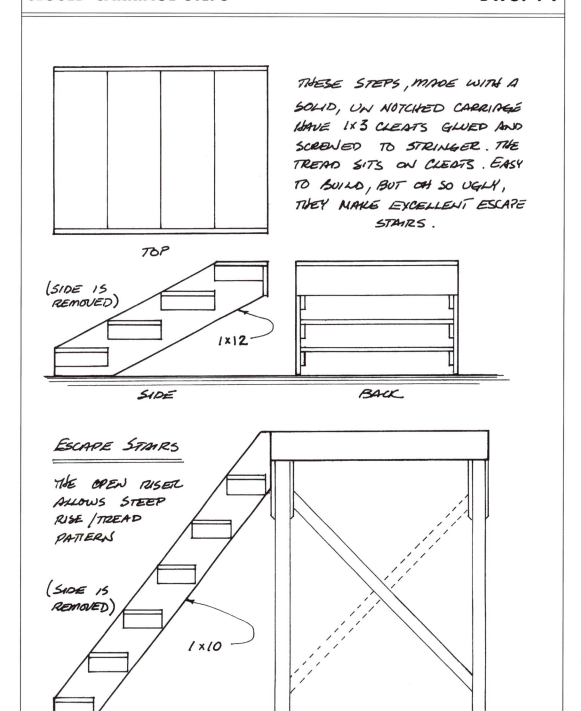

TOP

THESE STEPS, MADE WITH A SOLID, UN NOTCHED CARRIAGE HAVE 1X3 CLEATS GLUED AND SCREWED TO STRINGER. THE TREAD SITS ON CLEATS. EASY TO BUILD, BUT OH SO UGLY, THEY MAKE EXCELLENT ESCAPE STAIRS.

(SIDE IS REMOVED)

1X12

SIDE

BACK

Escape Stairs

THE OPEN RISER ALLOWS STEEP RISE/TREAD PATTERN

(SIDE IS REMOVED)

1X10

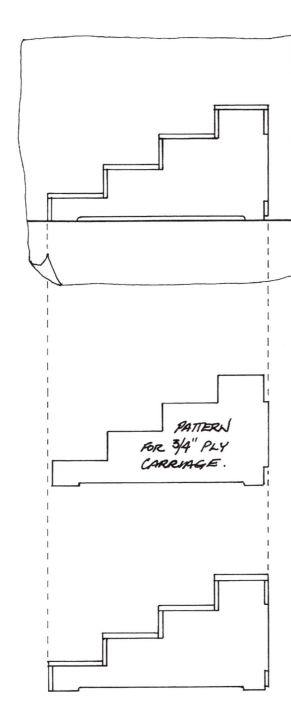

ON A PIECE OF PAPER, LAY OUT STAIRS WITH DESIRED RISE/TREAD RELATIONSHIP. THEN DRAW IN RISERS AND TREADS, NOTCHES FOR BACK SUPPORTS AND RAISED AREA AT BASE.

CUT OUT PATTERN FOR CARRIAGE. NOTE HEIGHT OF FIRST RISE AND WIDTH OF LAST TREAD.

PATTERN FOR 3/4" PLY CARRIAGE.

RISERS + TREADS

TO ASSEMBLE, ATTACH TWO BACK SUPPORTS THEN RISERS. APPLY TREADS.

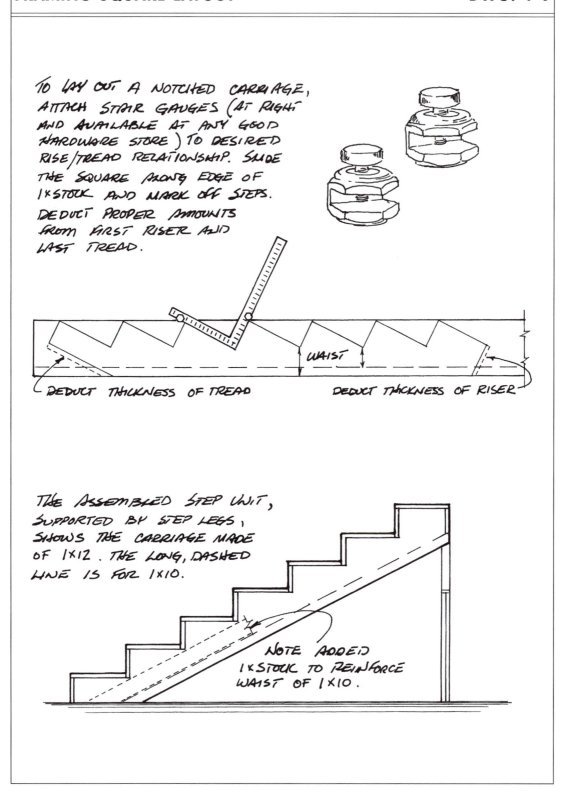

TO LAY OUT A NOTCHED CARRIAGE, ATTACH STAIR GAUGES (AT RIGHT AND AVAILABLE AT ANY GOOD HARDWARE STORE) TO DESIRED RISE/TREAD RELATIONSHIP. SLIDE THE SQUARE ALONG EDGE OF 1×STOCK AND MARK OFF STEPS. DEDUCT PROPER AMOUNTS FROM FIRST RISER AND LAST TREAD.

WAIST

DEDUCT THICKNESS OF TREAD

DEDUCT THICKNESS OF RISER

THE ASSEMBLED STEP UNIT, SUPPORTED BY STEP LEGS, SHOWS THE CARRIAGE MADE OF 1×12. THE LONG, DASHED LINE IS FOR 1×10.

NOTE ADDED 1×STOCK TO REINFORCE WAIST OF 1×10.

THE WAIST

Notice the mention of the "waist" in Drawing V-9. It must be at least 4″ wide. This is very important because it is the waist width which is actually carrying the weight; and the waist must increase in width as the stair unit grows in length.

If the waist appears weak, avoid a series of collapsing stairs by laminating an additional piece of 1 x stock to the inside of the stringer. This might affect a folding support leg if you are using one.

BUILDING STAIRS

The step unit at the top of Drawing V-6 shows a typical solid cut-carriage. It is probably the lightest-weight independent carriage. The ¾″ riser is very solid and gives good "meat" into which to attach the front of the tread as well as the back bottom of the tread. Notice the piece of 1 x 5¼″ stock at the back, beneath the top tread. This size will standardize with 1x stock platform construction, allowing stock stairs to work with stock platforms, and stock step legs.

MAKING DEPENDENT STAIRS INDEPENDENT

This sounds like a proposal for a federal program. Actually, by adding a folding leg (see Drawing V-12) to the back of a dependent unit, set-ups, shifts and strikes will be easier. These legs fold to the back of the unit and can be held against the stair with a tie-line tacked to the bottom of a tread. It is also possible to use stock platform legs, because the top support at the back of the step unit is 5¼″ wide, matching a stock platform (see Drawing V-6, bottom step unit).

FIGURING THE FOLDING BRACE

The folding brace need not exist, because it can be replaced with a 1 x 3 which is tight-pin hinged to the bottom of a tread and loose-pin hinged to the toggle in the back support carriage (see Drawing V-12). Simply remove the loose pin and fold the brace into the unit, and then fold the leg. The brace will be held in by the leg. If this simple, practical and cheaper-by-one-less-hinge method suits your needs, read no more. However, if you have a thirst for adventure, desire for the excitement of potential failure (unless incredible hurdles are jumped), and crave the smug satisfaction which wafts over you when you hold a crowd in awe with your prowess, do build a folding brace for the leg. The only advantage this brace has over the unbroken 1 x 3 is that it speeds set-up and strike time by a few seconds. You've been warned.

Obviously, accuracy is very important here, and you must lay out the components as carefully as possible. Either draft the unit on paper using a large scale, or lay the step unit onto its side with the flat-frame carriage leg hinged in place. Open the leg as it will be (90° to the floor) and hold it to the work table or floor for swinging the arc. Cut a 1 x 3 for the bottom brace which will fit the distance. Mount the hinges at each end and test it again. Snap a line from the pin of hinges A and B. Now swing the arcs to find the "magic middle" for the break. Using the distance between the pins of hinges A and C as a radius and the pin of hinge A as a point, swing an arc to intersect the snapped line (A'). Next, using the pins of hinges B and C as a radius and the pin of B as a point, swing another arc (B'). Divide the distance between A' and B' (X). Reset the compass with a radius from the pin of hinge B to the midpoint (X) between A' and B'. Swing this arc from the pin of hinge B to the brace. This is where the brace would be cut and hinged. Mount the brace and pray. After all, your future depends on this happening properly. If the brace chooses not to fold as neatly as desired, do not hang up your carpenter's belt and slink away into the sunshine, but remove the hammer and adjust (slightly) the offending hinges, or remove the mother and replace it with a loose-pin brace, or…

USING STOCK STAIRS

The Drawings (V-1, V-10, and V-11) show some examples of how modular stock stairs will work with other modules. The combinations become more flexible and, blush, more exciting with each new piece of stock.

ESCAPE STAIRS

"Escapes," as they are fondly called, do not have to be seen and can, therefore, be made differently (see Drawings V-11 and VI-13). They must not be made badly, however, because if anything, they take a worse beating than their onstage stepsisters.

The closed or solid carriage method (which resembles a ship's ladder) offers a quick and effective way of building escapes, especially for steep stairs (see Drawing V-7). Try not to have the treads overhang each other too much. This forces actors to back down the stairs to get good footing, and bulky costumes can further hinder progress. Climbing up is usually no problem. It is, of course, possible to use stock stairs for escapes when available and appropriate.

RAILINGS

Actors' Equity Association, the professional union for actors and stage managers, insists that all escape stairs and platforms have railings. While this law seems a giant pain in the work schedule, it is one of the most logical in their book. Actors leaving the stage are "blinded" from the stage lights, which is compounded by the contrast to the dark backstage area. This makes the actors quite dangerous. They must have railings and lights to help guide them, or they could fall and seriously damage the scenery, not to mention the costume. I have heard that once even an actor was damaged, but recovered without the assistance of a shop crew on overtime.

While we are ranting about railings, it is also noteworthy to mention the need to round all edges and ends of the stock used to make them. This busy-work, affectionately known as "baby-proofing," also saves splinters in hands, snagged costumes, torn curtains and tempers. A cornering tool, Surform rasp or small plane is

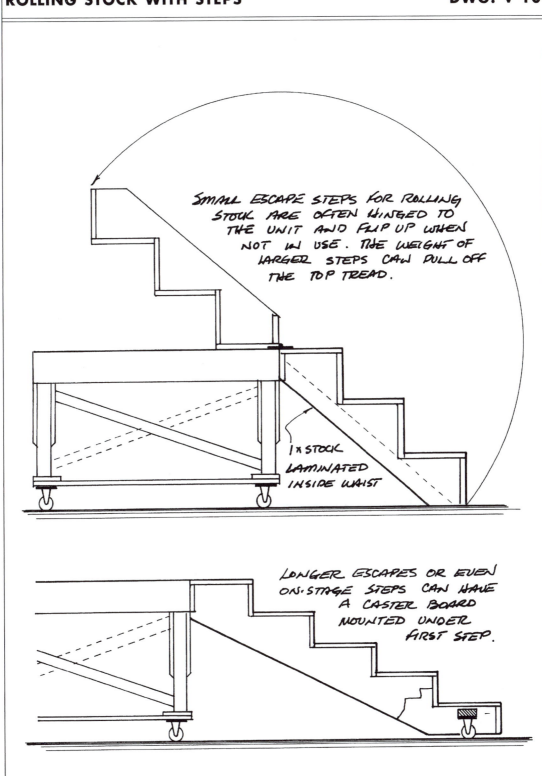

SMALL ESCAPE STEPS FOR ROLLING STOCK ARE OFTEN HINGED TO THE UNIT AND FLIP UP WHEN NOT IN USE. THE WEIGHT OF LARGER STEPS CAN PULL OFF THE TOP TREAD.

1 x STOCK LAMINATED INSIDE WAIST

LONGER ESCAPES OR EVEN ON-STAGE STEPS CAN HAVE A CASTER BOARD MOUNTED UNDER FIRST STEP.

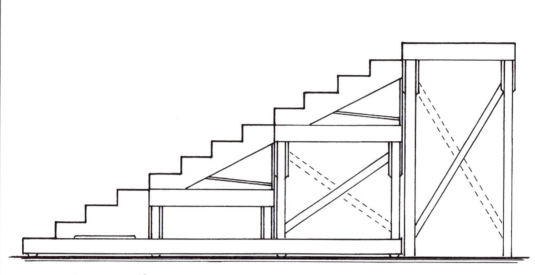

A LONG FLIGHT OF STAIRS MADE FROM STOCK UNITS.

THE DRAWING ABOVE SHOWS
BOTH STOCK STEPS AND PLAT-
FORMS UTILIZED IN THE FLIGHT.
A CASTERED WAGON CARRIES
MOST OF THE UNITS AND BE-
COMES THE FIRST STEP.

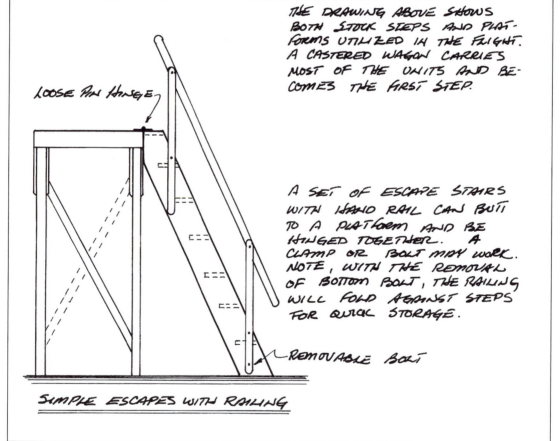

LOOSE PIN HINGE

A SET OF ESCAPE STAIRS
WITH HAND RAIL CAN BUTT
TO A PLATFORM AND BE
HINGED TOGETHER. A
CLAMP OR BOLT MAY WORK.
NOTE, WITH THE REMOVAL
OF BOTTOM BOLT, THE RAILING
WILL FOLD AGAINST STEPS
FOR QUICK STORAGE.

REMOVABLE BOLT

SIMPLE ESCAPES WITH RAILING

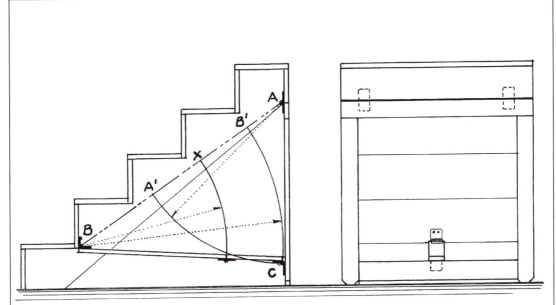

TO FIGURE THE HINGED, FOLDING BRACE, CONSTRUCT A LINE FROM THE
CENTER OF THE PIN ON HINGE A TO SAME ON HINGE B. WITH B AS
A RADIUS POINT AND BC AS A RADIUS, SCRIBE AN ARC THROUGH AB (B').
REPEAT WITH A AS POINT AND AC AS RADIUS (A'). HALVE A'-B' (X).
WITH B AS A POINT AND BX AS RADIUS, SCRIBE THE ARC WHICH WILL
INDICATE THE BREAK IN THE BRACE.

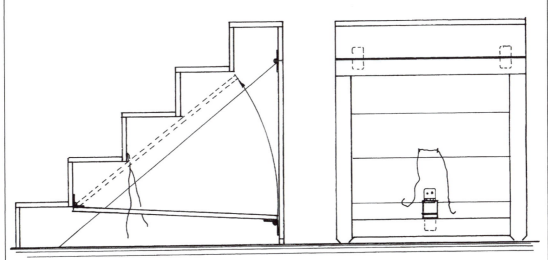

OPEN LEG UNTIL SQUARE. MEASURE FOR BRACE. ATTACH TO STEP WITH
TIGHT PIN HINGE AND TOGGLE WITH LOOSE PIN HINGE. THE CORD
SECURES AROUND TOGGLE, USUALLY IN A GRANNY KNOT. IT'S CHEATING.

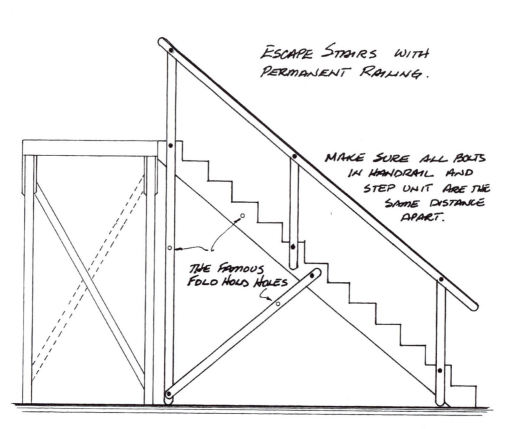

ESCAPE STAIRS WITH PERMANENT RAILING.

MAKE SURE ALL BOLTS IN HANDRAIL AND STEP UNIT ARE THE SAME DISTANCE APART.

THE FAMOUS FOLD HOLD HOLES

SOME SHOPS EXTEND CENTER VERTICAL IN RAILING TO FLOOR. THIS MAKES A LEG BUT THE ANGLE BRACE ALSO TAKES WEIGHT TO FLOOR IN ADDITION TO CROSS BRACING UNIT. BOTH CAN BE INCORPORATED

ESCAPE STAIRS IN REPOSE

FOLD HOLD HOLES LINE UP AND WITH BOLT, HOLD RAILING TO STEP UNIT.

THE RISER WITH CLEAT

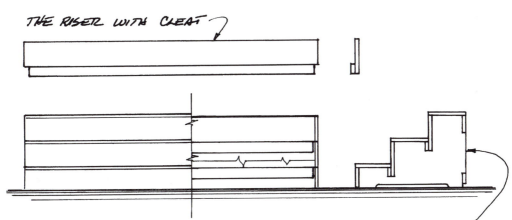

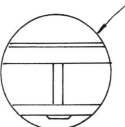

THE RISER CAN NOTCH AND EXTEND
BELOW THE TREAD. A CLEAT OF
1×STOCK, WELL-LAMINATED TO THE
RISER, CARRIES THE BACK OF THE
TREAD. THIS IS ESPECIALLY WEIGHT-
SAVING IN LONG UNITS.

CENTER SUPPORT
AT BACK IF
NEEDED.

TO REALLY CHEAT, RUN A STRINGER
OF 1×STOCK BENEATH THE RISERS AND
TREADS. CLEAT IT TO THE STEPS. THIS IS
QUITE TACKY BUT EFFECTIVE.

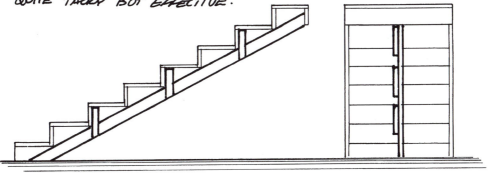

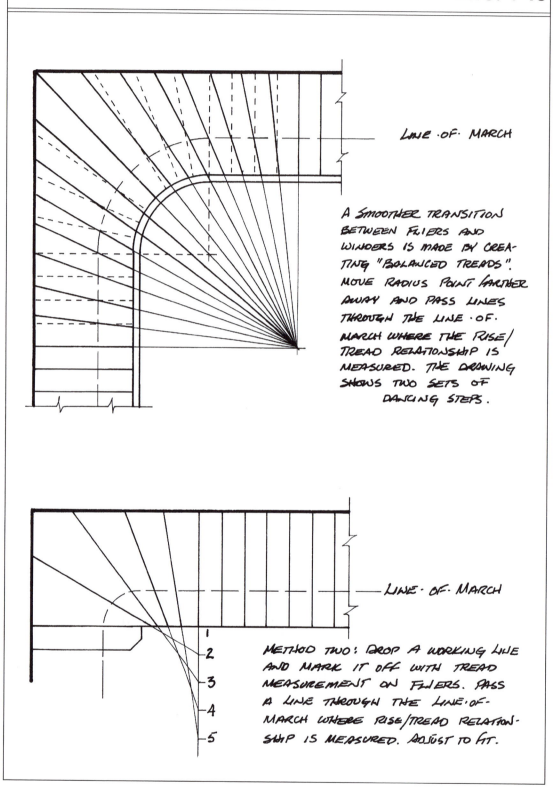

LINE·OF·MARCH

A SMOOTHER TRANSITION BETWEEN FLIERS AND WINDERS IS MADE BY CREATING "BALANCED TREADS". MOVE RADIUS POINT FARTHER AWAY AND PASS LINES THROUGH THE LINE·OF·MARCH WHERE THE RISE/TREAD RELATIONSHIP IS MEASURED. THE DRAWING SHOWS TWO SETS OF DANCING STEPS.

LINE·OF·MARCH

METHOD TWO: DROP A WORKING LINE AND MARK IT OFF WITH TREAD MEASUREMENT ON FLIERS. PASS A LINE THROUGH THE LINE·OF·MARCH WHERE RISE/TREAD RELATIONSHIP IS MEASURED. ADJUST TO FIT.

good for this job, though some shops automatically use the router with a bullnosing or roundover bit on all edges of the railing stock before it is assembled.

Railings are usually bolted to the stairs (and platforms used as escapes) for efficient removal at the end of the show. However, some are permanently mounted to the escape unit (see Drawing V-13), and fold and store with the stairs. The nut on the bolt must be on the outside of the rail to prevent snagging. Emergency railings can be C-clamped in place, but should be bolted as soon as possible to get rid of the overhanging clamp.

SOME SHORT AND LONG CUTS

The Drawing V-14 shows two ways to avoid using a center carriage, usually necessary in step units over three feet wide. The top method extends a notched riser below the tread in front of it, and laminates a 1 x cleat on the notched part to snug up under the tread and carry the weight placed on it.

Note also the support at the back of the unit; this will probably be needed in stairs wider than 4'-0".

The bottom drawing shows a "stringer" which is cleated to the risers and helps take the weight. It is really ugly, but workable.

It is perhaps beyond the scope of this handbook, but… there are times when simple winders (see Drawing V-3) solve the problem of rising high enough in a given space, but they create awkward steps. It is possible to "balance" the treads and spread out the sharp angles. This usually creates a stair unit which meets the dumpster after the show, but… oh, well. Drawing V-15 shows two ways to solve the problem. Note that the line-of-march, about one-third of the stair's width, is where the rise/tread formula should be measured.

Fancy ends on the bottom step are not uncommon in the real world. These decorative extensions are often added into a stock step in the theatre world. However, as Drawing V-16 shows, they could be standardized and kept in stock. Of course, the designer will always want the other end to be the fancy one.

A commode step is an extended bottom step (or several steps), and is useful in theatre not only because it reeks of elegance, but because it affords a workable raised area for actors, who often reek of their own accord. The layout for a commode step is really quite simple and can be adjusted to fit any given situation. Again, it is possible the step could be a separate platform placed before the flight of stairs.

FLAT FRAME CARRIAGES

Flat frame stair carriages (also called "gates") have a great advantage over all other step systems. They can be easily dismantled, the frames and treads stored separately, taking up little space. The component pieces are reusable, either as they were originally used or in a different tread configuration. The same carriages can be a straight run of stairs, a curved staircase, or serpentine or anything else desired by merely changing the shapes of the treads (see Drawings V-17, V-18 and V-19).

The disadvantages are worth noting. Flat frame carriages may initially take longer

FOUR (OF MANY) CURTAIL STEPS:

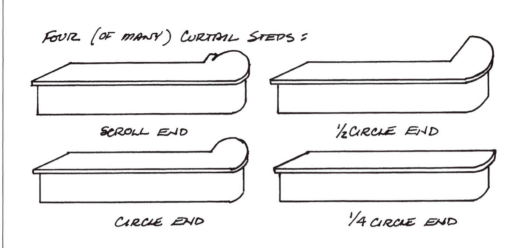

SCROLL END

½ CIRCLE END

CIRCLE END

¼ CIRCLE END

How to Lay out a Commode Step

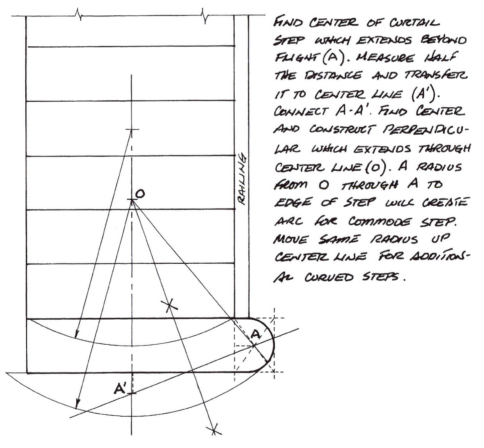

FIND CENTER OF CURTAIL STEP WHICH EXTENDS BEYOND FLIGHT (A). MEASURE HALF THE DISTANCE AND TRANSFER IT TO CENTER LINE (A'). CONNECT A-A'. FIND CENTER AND CONSTRUCT PERPENDICULAR WHICH EXTENDS THROUGH CENTER LINE (O). A RADIUS FROM O THROUGH A TO EDGE OF STEP WILL CREATE ARC FOR COMMODE STEP. MOVE SAME RADIUS UP CENTER LINE FOR ADDITIONAL CURVED STEPS.

to construct. Another disadvantage is that, when assembled, they are awkward to move about, though a specially constructed dolly can do away with this problem. It should be pointed out that this method is not good for small step units but is fine for longer runs of steps and curves. Another disadvantage is that actors cannot pass under them.

The same rules for easily navigable stairs (see Drawing V-4) apply for curved stairs as well as for straight runs. However, on curved stairs figure the rise/tread ratio between one-quarter and one-third the distance in from the narrow end of the tread. This is the old familiar "line-of-march." If you can't make the rules work, then don't make the stairs.

If you are going to build a set (or sets) of stock flat frame carriages, you must first decide what stock rise to use. It should correspond with other stock steps. It is not practical to build stairs wider than 4'-0" because of the 4 x 8 sheet of plywood which is used for the tread, but it can be done. Inasmuch as the stair configurations may be curved, it is inadvisable to build narrower than 3'-0", because on curved stairs the tread is often fairly narrow on the inside curve. Actors tend to seek a wider, more comfortable, part to walk on. They also tend to fall off if they don't find it. However, carriages less than 3'-0" can certainly be built for runs or large curves.

When planning the set of flat frame carriages, remember that it takes two carriages for each tread, one for the front and one for the back. As Drawing V-17 shows, the construction is quite simple, but must be exact. The total height of each carriage is less the thickness of the tread material, which is usually ¾". The 2'-0" step, for example, would have a front carriage which is 1'-11¼" high, and the next with a cleat at the same height. When the tread is placed on the top, it then equals the desired height of 2'-0".

You will note that there is no bottom rail on the frame. This is done to eliminate the rail which would sit on the floor and rock. Because the stiles go to the floor, the ends are nipped off with a 45° angle cut ¾" up on each edge (see Drawing II-34). This leaves each 3" stile with only 1½" resting on the floor, and prevents splitting the stile when skidding the frame on the floor. The corner blocks are flushed to the edge instead of holding them back the customary stock thickness; because nothing will need to butt to the stile and to gain extra strength. A standard corner brace is inserted into the frame when it fits.

The top rail is held to the stiles with a large block of ¼" 3-ply, cut so the grain runs vertically. This is the strongest way to reinforce the joint of the stile to the rail. The plywood block must run from the top of the rail to the bottom of the 1 x 3 cleat (see Drawing V-17).

The 1 x 3 cleat is for the back of the tread to rest on, and is glued and screwed down to the front of the frame over the ¼" plywood block, which is attached to the cleat from the other side. It is, therefore, necessary that the top of the preceding carriage be the same height as the cleat on the next carriage, and that the upcoming carriage have a cleat which will match its top. The distance between the top of the carriage and the top of the cleat is the agreed upon step rise. When a tread is laid on a cleat, the distance to the top of the frame is now short the rise by the thickness of

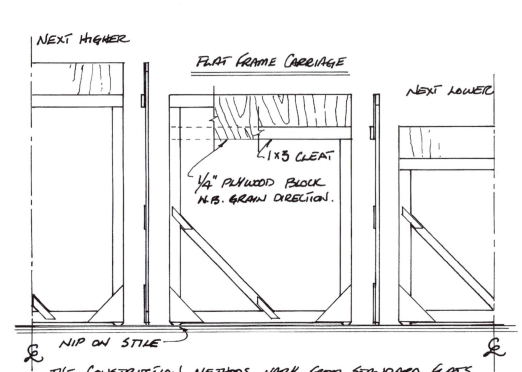

NEXT HIGHER

FLAT FRAME CARRIAGE

NEXT LOWER

1×3 CLEAT

1/4" PLYWOOD BLOCK
N.B. GRAIN DIRECTION.

NIP ON STILE

THE CONSTRUCTION METHODS VARY FROM STANDARD FLATS BOTH IN THE STILES WHICH ARE NIPPED AND GO TO THE FLOOR, AND THE RAIL WHICH IS FIXED WITH A BLOCK OF 1/4" PLY THAT EXTENDS TO THE BOTTOM OF THE CLEAT (WHICH ALSO ATTACHES TO IT FROM BEHIND).

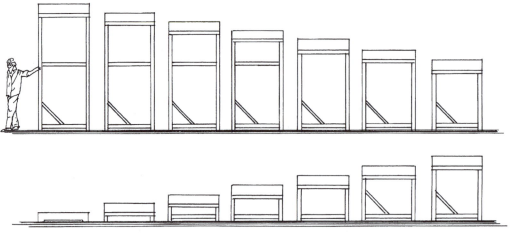

A FAMILY OF FLAT FRAME CARRIAGES FROM 8" TO 112".

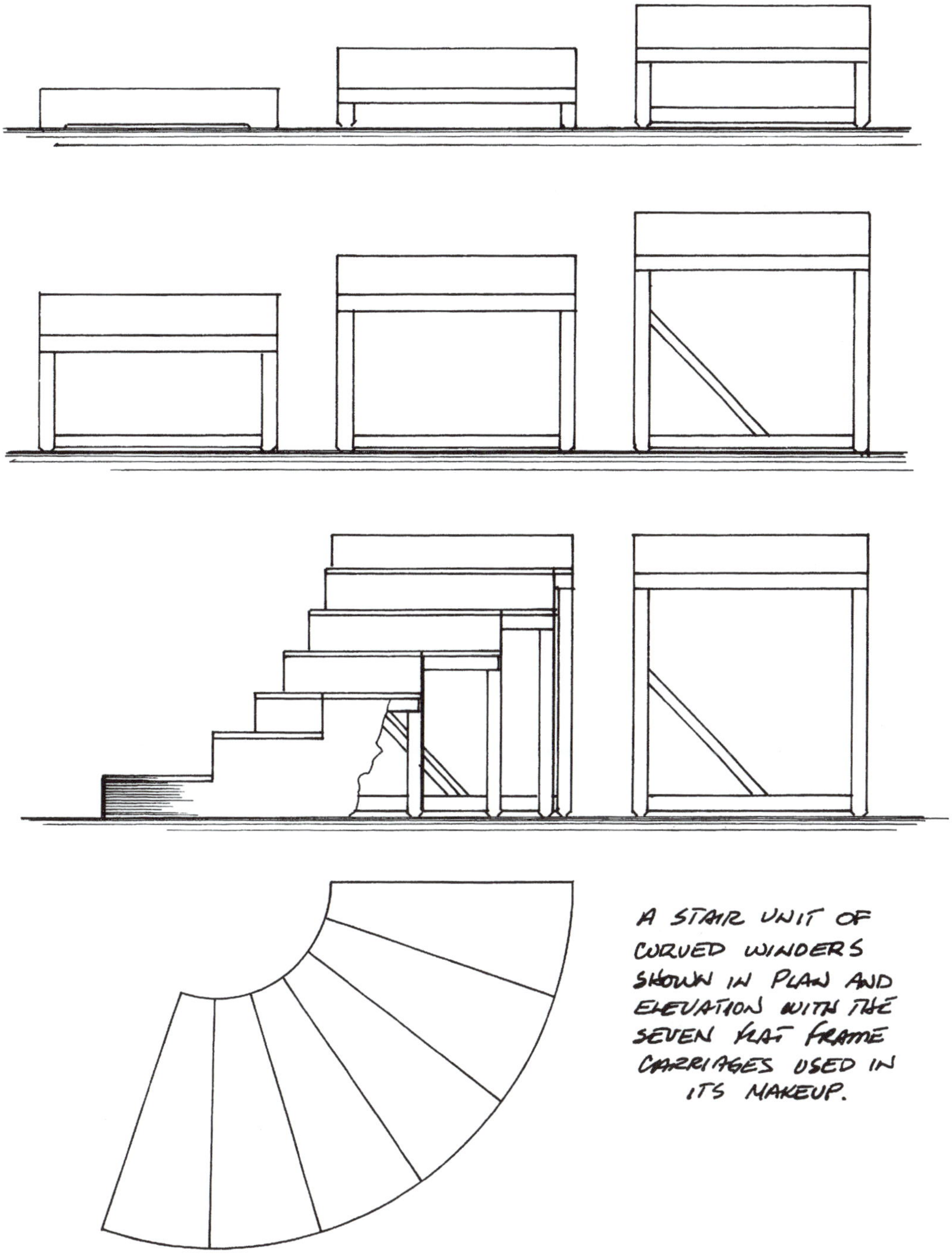

A STAIR UNIT OF
CURVED WINDERS
SHOWN IN PLAN AND
ELEVATION WITH THE
SEVEN FLAT FRAME
CARRIAGES USED IN
ITS MAKEUP.

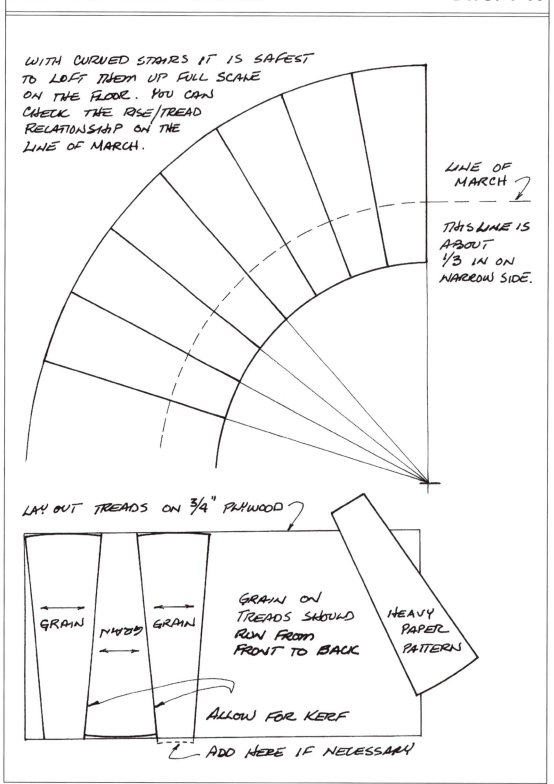

WITH CURVED STAIRS IT IS SAFEST
TO LOFT THEM UP FULL SCALE
ON THE FLOOR. YOU CAN
CHECK THE RISE/TREAD
RELATIONSHIP ON THE
LINE OF MARCH.

LINE OF
MARCH

THIS LINE IS
ABOUT
1/3 IN ON
NARROW SIDE.

LAY OUT TREADS ON 3/4" PLYWOOD

GRAIN

GRAIN

GRAIN

GRAIN ON
TREADS SHOULD
RUN FROM
FRONT TO BACK

HEAVY
PAPER
PATTERN

ALLOW FOR KERF

ADD HERE IF NECESSARY

the tread, but this distance will be made up when the next tread is placed on the top. Again, the distance from the top of the frame to the top of the cleat is the rise.

Make sure that the plywood block is well glued and attached to the stiles and rail. It not only fastens the joint, but acts as the facing piece for the step and also becomes the necessary sway bracing for the frame. The reason the block must extend below the 1 x 3 cleat and be glued and attached to it is because the weight of the actor must be distributed from the tread to the cleat and into the block, so it can go back to the stile and to the floor. The 1 x 3 cleat alone is not strong enough without the block's support.

A set of flat frame carriages can easily run up to 8'-0" without any worries of sway or wobble when properly braced and faced. The same general rules work for additional toggles as they do in standard flats. The distance need not be closer than 4'-0", but should not be farther apart than 6'-0". However, when a height is reached which would require a toggle, it is useful to standardize the position in the next frames. This simply gives another position to attach the frames together (see Drawing V-17). When the frames are assembled with their treads (see Drawing V-18) and squared up, a batten or battens should be attached to the 1 x 3 toggle at the bottom of the frames to hold them constant. Next, some cross-bracing will be needed between the larger frames of the run to hold them vertical. Once the treads hold the top constant and the battens hold the bottom, very little cross-bracing is needed to hold the stairs square. The completed unit will be amazingly solid and rigid. A facing of ⅛" untempered hardboard (or the like) will act as additional cross-bracing for the side, if it is attached to the frames.

Loft up and cut the treads as required and screw them to the carriages (see Drawing V-19). Do not nail; pounding can break the glued joints and weaken the frames. A piece of ¼" x ¾" strap iron can be drilled to act as a jig for the screws. If used on all treads, it facilitates set-up and saves additional holes in the cleat when the carriage is used again. If possible, when using plywood treads try to keep the grain running about 90° to the carriage or the cleat for maximum strength.

PART VI • SHOP MATH

Basic shop math is not the type of information which needs to be held in ready at all times, but it is handy to have it somewhere. Aside from the plane geometry which follows, it is nice to know that:

• The AREA of a RECTANGLE is one side multiplied by an adjacent side.

• The AREA of a CIRCLE is pi (3.14) multiplied by the radius squared ($A = \pi r^2$).

• The CIRCUMFERENCE of a CIRCLE is pi (3.14) multiplied by the diameter ($C = \pi d$), or you can follow Drawing VI-20.

If you are using these formulae to figure out how much paint to buy, just remember the paint company stretches everything including your budget. Always purchase 20–25% additional paint or plan to thin a lot.

And if you believe that there is no such thing as a line, what do you think they've been handing you all these years? The following pages contain examples of things nobody should have to remember, but…

TO BISECT A STRAIGHT LINE (A·B)
SET A COMPASS WITH A RADIUS
LONGER THAN 1/2 THE LINE.
SWING ARCS FROM A AND B.
A LINE THROUGH THEIR INTER-
SECTIONS WILL DIVIDE THE
LINE. THIS LINE IS ALSO PER-
PENDICULAR TO THE ORIGINAL
LINE.

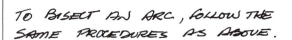

TO BISECT AN ARC, FOLLOW THE
SAME PROCEDURES AS ABOVE.

TO BISECT AN ANGLE, TAKE A
COMPASS AND FROM THE VERTEX,
SWING AN ARC WHICH CROSSES
THE LEGS (C AND D). FROM C
AND D, SWING ARCS WHICH WILL
INTERSECT (E). A LINE FROM
THE VERTEX TO E WILL DIVIDE
THE ANGLE INTO TWO EQUAL
PARTS.

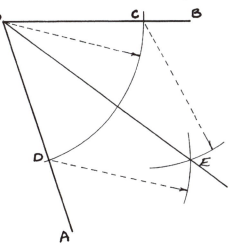

TO ERECT A PERPENDICULAR AT
A GIVEN POINT ON A LINE,
SWING ANY ARC FROM THE
POINT TO INTERSECT THE LINE.
FROM THESE POINTS SWING TWO
ARCS WHICH INTERSECT. A
LINE FROM THIS INTERSECTION
THROUGH THE ORIGINAL POINT
WILL CREATE A PERPENDICULAR.

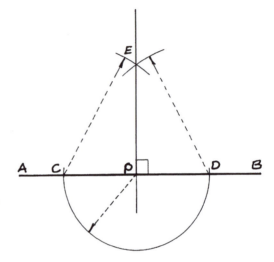

TO ERECT A PERPENDICULAR AT A
GIVEN POINT NEAR THE END OF
A LINE, PICK ANY POINT (C)
ABOVE THE LINE. SWING AN
ARC FROM C WITH THE RADIUS
C·P. IT WILL INTERSECT THE
ORIGINAL LINE (D) AND SHOULD
SWING PAST P. A LINE FROM
D THROUGH C AND EXTENDED
TO INTERSECT THE ARC WILL
FIX E. A LINE FROM E TO
P IS PERPENDICULAR TO THE
ORIGINAL LINE.

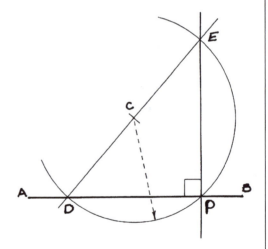

TO DRAW A PERPENDICULAR
TO A LINE FROM A POINT
AWAY FROM THE LINE, USE
THE POINT AS A RADIUS
CENTER AND SWING ANY
ARC WHICH WILL INTERSECT
THE ORIGINAL LINE (C AND D).
FROM THESE POINTS ERECT
A PERPENDICULAR BISECTOR
WHICH SHOULD PASS THROUGH
THE POINT.

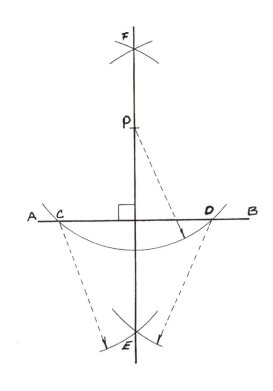

A VARIATION SOLVES THE
PROBLEM BY ESTABLISHING
ANY TWO POINTS (C AND D)
ON THE ORIGINAL LINE. ARCS
ARE SWUNG FROM C AND D
WHICH PASS THROUGH THE
POINT (P) AND BELOW THE
LINE, INTERSECT AT E.
A LINE FROM E TO P WILL
ESTABLISH THE PERPENDICULAR
TO THE LINE.

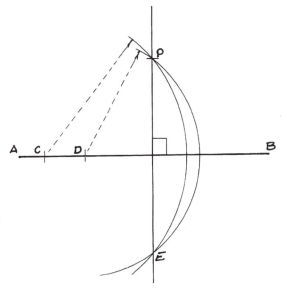

TO CREATE A LINE FROM A GIVEN POINT WHICH IS PARALLEL TO ANOTHER LINE, SET A COMPASS WITH A RADIUS SUFFICIENT TO SWING AN ARC FROM THE POINT AND INTERSECT THE LINE (C). FROM C, SWING ANOTHER ARC OF THE SAME RADIUS TO PASS THROUGH THE POINT AND LINE (D). RESET THE COMPASS WITH DP AS A RADIUS AND FROM C INTERSECT THE FIRST ARC (E). A LINE FROM THE POINT THROUGH E IS PARALLEL TO THE ORIGINAL LINE.

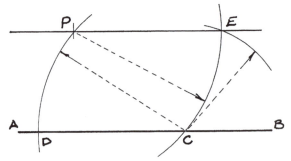

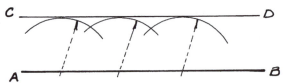

CREATING A LINE PARALLEL TO ANOTHER CAN ALSO BE DONE BY SWINGING MANY ARCS FROM THE ORIGINAL LINE. A PARALLEL LINE WILL "SIT" ON THE TOPS OF THE ARCS. MANY ARCS MAKE LIGHT WORK.

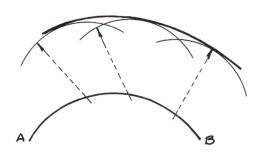

A LINE MAY BE DIVIDED
INTO ANY NUMBER OF EQUAL
PARTS USING A RULER.
PLACE "ZERO" AT ONE END
OF THE LINE AND THE
DESIRED DIVISION (7") ON A
PERPENDICULAR TO THE OTHER
END. MARK THE POINTS.
LINES, PARALLEL TO THE
PERPENDICULAR, WILL DI-
VIDE THE ORIGINAL LINE.
THIS IS OFTEN USED WITH
LUMBER OR FLATS WHICH
RECEIVE A PATTERN.

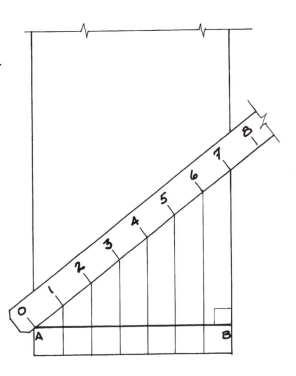

THIS VARIATION MERELY
PUTS THE DIVIDING INCRE-
MENTS ON AN ARBITRARY
LINE. THE ZERO MARK ON
THE RULER IS CONNECTED
TO THE END OF THE LINE,
AND LINES PARALLEL TO
THAT LINE CONNECT THE
OTHER POINTS. THE ORIGINAL
LINE IS AGAIN DIVIDED
INTO EQUAL PARTS.

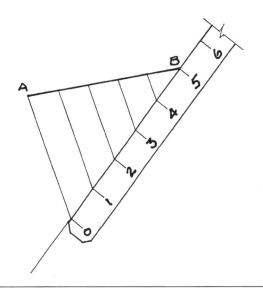

REDUCING OR ENLARGING LINEAR DIMENSIONS CAN BE DONE BY ESTABLISHING A HORIZONTAL LINE WHICH IS PERPENDICULAR TO THE OBJECT. ESTABLISH A POINT (O) ON THIS LINE WHICH IS APPROXIMATELY TWICE THE LENGTH AWAY FROM THE OBJECT AS ITS HEIGHT. LINES FROM O THROUGH POINTS ON THE OBJECT WILL INDICATE PROPORTIONAL CHANGES.

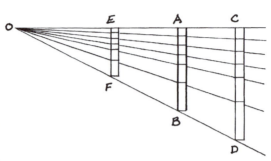

TO REDUCE OR ENLARGE ANY RECTANGULAR SHAPE, ESTABLISH A DIAGONAL THROUGH IT. BY CHANGING AB, AC WILL CHANGE PROPORTIONALLY AND CORRECTLY WHEN THE ENDS MEET ON THE DIAGONAL.

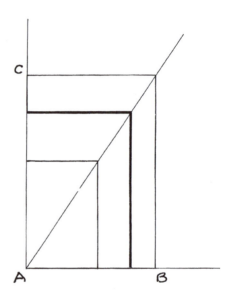

IRREGULAR SHAPES WILL REDUCE OR ENLARGE WHEN DIAGONALS INTERSECT EACH CORNER AND THE LINES ARE KEPT PARALLEL TO THE ORIGINAL.

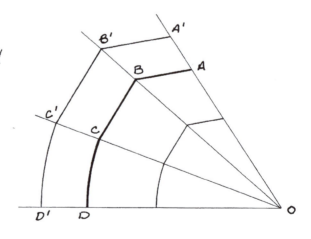

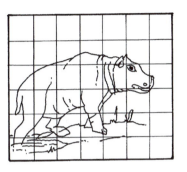

REDUCTION AND ENLARGEMENT BY THE GRID METHOD IS OFTEN USED WHEN PAINTING DROPS. BUT IT IS HANDY WHEN THE OPAQUE PROJECTOR OR THE OVERHEAD PROJECTOR BLOW THEIR LAST LAMP AT MIDNIGHT. ANY OBJECT OR DESIGN CAN BE ADJUSTED BY GRIDDING IT OFF IN ONE SCALE AND TRANSFERRING THE INFORMATION IN EACH RECTANGLE TO A CORRESPONDING RECTANGLE IN ANOTHER SCALE.

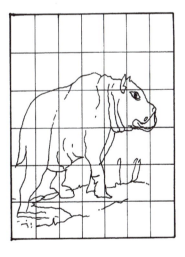

TO COPY A GIVEN ANGLE, DRAW ONE SIDE OF IT IN THE POSITION NEEDED. SET THE COMPASS AT ANY LENGTH AND SWING AN ARC FROM THE VERTEX TO INTERSECT THE LEGS. REPEAT THIS ARC ON THE LINE FOR THE NEW ANGLE. RESET THE COMPASS FOR THE CHORD CREATED BY THE FIRST ARC. TRANSFER THIS INFORMATION TO THE SECOND ARC. AT THE INTERSECTION A LINE MAY BE DRAWN TO THE END OF THE LINE TO CREATE THE VERTEX OF THE SECOND ANGLE.

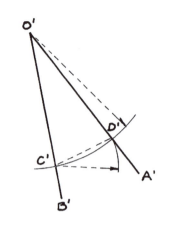

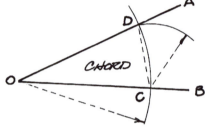

UNUSUAL SHAPES CAN BECOME "BOXED" OBJECTS AND EASILY MOVE ABOUT. DRAW RECTANGLES TO FIT THE MAJOR POINTS ON THE OBJECT. RE-DRAW THE RECTANGLES IN THE NEW POSITION AND RE-CONNECT THE POINTS TO ESTABLISH THE OBJECT.

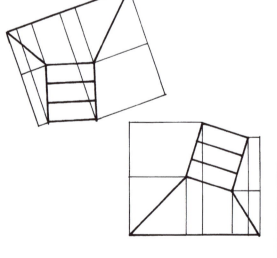

CREATING A TRIANGLE WHEN THE
SIDES ARE KNOWN IS ACCOMP-
LISHED BY SWINGING ARCS.
ESTABLISH THE BASE OF THE
TRIANGLE AND FROM EACH END
SWING ARCS WHOSE RADII ARE
THE LENGTHS OF THE KNOWN
SIDES. THE INTERSECTION OF
THESE ARCS IS THE VERTEX OF
THE TRIANGLE.

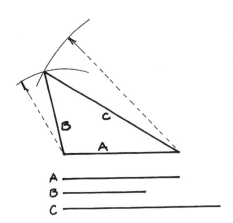

AN ISOSCELES TRIANGLE HAS THE
SAME RADIUS SWUNG FROM EACH
END OF THE BASE. THE INTER-
SECTION OF THE RADII FORMS THE
VERTEX.

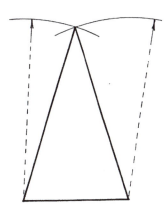

AN EQUILATERAL TRIANGLE IS
FORMED AS ABOVE. ALL SIDES
ARE EQUAL.

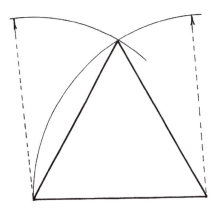

THE ETERNAL TRIANGLE SWINGS IN
DIFFERENT, OFTEN EROTIC CIRCLES,
WHICH INTERSECT AT THE VORTEX.

TO DRAW A RIGHT TRIANGLE WHEN THE HYPOTENUSE AND ONE SIDE ARE KNOWN, LAY OUT THE HYPOTENUSE AS A BASE. FROM THE CENTER OF THE LINE, SWING AN ARC FROM ONE END TO THE OTHER. RESET THE COMPASS TO THE KNOWN SIDE AND FROM ONE END SWING AN ARC TO INTERSECT THE FIRST ARC. CONNECT THIS INTERSECTION TO BOTH ENDS OF THE LINE TO COMPLETE THE RIGHT TRIANGLE.

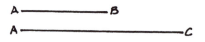

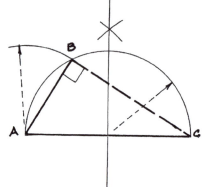

VISUAL PROOF IS OFFERED TO HELP PYTHAGORUS PROVE THAT THE SQUARE OF A HYPOTENUSE OF A RIGHT-ANGLED TRIANGLE IS EQUAL TO THE SUM OF THE SQUARES OF THE OTHER TWO SIDES.

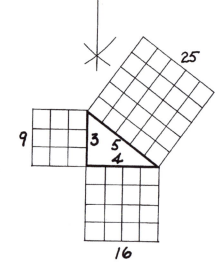

USING THE 3·4·5 METHOD TO CHECK ANY RIGHT ANGLE IS QUICK AND EASY, ESPECIALLY ON LARGE SCENIC UNITS.

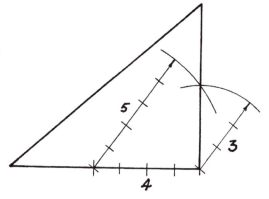

CREATING A PYTHAGOREAN TRIANGLE
WITH A 50-FOOT TAPE MEASURE
IS A FAST WAY TO ESTABLISH
THE CENTERLINE ON STAGE.
SNAP A LINE ON THE FLOOR
WHERE THE PLASTERLINE SHOULD
BE. FIND THE CENTER AND MARK
IT. MEASURE OFF 15'-0" AND
MARK THAT. PUT THE ZERO END
OF THE TAPE ON THE 15'-0" MARK
AND HOLD IT. ANOTHER PERSON
HOLDS THE 50'-0" LINE TO THE
CENTER MARK. A THIRD PERSON
MAKES A LOOP IN THE TAPE BY
PLACING THE 25'-0" POINT TO THE
30'-0" POINT. WHEN THE TAPE IS
STRETCHED TIGHTLY, A RIGHT
ANGLE IS CREATED FROM THE
CENTER MARK.

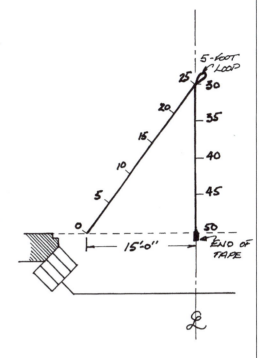

THE GOLDEN RECTANGLE
IS BASED ON A SQUARE
AND THE RECTANGLE CREA-
TED BY ITS DIAGONAL.
IF THIS "IDEAL" SHAPE
IS NOT TO YOUR LIKING
THE OPTIONS ARE ENDLESS.

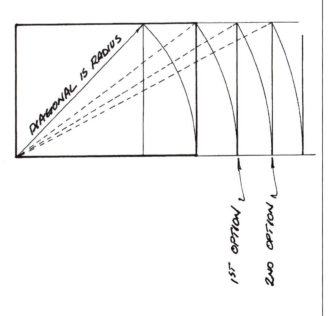

TO SQUARE A CIRCLE OR EVEN
ENCIRCLE A SQUARE, IT IS
IMPORTANT TO ESTABLISH THE
DIAGONAL OF THE SQUARE.
THE RADIUS IS HALF THE LENGTH
OF THE DIAGONAL.

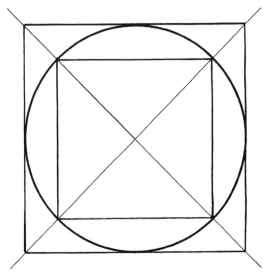

TO DRAW A SQUARE IN A SEMI-
CIRCLE, ERECT A PERPENDICULAR
AS LONG AS THE DIAMETER
OF THE SEMICIRCLE. THIS SHOULD
BE TANGENT TO ONE END. A
LINE FROM THE CENTER OF
THE SEMICIRCLE TO THE END OF
THE PERPENDICULAR WILL INTER-
SECT THE ARC. THIS POINT IS
ONE CORNER OF THE SQUARE.

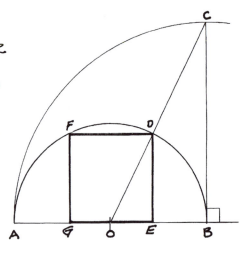

TO CONSTRUCT A PENTAGON WITH A GIVEN SIDE, LAY OUT THE GIVEN SIDE (A·B). CONSTRUCT A PERPENDICULAR (AC) WHICH IS ONE HALF A·B. DRAW A LINE FROM B TO C AND EXTEND IT. CD IS THE SAME LENGTH AS AC. RESET THE COMPASS FOR THE LENGTH A·D. WITH A AND C AS CENTERS, SWING ARCS WHICH INTERSECT (O). WITH THE SAME RADIUS AND O AS THE CENTER, CONSTRUCT A CIRCLE. THE CHORD AB (OR THE GIVEN SIDE) CAN NOW BE STEPPED OFF AROUND THE CIRCUMFERENCE (E, F AND G). CONNECT POINTS FOR PENTAGON.

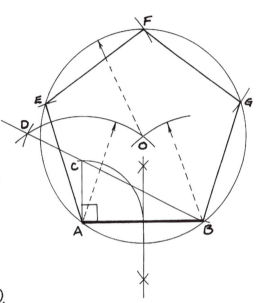

TO DRAW A PENTAGON IN A GIVEN CIRCLE, FIND THE CENTER (O) AND CONSTRUCT A DIAMETER (A·O·B). BISECT O·B TO FIND D. FROM D, WITH A RADIUS OF DC, SWING AN ARC TO INTERSECT A·O (E). WITH C AS A CENTER AND C·E AS A RADIUS, DRAW AN ARC TO INTERSECT THE CIRCLE (F). THE CHORD C·F IS ONE SIDE OF THE PENTAGON AND THE OTHERS MAY BE STEPPED OFF AROUND THE CIRCUMFERENCE.

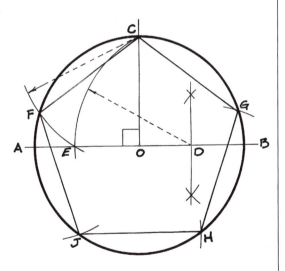

TO DRAW A REGULAR HEXAGON IN A GIVEN CIRCLE, STEP OFF THE CIRCUMFERENCE WITH THE RADIUS. CONNECT THE POINTS.

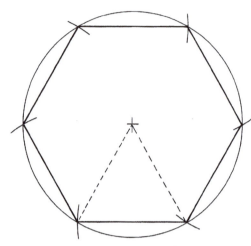

TO DRAW AN OCTAGON IN A SQUARE, DRAW DIAGONALS THROUGH THE SQUARE. SET A COMPASS WITH A RADIUS EQUAL TO THE DISTANCE FROM CORNER TO CENTER (1/2 THE DIAGONAL). FROM EACH CORNER SWING ARCS WHICH INTERSECT THE SIDES. CONNECT THESE INTERSECTIONS FOR AN OCTAGON.

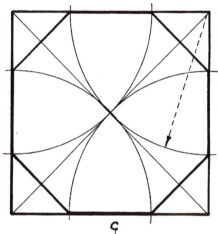

TO DRAW AN OCTAGON IN A CIRCLE, CONSTRUCT A DIAMETER (AB) AND A PERPENDICULAR BISECTOR (CD). PLACE A SQUARE AROUND THE CIRCLE WHICH HAS SIDES PARALLEL TO THE DIAMETER AND BISECTOR. DRAW DIAGONALS IN THE SQUARE WHICH INTERSECT THE CIRCLE. CONNECT THE INTERSECTING POINTS.

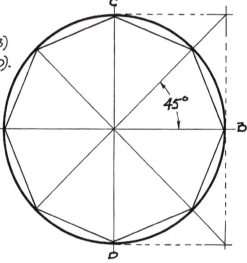

TO DRAW ANY MULTISIDED REG-
ULAR POLYGON WITH A KNOWN
SIDE, LAY OUT THE SIDE (A-B).
EXTEND IT AND WITH AB AS
A RADIUS CREAT A SEMI-
CIRCLE (C.C.A.B). USING
DIVIDERS, STEP OFF THIS ARC
INTO THE SAME NUMBER OF
EQUAL PARTS AS THE DESIRED
NUMBER OF SIDES ON THE
POLYGON (THE EXAMPLE IS A
HEPTAGON). CONNECT A-2.
CONNECT PERPENDICULAR BI-
SECTORS ON A-B AND A-2.
USING THEIR INTERSECTION (O)
AS A POINT AND A-O AS A
RADIUS, CONSTRUCT A CIRCLE. THE
REMAINING SIDES WILL STEP
OFF ON THE CIRCUMFERENCE.
=

TO DRAW ANY POLYGON IN A
GIVEN CIRCLE, ESTABLISH A
DIAMETER (A-B). DIVIDE IT
INTO EQUAL PARTS OF THE SAME
NUMBER AS THE DESIRED POLY-
GON (THE EXAMPLE IS A HEPTAGON).
ERECT A PERPENDICULAR FROM
THE CENTER OF THE DIAMETER.
IT SHOULD RISE 7/8 OF THE
DIAMETER (C). FROM C, DRAW
A LINE THROUGH 2 AND EX-
TEND IT TO INTERSECT THE
CIRCLE (D). AD IS ONE SIDE
OF THE POLYGON AND THE
REST MAY BE STEPPED OFF
ON THE CIRCUMFERENCE.

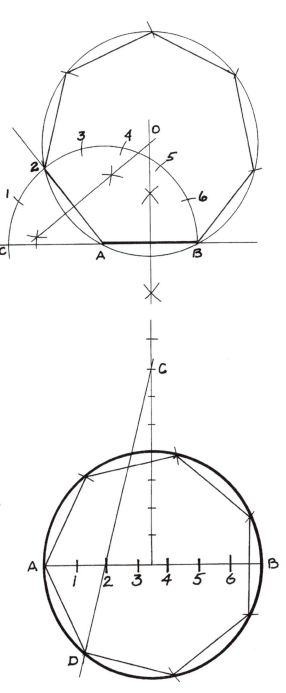

TO FIND THE CENTER OF A CIRCLE, PICK ANY 3 POINTS ON THE CIRCUMFERENCE (A, B AND C). CONNECT THE POINTS AND CONSTRUCT PERPENDICULAR BISECTORS. THE BISECTORS WILL INTERSECT AT THE CENTER OF THE CIRCLE.

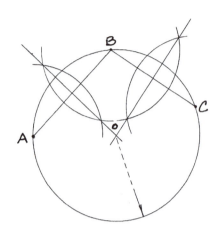

THE CENTER OF A CIRCLE CAN ALSO BE FOUND BY DRAWING A LINE (AB) ABOUT ¼ DOWN FROM THE TOP. DROP PERPENDICULARS (A-C AND B-D) FROM THE LINE. DIAGONALS FROM THE FOUR POINTS WILL CROSS IN THE CENTER.

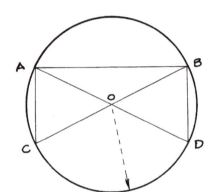

<u>HOW TO CUT THE ANGLE</u> =
TO FIND THE CORRECT CUT-ANGLE FOR A SEGMENTED FORM, DIVIDE 360 BY THE NUMBER OF PIECES. DIVIDE THIS RESULT BY 2.

THE EXAMPLE IS A DECAGON. 360 DIVIDED BY 10 IS 36. 36 DIVIDED BY 2 IS 18. THE INCLUDED ANGLE IS 36 DEGREES AND THE CUT ANGLE IS 18 DEGREES.

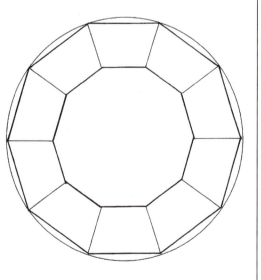

TO DRAW A TANGENT TO A CIRCLE
AT A GIVEN POINT (P), CONSTRUCT
A LINE FROM THE CENTER OF
THE CIRCLE (O) THROUGH THE
POINT. A PERPENDICULAR BI-
SECTOR AT P IS TANGENT TO
THE CIRCLE.

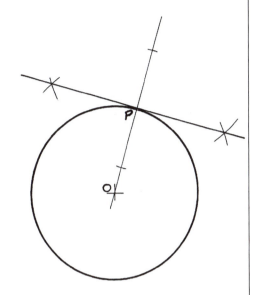

TO DRAW A TANGENT (OR TWO)
TO A CIRCLE FROM A POINT (P)
AWAY FROM THE CIRCLE, FIND
THE CENTER OF THE CIRCLE (O).
CONNECT O·P. BISECT O·P (X)
AND CONSTRUCT A CIRCLE FROM
X WITH A RADIUS X-P. A LINE
FROM THE INTERSECTIONS OF
THIS CIRCLE ON THE ORIGINAL
(A AND B) WHEN CONNECTED
TO P WILL BE TANGENT.

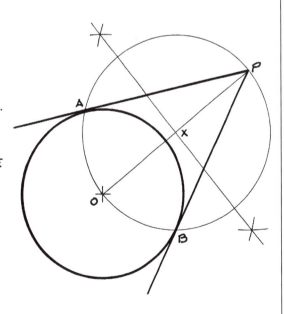

TO DRAW AN ARC TANGENT
TO TWO STRAIGHT LINES, AT
AN ACUTE ANGLE, ERECT
PERPENDICULARS AT THE END
OF THE LINES. THEY WILL
INTERSECT AND FORM THE
RADIUS CENTER FOR THE
TANGENT ARC.

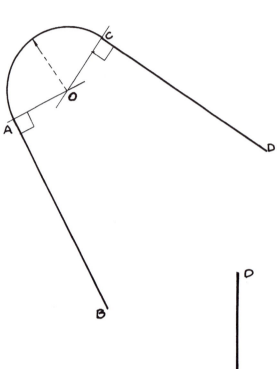

AN ARC TANGENT TO LINES
AT A RIGHT ANGLE CAN
BE CREATED AS ABOVE.

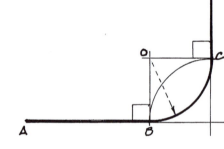

AN ARC TANGENT TO LINES
AT AN OBTUSE ANGLE CAN
BE CREATED UTILIZING A
DITTO OF THE DITTO ABOVE.

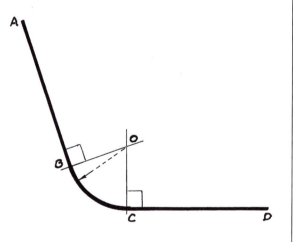

OGEE CURVES ARE CREATED BY
TANGENT ARCS. PICK THE POINT
YOU WANT THE CURVES TO CHANGE,
(E). CONNECT POINTS WHERE THE
CURVES BEGIN (B AND C). BISECT
B-E AND C-E. ERECT PERPEN-
DICULARS AT B AND C. THEY WILL
INTERSECT BISECTORS AND GIVE
RADIUS CENTERS FOR CURVES.

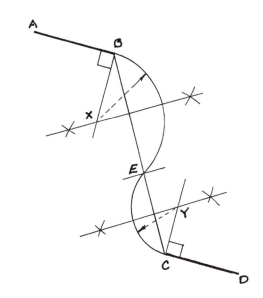

TO DRAW AN ARC WITH A GIVEN
RADIUS TANGENT TO GIVEN ARCS
OF OTHER RADII, AND THE
CENTERS OF THE GIVEN ARCS
(AO AND BO). SWING ARCS EQUAL
TO THE SUM OF THE RADIUS OF
THAT ARC AND THE RADIUS OF
ARC TO BE DRAWN. THESE WILL
INTERSECT AT THE RADIUS
CENTER OF THE ARC TO BE DRAWN
AT CO.

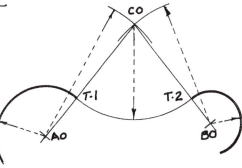

TO DRAW AN ARC WITH A
GIVEN RADIUS TANGENT TO
ANOTHER ARC AND A STRAIGHT
LINE, DRAW LINES PARALLEL
TO THE ORIGINAL LINE AND
ARC. THESE LINES SHOULD BE
DISTANCED THE AMOUNT OF
THE GIVEN RADIUS. THEY
WILL INTERSECT A PERPEN-
DICULAR FROM THE END OF
THE LINE. THIS INTERSECTION
IS THE RADIUS CENTER FOR
THE TANGENT ARC.

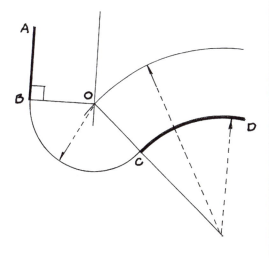

TO STEP OFF THE AP-
PROXIMATE LENGTH OF
AN ARC ON A STRAIGHT
LINE, CONSTRUCT A LINE
TANGENT TO ONE END
OF THE ARC (AC). WITH
THE DIVIDERS SET TO A
SMALL AMOUNT, STEP OFF
THE ARC. WHEN NO MORE
STEPS WILL FIT, SWING
THE DIVIDERS TO THE
LINE AND STEP OFF THE
SAME NUMBER.

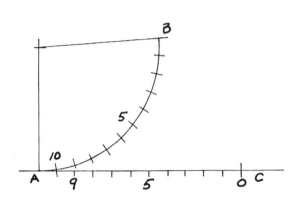

TO CONSTRUCT THE AP-
PROXIMATE LENGTH OF
THE CIRCUMFERENCE OF A
CIRCLE, ERECT A DIAMETER
(A·O·B) AND CONSTRUCT
PERPENDICULARS AT THE
BASE, CENTER AND TOP.
SET COMPASS WITH THE
RADIUS OF CIRCLE. FROM
X STRIKE AN ARC THROUGH
THE CIRCUMFERENCE (Y) AND
EXTEND IT TO FIND D.
MEASURE OFF, FROM B,
3 RADII TO FIND C. A
LINE FROM C TO D IS ½
THE CIRCUMFERENCE.

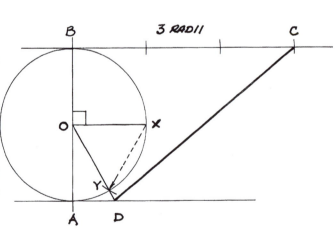

N.B. LINE C·D HAS A DEVIATION OF
LESS THAN 1 IN 100,000 SO USE
IT WITH GREAT CARE.

TO DRAW THE INVOLUTE
OF A TRIANGLE (1·2·3)
EXTEND THE SIDES OF
THE TRIANGLE. SET A
COMPASS WITH THE RE-
QUIRED RADIUS (1-3)
AND DRAW AN ARC
UNTIL IT INTERSECTS
THE EXTENSION LINE.
RESET THE COMPASS
AND CONTINUE AROUND
THE TRIANGLE.

TO DRAW THE INVOLUTE
OF A SQUARE, EXTEND
THE SIDES AND FOLLOW
THE PROCEDURES ABOVE.

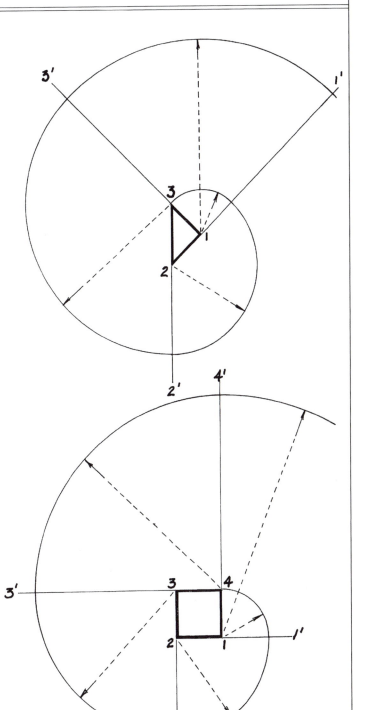

AN ELLIPSE IS A CURVE FORMED BY A POINT MOVING IN A PLANE SO THAT THE SUM OF ITS DISTANCE FROM TWO FIXED POINTS, OR FOCI, IS CONSTANT. THE FOCI ARE ON THE MAJOR (LONGER) AXIS. A PERPENDICULAR BISECTOR OF THE MAJOR AXIS IS THE MINOR (SHORTER) AXIS. THE FOCI ARE LOCATED BY SWINGING AN ARC WITH A RADIUS 1/2 THE MAJOR AXIS FROM THE TOP OF THE MINOR AXIS.

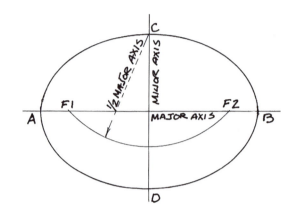

TO CREATE AN ELLIPSE WITH A CORD, PUT NAILS AT F1 AND F2 AND AT C. FIX THE CORD INTO A TIGHT LOOP. A PENCIL REPLACING THE NAIL AT C CAN BE PULLED AROUND. KEEP THE TENSION TIGHT AS THE CORD MOVES AROUND THE FOCI NAILS.

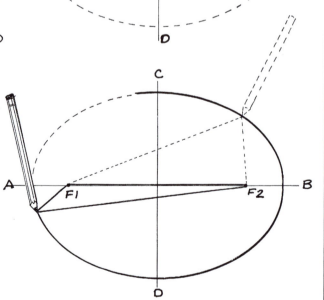

TO DRAW AN ELLIPSE WITH THE TRAMMEL METHOD, CUT OUT A STRIP OF BOARD.* MARK THE EDGE A-O WHICH IS ½ THE MAJOR AXIS AND C-O WHICH IS ½ THE MINOR AXIS. PLACE C ON THE MAJOR AXIS AND A ON THE MINOR AXIS. MOVING THE BOARD ALONG BOTH AXES, POINT O WILL TRACE THE ELLIPSE.

* CARDBOARD FOR SMALL WORK, PLYWOOD OR 1 X STOCK FOR LARGER ELLIPSES.

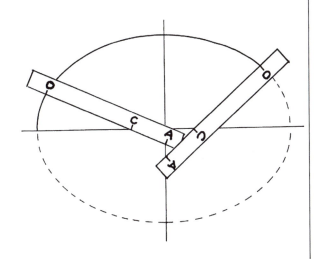

A FLAT FRAME SQUARE AND A STRIP OF WOOD WITH POINTS A AND C REPLACED WITH PINS AND POINT O, NOW A PENCIL, WILL QUICKLY TRACE AN ELLIPSE.

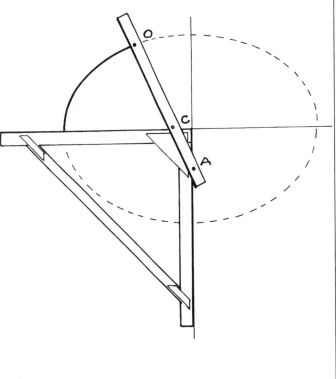

PART VII • SHOP TALK, SHOP TRICKS AND SHOP MADE TOOLS

USING UP SCRAP MATERIAL

Waste not, want not. Oh, were it only so! However, it is possible to keep the dumpster hungry by using up most scrap. Below are some suggested recipes for leftovers.

PLYWOOD SCRAP

Panel materials, including ¾″ plywood, ¾″ particle board (ugly stuff) can be used for caster boards (see Drawing IV-15); ¼″ plywood scraps can often be re-cut to make stock fasteners (see Drawing II-4). Wait until you have a goodly amount of scrap for the conversion because it usually ties up the equipment in the shop. Plywood which is ¼″ thick by 5¼″ wide (with the grain direction) should be saved for curved platform construction (see Drawing IV-7).

1 X STOCK SCRAP

Any 1 x stock which is 3½″ wide (this could also be ¾″ plywood or ¾″ particle board) is good for making up caster boards These can be laminated up and stored away until needed (see above).

Shorter pieces of 3″ wide 1 x stock make good picture battens (see Drawing II-45). These are standardized to stock flats and can be stored in readiness—a great time-saver when you need just one more.

The same 3″ wide 1 x stock, also in shortish pieces, is just what the doctor ordered for step legs (see Drawing IV-10). Time, or a prophetic look into the future, will tell you approximately how many of these you will need down the road. There are rarely enough. Laminate them in those "off days."

Pieces of 2″ wide 1 x stock which is 3′-0″ long can be made into corner braces (see Drawing II-3 and text). These are always needed and can be easily stored away. Toggles from broken and discarded flats can also be used up in this way.

Tailing strips which are usually broken up and tossed, make excellent paint stir sticks. Standardize their length to fit the size buckets you use and to facilitate storage. There is nothing as luxurious as a fresh, disposable paint stick.

SAWDUST

Keep a box under the table saw to catch sawdust. A bucket of sawdust in the paint area is ideal to soak up any spilled paint. It also makes the floor a lot less slippery. Just sprinkle it on any puddle and sweep it about. Pick it up before the paint dries, so it doesn't stick to the floor.

A pail of wet sawdust makes an excellent and inexpensive sweeping compound. It keeps the dust down when cleaning up the shop. Boy, it could probably stretch hamburger for meat loaf, too.

FIREWOOD

Small scraps of wood can be packed into boxes and bags and given as holiday mementos to all mucky-mucks in high positions who have fireplaces. It is excellent starter wood for fires and conversation later in the year when you need more funding for productions.

SHOP-MADE TOOLS

Most shop-made tools are designed to make working with power tools a safer experience, or at least one which keeps fingers connected to the palm.

Drawing VII-1 shows the push stick, one of the simplest, but most necessary of all tools. Push sticks should be made up in quantity and discarded when the bottom becomes too "chewed up" by the saw blade. To add a real touch of class, rout all edges (except the notch at the bottom) with a round-over bit.

The two trimming guides (see Drawing VII-2) are both handy. The guide for the circular saw is a great time saver because the edge of the plywood is also the edge of the kerf cut by the saw and can be easily aligned to the cut line on the board. Of course, different circular saws will each need their own guides.

Also in Drawing VII-2 is a guide to remove the bow from a piece of wood. It will need to be as long and as wide as the wood to be "de-bowed." Once the outer bow has been trimmed off, the saw must be reset and the piece fed through with the flat edge against the fence. This certainly beats snapping a line and free-handing the piece through the saw.

The scarf taper jig (see Drawing VII-3) is designed to be used with a portable circular saw. The length of the taper is up to you. Approximately 18″ is ideal. The first cousin of this jig is the taper jig discussed in Drawing IV-19.

The "hand," also called a "feather board" or "finger board," is certainly worth the little effort it takes to construct (see Drawing VII-4). When clamped to a table, the "fingers" will keep constant tension on a board and help ensure a good cut. Notice the curved top allows two different approaches, thus giving more flexibility.

The V-block (see Drawing VII-4) is fairly self-explanatory. It will prevent round stock from turning, which can break the drill bit, throw the piece off the table or give the operator a good whapping. This jig can be used against the fence of the radial arm saw for cutting doweling and full round.

Drawing VII-5 shows three helpers for curved lines. If you cannot find trammel points, a piece of 1 x 1 will easily substitute. Drill a hole through one end to accept the pencil and drive a nail for the pivot point. Granted, it's crude, but effective.

The folding work stands in Drawing VII-6 are included because they might inspire a home-made version. They are a variation on the continental parallel (see Drawing IV-23 and following), but have been refined to a great extent. Whether or not you decide to build your own, or investigate buying some, these clever tables may be the ideal solution for any shop which, like Omar, must steal away into the night and (to mix similes) rise, phoenix-like, the next day.

Some of the other shop made tools already discussed include the marking gauge (see Drawing II-8), the whiskey stick (see Drawing II-29), and the bolt hole jigs (see Drawing IV-12). The folding sawhorses (see Drawings II-32 and II-33) certainly qualify as a shop-made tool. And, to push a point, the flat frame square (see *Shop Math,* Drawing VI-23) should probably be included.

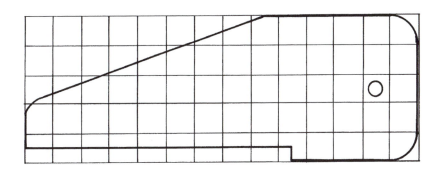

THE PUSH STICK DRAWN ABOVE (IN A ONE-
INCH GRID) IS BUT ONE OF MANY DESIGNS
AVAILABLE. HOWEVER, IT DOES DO SEVERAL
THINGS QUITE WELL. IT IS TALL ENOUGH
TO RIDE ABOVE MOST FENCES AND THEREFOR
NOT "SNAG" FINGERS PLUS IT KEEPS THE
HAND WELL ABOVE THE BLADE. THE HALF-
INCH NOTCH AT THE BOTTOM ALLOWS GOOD
PRESSURE ON THE BOARD THUS HOLDING
IT TO THE TABLE.

TO USE THIS STICK
AS A "HAND" TO HOLD
A PIECE AGAINST THE
FENCE, HOLD THE
NARROW END IN ONE
HAND AND PRESS THE
ROUNDED BUTT END
AGAINST THE WOOD.
THIS WILL APPLY
PRESSURE AND ALSO
ALLOW THE BOARD
TO GLIDE PAST.

CIRCULAR SAW GUIDE

A PIECE OF ¼" PLYWOOD OR HARD-
BOARD WITH A 1X3 LAMINATED
TO ONE EDGE CAN BE CLAMPED
TO PANEL TO BE CUT. SOLE
PLATE OF SAW RIDES
AGAINST 1X3
AND BLADE
CUTS AT
EDGE OF
PLYWOOD.

ANTI-BOW GUIDE

BOWED BOARD

PLACE BOWED BOARD ONTO GUIDE. SET
FENCE ON TABLE SAW TO TRIM EDGE.
FLIP BOARD, RESET FENCE, AND TRIM TRUE.

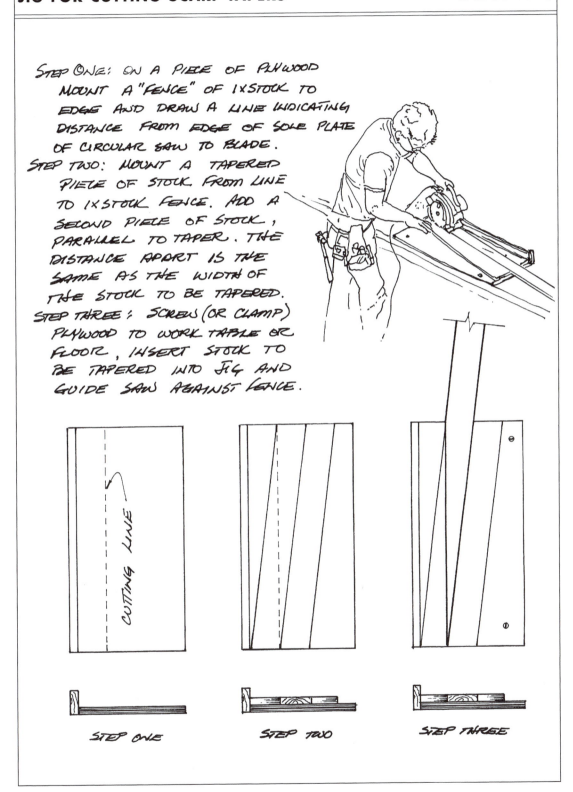

STEP ONE: ON A PIECE OF PLYWOOD MOUNT A "FENCE" OF 1X STOCK TO EDGE AND DRAW A LINE INDICATING DISTANCE FROM EDGE OF SOLE PLATE OF CIRCULAR SAW TO BLADE.

STEP TWO: MOUNT A TAPERED PIECE OF STOCK FROM LINE TO 1X STOCK FENCE. ADD A SECOND PIECE OF STOCK, PARALLEL TO TAPER. THE DISTANCE APART IS THE SAME AS THE WIDTH OF THE STOCK TO BE TAPERED.

STEP THREE: SCREW (OR CLAMP) PLYWOOD TO WORK TABLE OR FLOOR, INSERT STOCK TO BE TAPERED INTO JIG AND GUIDE SAW AGAINST FENCE.

CUTTING LINE

STEP ONE   STEP TWO   STEP THREE

A WOODEN "HAND" IS ONE OF THE HANDIEST OF SHOP-MADE TOOLS. WHEN CLAMPED TO A TABLE, ITS "FINGERS" PRESS AGAINST THE STOCK AND HOLD IT AGAINST THE FENCE. MAKE AS NEEDED, BUT KEEP THE WORKING END CURVED AND THE FINGERS ABOUT 1/4" WIDE, AND THE KERF OF THE BLADE BETWEEN.

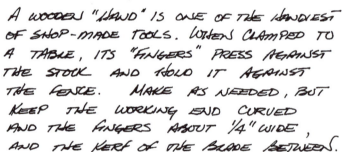

THE "V" BLOCK IS QUICKLY MADE AND ABSOLUTELY NECESSARY WHEN TRYING TO DRILL ROUND STOCK. A 4×4 WILL ACCEPT THE "V" OR LAMINATE TWO PIECES OF 2×4 WITH A CHAMFER ON EACH PIECE.

UNUSUAL CURVES CAN BE
"SMOOTHLY" DRAWN BY
FORCING A NARROW
PIECE OF PLASTIC OR A
THIN, KNOT FREE TAILING
STRIP TO CONFORM TO THE
CURVE. A FEW NAILS AND
HELPFUL HANDS MAKE THIS A
BREEZE.

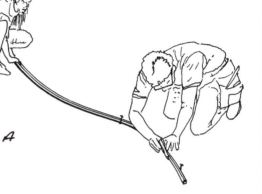

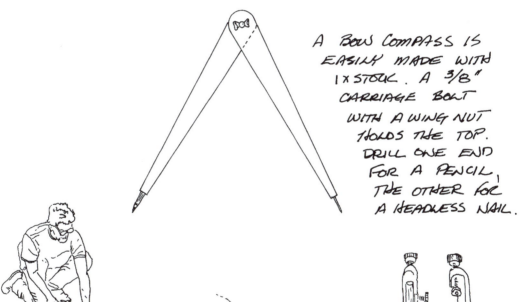

A BOW COMPASS IS
EASILY MADE WITH
1 X STOCK. A 3/8"
CARRIAGE BOLT
WITH A WING NUT
HOLDS THE TOP.
DRILL ONE END
FOR A PENCIL,
THE OTHER FOR
A HEADLESS NAIL.

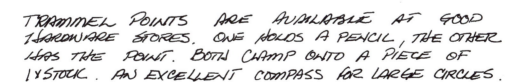

TRAMMEL POINTS ARE AVAILABLE AT GOOD
HARDWARE STORES. ONE HOLDS A PENCIL, THE OTHER
HAS THE POINT. BOTH CLAMP ONTO A PIECE OF
1 X STOCK. AN EXCELLENT COMPASS FOR LARGE CIRCLES.

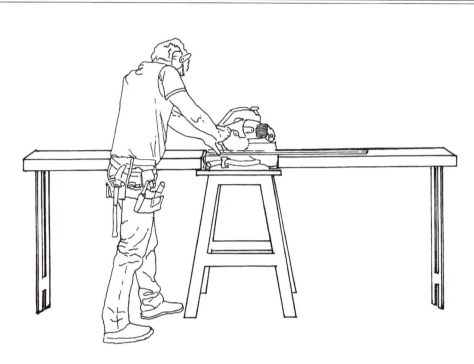

THE DRAWING SHOWS THREE PORTABLE TABLES DESIGNED AND BUILT FOR THE CONSTRUCTION SITE. ABOVE IS A CHOP SAW TABLE WITH WINGS. BELOW IS A BASE FOR A SMALL TABLE SAW. THE TAKE OFF TABLE ALSO HOLDS A ROUTER, MAKING IT INTO A SHAPER. ALL THREE TABLES ARE SOLID, FOLD FOR STORAGE, AND ARE LIGHT.

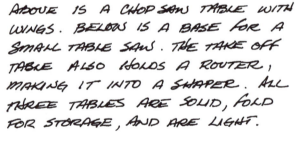

PART VIII • PAINT

INTRODUCTION

From the get-go as we try to saddle Ol' Paint it must be understood that this section is not about being a painter. The skills and training required to be a scenic artist must be learned elsewhere. There are a number of excellent books, some fine schools and a lifetime of opportunities which can be explored. This chapter will, hopefully, fill in enough basic background to allow a paint area to be planned, organized for production, and utilized in an efficient, safe and cost effective manner.

Also, from the get-go let me stress that all paint is potentially hazardous to your health and to those in the area where it is used. I have tried to contain the warnings but like the toxicity of paint they often pop up.

A BIT OF HISTORY

Today's commercial paint is a relatively new concept in product marketing. From earliest times man has decorated with paint. In the Middle Ages the formulas for tempera with its egg binder were jealously guarded secrets of craftsmen. White lead paint became widely available in the seventeenth century, but more people seemed to paint their faces than their homes. It was the later large-scale manufacture of linseed oil from the flax plant and pigment-grade zinc oxide which allowed paint manufacturers to become an industry. However, it was not until 1880 when Henry Sherwin put the first standard-formula, quality-controlled, ready-mixed paint on the market that people no longer had to purchase powdered white lead and pigments and add their own linseed oil and turpentine. It was the skill required to mix paint, not the largely ignored dangers encountered in using it, which gave rise to an army of professional house painters who survived well into this century. After WWII there was the introduction of less toxic, water-based paints. Scenic artists, like most theatre people, at the forefront of tradition, continued to mix their own paints from bins of colored pigments and pots of heated glue. Many are still doing so, and indeed, the color range of powdered pigments has rarely been surpassed.

Ironically, the upheavals of war contributed more to the progress of paint and dye stuffs than any aesthetic movement. The German monopoly on chemically derived pigments forced other countries to re-invent the color wheel when World War I began.

Aspirin was another important theatrical staple wrenched from German supremacy at the same time. Logically, the Russian paint industry began in October, 1917 but for years red was the only primary. In addition to new materials to replace ones temporarily unavailable because of hostilities, labor shortages forced more machinery to be utilized and a better, more consistent product resulted.

The Second World War was even more disruptive to paint manufacture but resulted in many new binders including the perfection of alkyd resin, a type of polyester. Water based paints, prior to 1900, were mainly lime wash (lime, tallow, and water) but distempers (powdered pigments to be mixed with various sizes) were in common use. Milk was mixed with quick lime to help make whitewash and this developed into a line of casein paints. To make paint more water resistant, dying oils were added. During WWII, German industries searched for an alternative to using oil, in dwindling supply and urgently needed elsewhere, and chemists invented polyvinyl acetate (PVA), a new binder for paint.

In 1935, the Germans also invented Buna, a synthetic rubber, which was utilized in the United States immediately after the War in the manufacture of "rubber-base" paint, commonly called latex paint. However, PVA paints have surged ahead and captured a large part of the market. These are the acrylic paints sold everywhere. The Second World War also saw the invention of epoxy resins and polyurethanes, both of which have found their way into the paint industry and emit fumes of death and destruction. Well, okay, they smell and are more dangerous.

PAINT CHOICES

The wide variety of paints available today, and their specialized uses, present choices for the scenic artist which would amaze and perhaps bewilder the painter of even half a century ago. All paint consists of pigment (color), binder (the glue) and medium or vehicle (the liquid). The binder and medium combine to become the vehicle which carries the other ingredients. Pigment is color to most but it is a bit more complicated. Pigments are small particles suspended in the binder and medium. Pigments are derived from earth (e.g., yellow ochre), minerals (e.g., malachite) and dyes (organic, and, since the mid-19th century, often synthetic). Pigment can be created from an inert ground, whitening for example, over which dye is precipitated. The particles are suspended in the medium and binder, but the dye can bleed out and become soluble in the liquid. This partly explains why paint will wash out of clothes but also leave a stain. Of course, most paint chemists combine the above in various ways to achieve the desired color. Poisonous ingredients for the color accepting inert ground (like lead white, unavailable since 1973) are no longer used, but the dust and peeling "ghetto potato chips" found in older paint jobs are still lethal.

PAINT TIP How much paint is needed to complete a job? The question is complex and the answer is always "a bit more." In truth, even the most experienced painter can be caught short. There are many variables—surface, viscosity of paint, applicator, temperature, humidity, person painting, buckets kicked over and the like. A rough starting point would be 300 to 400 square feet of coverage per gallon. Usually scenic paint is thinner than house paint—water is a budget conscious extender—and while it does affect the long-lasting strength of the paint, the fleeting life of most scenery is not adversely affected by thinning the paint.

To get large quantities of paint ready for the job, it is often advisable to box the paint (Drawing VIII-1). Boxing paint also helps ensure a consistency of viscosity and color. To box paint, select at least three buckets which will more than hold the total amount of paint. Fill each part way and then add the contents of the first bucket to the others. Add part of bucket two back into the first bucket and to the other. Pour bucket three into one and two. Continue alternating until the paint is thoroughly mixed about. Pouring through a large kitchen strainer (available at restaurant supply houses) or window screen will help mix different paints and also trap any debris, sawdust, dirt, dried paint film or stray animals. Always wet the strainer or screen first. This will facilitate cleanup. Boxing paint in five-gallon buckets can take its toll on the back. Lift carefully. "A pint's a pound the world around," however, a gallon of paint weighs between 8 and 11 pounds—go figure.

Many painters prefer to avoid the back strain which can result from boxing paint and utilize one of the many commercial mixing wands which fit into a power drill. They do fast and excellent work but make sure the drill is powerful enough for the job. Take particular care to avoid paint spills with an electric drill. Keep the plug off the floor and away from mixing area. It is best to devote an old "clunker" drill to the paint area because it will inevitably be repainted to match each bucket of paint. Scenery people frown on such decorative additions.

The large strainer used in boxing paint is still invaluable for removing unwanted debris from paint. In addition to those mentioned above, the strainer will retrieve shop items including nails, staples, bolts and screws, lunch and the furniture from the designer's model.

PAINT TIP Fiberglass window screen makes an excellent cleaning aid. When crumbled up like a sponge it will "chew" away and rinse away dried and hardened paint in buckets and on the handles and ferrules of brushes. It is not as destructive to plastic buckets as a stainless steel wire brush. The wire brush can also be quite abrasive on natural bristles. The screen is also an excellent strainer for removing crudities from paint. It is not, however, a fine enough mesh for straining paint for spray guns.

Spilled paint (gawd forbid this ever happens) is easily handled in the shop with damp sawdust. Keep a bucket handy. When paint is spilled, first try to contain the language. Next attempt to scoop up as much paint as possible with the brush and put it back, either in the original bucket or a handy substitute. If the paint is contaminated with saw-dust, etc., a quick strain often revives it. After the bulk of the spill is removed, dump the damp sawdust over the area and work it about with a broom. Sweep up the paint saturated sawdust immediately or the binders in the paint will adhere the sawdust to the floor.

PAINT FINISHES

The finish, amount of sheen, of paint is achieved in the manufacture. Paint is formulated with proscribed flatting agents and the result is noted on the label—e.g., flat, eggshell, gloss, etc.—and on ideal surfaces will give the promised finish. There are four common finishes which scenic artist often need to duplicate. A flat finish which produces a matte surface has no sheen. This is easy to achieve. The word "flat" on the can will usually give this—unless of course, it must remain flat and then it will shine like crazy. Rubbing and buffing flat paint will help it shine. Flat finishes have the great advantage of not reflecting stage lights and thus remaining in the background.

"Eggshell" has a slight gloss and works well on stage if the surface must be cleaned or wiped down. It will shine more under lights and reveal any imperfections in the surface of walls, etc.

"Semi-gloss" is what it purports to be—a step below "gloss." Paint with high gloss finish can glisten under stage lights but is often required.

If a higher or lower gloss is needed, there are excellent translucent and transparent water-based finishes of various shine available. These can replace solvent based shellac, lacquer and other gloss coverings. If there is too much shine on a finish, clear, matte varnishes are available. There are also excellent "satin" products. These are usually milky in the can but dry clear and are applied after the original paint job has dried. They will also change the color underneath, usually deepening and intensifying it. One great advantage of applying the sheen after painting is the ability to utilize paints already in stock. It is generally not advisable to mix liquid clear finishes with paint in the can. This will change the sheen of the finish but also creates a glaze paint which will not cover as well. Of course, if you wish to tint a glaze, please feel free. Clear finishes can be applied by brush, roller or spray. They can be thinned somewhat (which can affect the total amount of sheen) and applied in several coats to build up a richer finish.

SCENE PAINT

Most paints designed and sold to theatres are water-based. In addition to "latex" and "acrylic" there is still a wide variety of paints with other binders. The once-standard scenic paint was powdered pigments. These are still available and have a wide variety of available color. The binders required range from animal glues (from hides to hooves) through "rubber" derived binders and more modern chemically derived polymer binders. The older binders usually require separate preparation involving soaking and cooking in a glue pot (a double boiler-like device) before they can be diluted with water to create a "size" which is then added to the powdered pigment. There are scenic artists who still prefer these paints but their years of experience allow them to avoid the pitfalls inherent in this system.

The preparation of powdered scene paint can be messy and requires some knowledge and experience. It is critical to wear a HEPA (High Efficiency Particulate Attenuating—that's a hepa syllables) face mask when mixing the powder. Inhaling the dust is dangerous particularly with the dye base powders. Once the paint is prepared it is relatively safe. Be forewarned, however, that many of the binders quickly spoil and the resulting odor would gag a dog on a gut wagon.

The trickiest part of mixing powdered pigments is possibly finding the correct strength of size water: not enough and the dried paint will rub off; too much and there will be a "glue shine" on the surface. Of course, different colors will require different amounts of binder. The results can be beautiful.

> **PAINT TIP** When buying cartridges for face masks (which should be fitted for each worker) purchase a combination HEPA-organic vapor cartridge which should cover the painter for just about every hazardous task.

To make scenic paint more "user friendly," manufacturers (no doubt with prodding from both costume and lighting designers) began distributing casein paint. Casein paint is available in powdered form (pigment and binder already combined) but is more commonly found pre-mixed to a thick paste in cans and buckets. The painter need only scoop out the needed color and dilute with water to the desired consistency. The binder in casein was originally a protein made from dried curds of skim milk. This crumble was powdered and a few secret ingredients were added (ammonium carbonate or ammonium hydroxide) which can emit a vapor to open the sinuses and roll your socks down. Today, the cow is no longer required as the casein binder is chemically manufactured. When dry, casein paint is relatively durable with a flat finish. Casein paints dilute a great deal compared to other types, a fact which is reflected in their higher cost.

As mentioned earlier, paint is pigment, binder and medium. The quality of the paint will vary. As a general rule of thumb, "you get what you pay for." Cheap paint is "stretched" by adding excessive amounts of whiting, clay or other hamburger-helper. This makes a very heavy can of paint which requires several heavy coats to cover, and in addition to excessive labor, saves nothing.

As a general rule of thumb, scenic paint is applied in a much thinner coat than house paint. Good paint (even house paints) can be thinned and still cover well…an obvious savings.

ROLL ON MACDUFF —

ROLLING FLOORS IS MUCH EASIER WITH A DEEP ROLLER TRAY OR BUCKET WITH A SPREADER SCREEN. NOTE 2" PIPE SLIPPED OVER EXTENSION POLE HANDLE. THIS WILL ELIMINATE PRESSING ON ROLLER.

BOXING PAINT —

CAUTION: VERY SOPHISTICATED! USE AN OPTIONAL STRAINER. POUR CONTENTS OF FIRST BUCKET INTO BUCKETS TWO AND THREE. NEXT, POUR BUCKET TWO INTO ONE AND THREE. NOW POUR BUCKET THREE INTO ONE AND TWO. REPEAT AS REQUIRED. PHEW!

WHERE TO BUY PAINT

If the theatre is located in a major city (OK, New York) there are probably local suppliers for all painted needs. Most theatres are outside this area and stocking paint becomes more of an issue. Local paint stores are an excellent source for paint and related supplies. Often there are industry ties and it is not difficult for "specialty" paints to be ordered. Local suppliers are a valuable resource—build a good relationship here. Of course, paints created expressly for the theatrical trade are available through catalogues. But in areas of extremely cold winters many distributors are hesitant to ship paint because freezing can destroy the binders. This could help determine the paint system or systems you decide to use.

The local paint store stocks a lot of white paint which is colored to customer choice with Universal Tinting colorants, a thick, concentrated pigment. These colorants, while not inexpensive, are reasonably priced and can be purchased and stocked in a paint shop. Designed for house paint they will mix into paints which have either an oil- or water-based binder. The colorant is available in handy squeeze bottles or cans. The squeeze bottle seems made for the scenic artist. The greatest advantage of using a local paint store is that they incur the cost (and space required) to stock a variety of useful paint products. While you pay for this service it is often worth it.

ON THE STORING OF PAINTS

Paints are a lot like people. Moderate temperature is best. Avoid storing paint near heat—direct sunlight, next to a furnace or radiator—especially solvent-based paints. Water-based paints dislike heat too, but are ruined if they freeze. The binders break down and costumers have been known to kill. Because of the more stringent health regulations many of the dangerous preservatives once common in commercial paints have been removed or reduced. Paint will now rot quite quickly, especially after being opened and even more so after being thinned with water. Some shops add Lysol or formaldehyde to retard spoilage. Formaldehyde may be carcinogenic and if the smell doesn't get your nose, cancer will. It is best to use paint fairly quickly. Whatever type of paint becomes "stock" in a shop, it is best to try to limit the variety. The intermixing of diverse paints, solvent and water-based notwithstanding, is fraught with unknown results. Sometimes they cooperate, but never when they must.

BRUSHES

Paint brushes are still the most common painting tool. There are as many varieties and variations of brushes as there are of wrenches, but a brush almost always consists of a handle, bristles and a ferrule which holds the bristles to the handle. Drawing VIII-2 exposes the most intimate workings of a quality brush. Note that the bristles are grouped, in this case, in rows, and set into a resinous often epoxy substance. The bristles are sometimes separated by plugs which "open-up" the interior of the brush for more surface to hold and evenly discharge paint. The bristles and plug(s) are glued to the block or heel of the handle and bound on by a ferrule.

The ferrule is commonly a rust-proof metal, usually stainless steel or brass, but if you're into leather, fret not—leather ferrules are available on some brushes.

There are two groups of bristles: natural and man-made. The natural bristle is from animal hair, either from the body or snout. The bristle of Chinese pigs has long been treasured for its great length, strength, superior flexibility and ability to hold paint, releasing it in a steady flow when the brush is dragged across a surface. The natural bristle, like human hair, is a filament with a bit of "tooth" and an end which is "split." Hair salons reap fortunes trying to eliminate this dreaded split end, but it is great on brushes, and cheaper for pigs. The split end prevents the liquid from sliding off the hair and creating a drip. Man-made bristles are "flagged" by beating or "exploded" by blasting to fray the tip of the filament to try to duplicate nature's helpful but unfashionable split end. Natural bristle also tapers. It is thicker where it attaches to the body of the animal and thinner at the tip. This taper is somewhat duplicated in man-made bristles by stretching the filament in the manufacturing process.

As a general rule of thumb, natural bristles are best for solvent based paints, varnishes and shellac. Man-made bristles, nylon or polyester, are best for man-made paint—acrylics and polyvinyl (both often generically called "latex"). Because these water based paints are thicker, they "clog" onto the less resilient natural bristles. The water is also absorbed into the porous bristle which swells it, softens it and can aid in loosening it from the resinous base which holds it. However, because much scenic painting uses thinned down commercial paints or naturally thinner scenic paint, the natural bristle brushes can be used. They do have a superior ability to hold a charge of thinner paints, but will become saturated and limp-out after a long day of use.

A good brush will do a good job and last a long time if properly selected and maintained. When selecting brushes, pick a bristle which is designed for the type of paint being used. Hold the brush by the handle as you would when painting. It should be comfortable in your hand and have good balance. Make sure the ferrule is solidly attached. The ferrule will take a beating when spattering. Gently pull the bristles. If you have a hand full of hair, put the mangy brush back. The bristles must be solidly fused inside the ferrule. Press the brush in your hand and observe how the bristles spread. They should fan out evenly from the ferrule and when the brush is lifted, the bristles should return to their original position. Examine a single bristle. Is the tip flagged? When you stroke the bristles between two fingers, is there a slight bit of "tooth" on the filament? This will help hold the paint. Is the brush much more expensive than you can afford? If so, it is probably a good brush.

Paint brushes are made in a wide variety of sizes and shapes for the construction industry. Each brush is designed for a specific job. Theatre people usually don't care about the original job, but should select brushes which will ensure their needed finish. Commercially available brushes can be found in any good paint store but inferior brushes lurk about everywhere else from grocery stores to cut-rate chains. They have even invaded some good paint stores…there goes the neighborhood. The best brush handles are wood and vary in shape and length. Quality plastic handles are becoming more common. The ferrules also vary in shape, metal and method of attachment—nails, rivets or crimping. Some ferrules are joined with a folded edge, some are soldered. The bristles, as discussed earlier, can be natural, man-made or even a

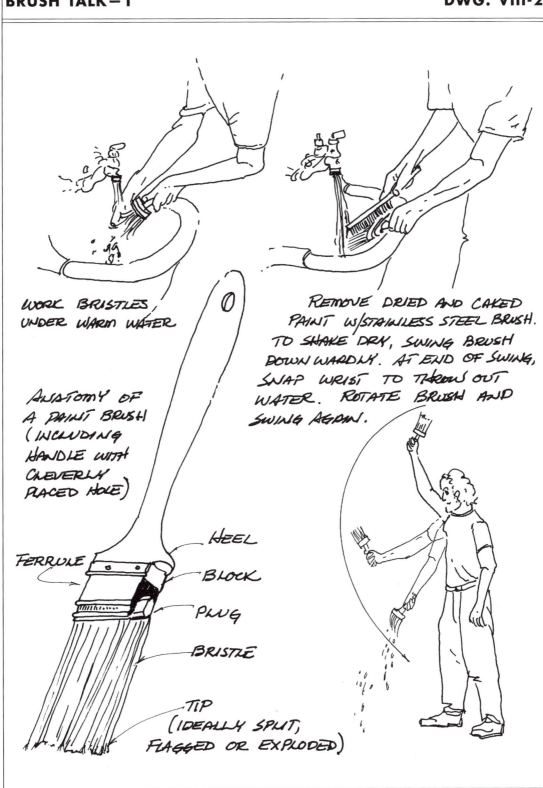

WORK BRISTLES UNDER WARM WATER

REMOVE DRIED AND CAKED PAINT W/STAINLESS STEEL BRUSH. TO SHAKE DRY, SWING BRUSH DOWNWARDLY. AT END OF SWING, SNAP WRIST TO THROW OUT WATER. ROTATE BRUSH AND SWING AGAIN.

ANATOMY OF A PAINT BRUSH (INCLUDING HANDLE WITH CLEVERLY PLACED HOLE)

FERRULE

HEEL

BLOCK

PLUG

BRISTLE

TIP (IDEALLY SPLIT, FLAGGED OR EXPLODED)

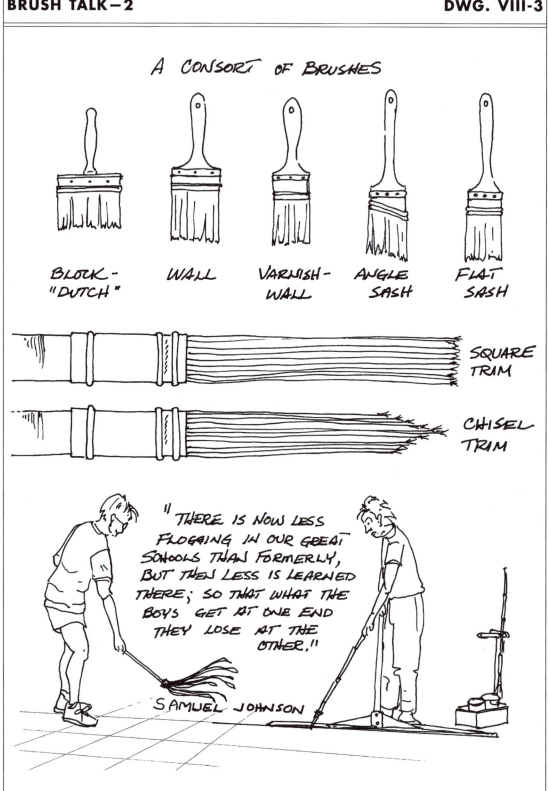

A CONSORT OF BRUSHES

BLOCK-"DUTCH"   WALL   VARNISH-WALL   ANGLE SASH   FLAT SASH

SQUARE TRIM

CHISEL TRIM

"THERE IS NOW LESS FLOGGING IN OUR GREAT SCHOOLS THAN FORMERLY, BUT THEN LESS IS LEARNED THERE; SO THAT WHAT THE BOYS GET AT ONE END THEY LOSE AT THE OTHER."

SAMUEL JOHNSON

combination. The shape of the cluster of bristles can be fairly flat on the tip end or they can be set with the end chiseled or tapered (Drawing VIII-3). The end profile can be straight across or angular, either flat or chiseled. The bristles could be grouped into a round or oval shape. Natural bristles are set by hand and "built" from the tip. The shape of the end of the brush is laid up because each bristle must terminate with the natural flagged end. This is one reason why natural bristle brushes are so expensive. Once the desired shape is created, the block end is trimmed, set into a resinous substance to bond the bristles together, and is then attached to the block or the heel of the handle. All this is bound together with the ferrule. Brushes of man-made bristle, normally nylon or polyester of various colors, can be set and attached to the handle before the tip is shaped. After being cut and chiseled to the desired shape, the end of the brush is then subjected to beating or blasting to abrade the ends of the bristle. It hurts to be beautiful.

PAINT TIP   General Doozendont says, "It is hard on a brush to switch back and forth between solvent-based and water-based paints." Because small amounts of residue from either solvent can bind with the opposite and make cleaning difficult, it is better to use separate brushes.

PAINT TIP   Don't store brushes or let them soak or dry standing on the bristles. This will permanently bend the bristles and give a new challenge to painting. Sometimes this deformation can be magically healed in brushes with man-made bristles by holding the brush in hot water— just below boiling—for a few minutes. As with people, this will some-times straighten them out. Reshape the bristles by wrapping the brush in heavy paper to hold the shape. No guarantee of success.

SIZES AND SHAPES

Dutch brushes and primers (see Drawing VIII-3) are large brushes which measure 5″ or 6″ across the ferrule and can be at least 1″ thick. Dutch brushes can be even larger: 7½″ wide and up to 2″ thick. They have long (4½ to 5¼ inches) bristles. Dutch brushes are also called calcimine brushes. Calcimine is a rough coating for walls and ceilings containing, as a major ingredient, Dutch White, which can be anything from various species of clay to pure white lead. Thus, when house painters mixed a Dutch paint, they obviously applied it with a proper Dutch brush. The smaller brushes, still available today are designed for ceilings and large wall areas. Their high cost and the introduction of the roller will probably see their ultimate demise. A pity because they hold a good charge of paint and can make quick work of large areas. These large brushes are most valuable for priming and laying in large fields of color. The 4″ wall brush is still popular with professional house painters, manufactured in some quantity and therefore available in many choices and at a price which only requires a mortgage on first children. Smaller versions of this brush, those both narrower and thinner, are called "trim" brushes.

Related to the trim brush is the "sash" brush designed for painting the narrow sashes on windows. The bristles are set both flat and angled which gives the latter the mysterious name, "angular sash brush." Common sizes for sash brushes range from 3″ down to 1″. The angular sash is excellent for its original use and for cutting-in paint to a proscribed line, lining along various trims and the like.

A long-handled oval brush now utilized almost completely by scenic artists is called a "Fitch." Because the house painter no longer uses fitches they are difficult to find and are usually sold by theatrical suppliers and are, as one might think, unreasonably expensive. Fitches appeared in the latter part of the 19th century. Originally made from the fur of the polecat or fitchew, these smaller, often oval shaped brushes have a ferrule that tapers toward the longish handle and the bristles flare out slightly. Even by 1873, Spon, in his book, *Workshop Record*, called small hogs-hair brushes which resembled the earlier fitch, by their now common name. If you wish to ferret out some for your shop, try a theatrical supply house. Scenic fitches range from large and expensive 3″ and 2″ sizes called "foliage brushes" to narrower brushes, down to ¼″. The narrower fitches are called "liners" for obvious reasons…you can cruise when using them. The best fitches are made of white china pig bristles and despite their cost are an invaluable addition to a scenic artist's kit. We will not discuss their caboodle.

Foam brushes make any professional painter bristle with indignation, but the sponge-on-a-stick can be useful for on-site touch up, quick and dirty lining work, or in situations where water may not be available. Their inexpensiveness and inability to last through repeated jobs make them an ideal disposable painting tool. They will, indeed, self-destruct on many surfaces. The width of a foam brush can be diminished to any desired size with a pair of scissors, mat knife or good teeth. Many scene painters carry an assortment of these ugly little brushes, carefully concealed from the mocking of co-workers.

SPECIALTY BRUSHES

As any professional painter, and certainly professional scenic artist, will tell you, there are many brushes available which are not found in most local paint stores. There are stencil brushes with short, tightly packed bristles in a round ferrule, designed specifically for pushing paint through a stencil. These are often used for other "tricks of the trade." Script and Stripers have extra-long bristles which are set to taper to a fine point. This allows thick and thin lines with the same brush—ideal for scrollwork and lettering. These softer bristle brushes are most useful in painting marble veins. There are brushes specifically for stains and varnishes created for the professional woodworker which transfer well into a scenic shop. Their long term-usefulness is determined by the protection of the scenic artist. Disposable brushes with natural bristles are called "chip brushes" and will service many uses with normal care. The variety of brushes is far vaster than these notes. Check with your local paint store. They will have many catalogues offering much more than they normally stock. Specialty companies will offer a selection to bankrupt a Rothchild. For the individual scenic artist an investment in quality brushes will pay handsome dividends (in addition to being a tax deductible expense). For the general paint shop, any brush will last only as long as its proper use and upkeep.

PAINT TIP If you do not have water or solvent available to wash a brush, wrap it in aluminum foil, plastic warp or even a newspaper to retard drying by air contact. Wash well as soon as possible. This wrapping method will not hold more than a few hours.

BRUSH CLEANING

A considerable investment can be made in brushes and proper cleaning is mandatory to maintain both the buck and the brush. If you are using solvent-based paints, employ the proper solvent for cleanup. In a well ventilated area, and wearing proper protective clothing and masks, fill a container with enough solvent to reach the ferrule. Insert the brush and press it about, turning and twisting the handle to loosen and dissolve the paint. A paint brush comb will help loosen hardened paint. When the solvent has become saturated with the paint, move to a new container with fresh solvent. Most solvent based paints will require three or four changes of cleaner to remove enough paint so the solvent is barely tinted by the residue in the brush. Do not pour solvents down the sink drain. In addition to endangering the water supply, solvents are often incompatible with water and will clog the drain. Because the fumes are combustible some rather explosive results have been recorded. Store used solvents according to their saturation of removed paint. Paint will settle in used solvent. Careful decanting will contain the sludge in the bottom and the poured off top can be re-used. This can be done many, many times. It is economical to begin washing a brush in used solvent and change to progressively less contaminated batches when cleaning. Once the brush is clean, smooth the bristles back to their original shape. Hang the brush up by the handle. For disposing of no longer usable solvents (or paints) read the section following.

Cleaning water based paints is somewhat easier and certainly less hazardous to your health and the work environment. Warm water is best. Cold water "hardens" the paint and hot water can warp the bristles and soften the binders in the ferrule. Warm water helps loosen the paint and float away the residue in the brush. Hold the brush under running water and work the bristle with your hand (Drawing VIII-2). The water should be comfortable. NEVER run the water directly into the end of the brush. This will force the bristles to bend back. As they try to resume their shape, the rushing water can knot them which will result in a definite bad-hair day. A good working over with a paint brush comb may help eliminate the problem if it happens. To remove dried or hardening paint from the ferrule or on the bristles, judiciously use a stainless steel wire brush. Hold the paint brush against the edge of the sink and with the metal brush work from the ferrule down to the tip of the bristles. This will loosen paint on the ferrule and help dislodge any remaining in the bristles near the ferrule. Excessive use of the steel brush can abrade the bristle and allow it to curl. Make certain the brush is clean. The water should run clear; when it is, place a bit of soap on the bristles. Some shops keep a cake of soap for this use. Others use a bucket with slightly thinned dish soap. Murphy's Oil Soap is also a favorite. Work the brush with your hands to develop good suds which will lift out any remaining paint. When you are sure the brush is clean, rinse well, and shake out any excess water. Never, never, never beat the brush against the side of the sink or any solid object. This shock will break apart the ferrule and can crack the resinous bond with the bristles. Reshape the bristles and hang up by the handle. Yes, on natural bristle brushes, a periodic short soak in hair conditioner makes them feel extra pretty. The necessity of washing brushes properly cannot be stressed enough. When hurriedly and superficially cleaned, the residue of paint left near the block and plugs dries and becomes impossible to remove. This build-up will continue and eventually, but rather quickly solidify, robbing the bristles of their long flexibility and forcing them to separate, thus losing the shape. When a paint brush more closely resembles a toilet brush the condition is called "finger" and is about as useful. Much of the drying and hardening of paint in the plugs can be eliminated if the brush is soaked in warm water for a few minutes before painting. This will wet up the area and retard any stray paint trying to settle in for a long winter's nap. Make sure you shake out all excess water before starting to paint (see Drawing VIII-2). Swing the brush downward and sharply snap the wrist. Rotate the brush 180 degrees in your hand and swing again. The number of sharp snaps and concomitant rotations are left to the discretion of the painter. Do not soak brushes for long periods of time, either before beginning, between jobs, or certainly over night. Natural bristles will swell, become limp and even expand enough to break the resinous binder and even the ferrule. Wood handles will also absorb water and swell. Many a well-fit ferrule will be split open if brushes soak too long. When the brush dries, the handle shrinks and the bristles begin to wobble within the ferrule. The ferrule can even part company with the handle. Not a pretty sight. No amount of counseling with a hot glue gun or construction adhesive will ever repair this once ideal marriage. It is obvious that the time and care required for cleaning must be built into the work schedule. The expenditure here will certainly pay off. A good brush will last many, many years and, as with other tools, become the hard working extension of skilled hands.

DISPOSING OF PAINT

"After the ball is over, after the dance is done…" what does one do with left over paint? If another show is coming up, perhaps it can be used. Certainly similar values or colors of like paint can be boxed together for a future primer or base coat. Darker colors make an excellent start for back paint.

If it is the end of a season and the paint won't store for the break—too hot, too cold or no place available—try to give the paint away. This is most feasible if the paint is in its original cans which have all the correct safety information.

If no one wants the free paint or it is long separated from its original can, you can dispose of it. If the paint is "latex" simply remove and discard the lid. Place the can away from children and pets and let the paint dry completely. It will harden in the can and can then qualify as household refuse. You can "hurry" this process by mixing the paint with sawdust or cat litter and letting the "goo" dry. Do not pour paint down drains. It can clog the drain and will and eventually affect drinking water.

Solvent-based paints (those alkyd or oil based problem children) require additional care in their disposal. The paints and accumulated fumes are ignitable. NEVER pour these down drains (especially one on a septic tank), into storm sewers or even on the ground. The chemicals eventually leach down and damage the water table. Most solvent based paints qualify as a Household Hazardous Waste, and if your community has special days for collecting such things, take advantage of the service. If not, contact a local or state government environmental control agency for assistance.

Paint thinners, turpentine, mineral spirits and solvents should *not* be poured down drains or on the ground. Always try to allow paint to settle in the container and carefully decant the re-usable liquid. The sludge can be poured into cat litter, spread out in a well-ventilated area, and allowed to dry *completely*. Again the same people who helped dispose of the solvent-based paints can assist with the disposal of these remains.

Check in the Yellow Pages under "waste disposal" to see if a local company or agency can offer help. Never, never, never pour paints or their solvents down a drain. In addition to back-firing on those who remain seated during the entire performance, it will affect the water quality and those after work martini-on-the-rocks will be more lethal than expected.

SOLVENT "BORN AGAIN" CLEANERS

A note on solvent-based brush cleaners is in order. These cleaners are strong, will eventually eat through dry, hardened paint on the bristles, the ferrule and handle, and return flexibility to the most catatonic brush. However, the cleaner may permanently weaken some man-made filaments leaving them listless, limp or permanently awry. It can do even meaner things to natural bristles. Use these cleaners with caution and help speed up the process with a paint brush comb or old kitchen fork, so the paint is quickly loosened and the bristles are subjected to a minimum of saturation. Take care to avoid personal contact—these cleaners are toxic.

Another cleaning solvent available is lacquer thinner. This will attack the dried residue clinging to bristles and packed around the plugs. It is also excellent for cleaning spray gun parts. However, great care must be exercised. Read the warnings on lacquer thinner and re-read the section on solvents and the section on disposing of paints.

Like Dr. Frankenstein you can create a monster using potentially dangerous cleaners. It is always better to wash out brushes promptly and properly. But there is something about playing god when you see an expensive brushed heeled-up hard, its once supple filaments hideously bent, warped and curled in crooked disarray. Does it bring out the goodness in you or guilt from bad handling in *les temps perdu*?

PAINT TIP Most glue used in scenic construction, particularly in covering flats, is not really compatible with paint, even if both are water solvent. To protect tempers, not to mention scenic brushes, have separate, inexpensive brushes or rollers for glue. One method which helps identify and isolate the glue stuff is to paint brush handles and glue buckets a bright blue. Eventually, "blue buckets are glue buckets— blue brushes are glue brushes" will sink into the consciousness of some shop personnel; that it remains unconscious for others still requires vigilance. Separate buckets with lids allow the shop glue to remain for extended periods and eliminates the constant washing of glue buckets. One additional advantage resulting from separate and clearly marked glue buckets is the avoidance of pouring glue into paint (or vice versa). Certainly the inadvertent admixture lessens the effectiveness of both. Some paints and glues even react chemically and make something akin to cold tapioca or ripe cottage cheese.

A BIT MORE HISTORY

Paint rollers were patented by 1890. The rollers were covered with lambskin, "and the like," but were not commercially successful. In early 1940, Earl Thomas of Thomas Products Co. was making a roller covered with stipple carpet used by decorators to create patterned wall finishes on plaster. After 1943, this small specialty company working out of a garage also made lambskin rollers for applying base coats. When WWII ended, victorious America utilized the German formula for a man-made rubber-based paint, and Kem-Tone hit the market. Rollers worked well with this new paint. By 1946, several companies began manufacturing rollers. Added impetus came from the post-War redecorating boom and the style-setting decorators' use of very deep colors. These easily showed brush marks. Union painters were contractually forbidden to use labor saving rollers but would literally "pull the blinds" and secretly roll on the intensely desired colors—leaving no brush marks. It was not until the mid-sixties that rollers were not disallowed in union contracts.

Solid core wood rollers also appeared after the War. When large ships were in dry dock many were painted from barges using rollers with long extension handles. Contractors ordered the solid roller so disgruntled union painters could not inadvertently step on the roller, crush it and thus render it useless. The union only wanted to prove the need for larger crews with the more traditional and reliable brush. Europe and the Far East discovered the roller and painting the ships of the world moved away from union control.

ROLLER COVERS AND HANDLES

Paint rollers are, certainly for the non-union painter, a mid-20th century invention. Originally made by laminating lamb's skin around a roller, they are now available in a wide variety of napped coverings, various widths and even shaped foam. Natural lamb covered rollers are still manufactured for solvent-based paints. Many synthetic napped versions are available at reasonable prices. Avoid cheap rollers. They will shed their coverings during the paint job and the cheap cardboard tube has been known to collapse. Less expensive rollers are excellent for jobs where cleanup is problematic, which would certainly include all solvent based paints, because it is easier, safer, and often cheaper to simply throw away the used cover. For water wash-up paints, however, better quality roller covers will last many, many jobs and cleaning is not too difficult with a roller spinner which quickly rotates the roller and "throws" the paint out of it. Roller spinners are available at any good paint store and are worth the investment. Keep an oil can handy to lubricate the internal parts if they become rusty. Rollers must be carefully washed or they become cement-like columns. The nap or depth of pile available on normal covers ranges from long (1 to 1¼ inches) through medium (½ to ¾ inches) to short (¼ inch). Obviously, the thicker the nap, the more paint it will hold and the more readily the roller will cover uneven surfaces. Thick napped rollers may also discharge too much paint on smooth surfaces, leave drips, sagging runs, lines and a stippled finish, very much like a well filled pair of polyester pants. Disposable rollers and those covered with foam rarely cover as well as a properly selected quality napped roller. Rollers come with their own set of accouterments: roller pans or trays, wire or plastic spreader screens made for both roller trays and buckets, and handle extenders. A good roller pan should comfortably fit the roller and have a well deep enough to hold sufficient paint for extended rolling. The investment in a quality roller handle cannot be stressed strongly enough. Because the handles are interchangeable with many roller covers, they receive constant use. A heavy, contoured handle on the roller frame which fits the hand well will drastically cut down on fatigue. The end of the handle should be threaded for an extension pole The end caps which support the roller and allow it to rotate should be nylon or some other material which resists paint and will spin smoothly on the handle's metal shaft. A sturdy spring cage extending between the end caps indicates a superior roller handle. The threaded handle end is designed for an extension pole. Poles are available in many lengths and in a variety of materials. Some poles are even adjustable. Invest in quality extension poles. They will save frayed tempers at cleanup time when none of the push brooms in the shop has a handle.

PAINT TIP One trick-of-the-trade which will save the painter's back when rolling floors or painting acreage (large amounts of scenery in a similar flat position) is to slip a length of 2″ iron pipe (approximately 18″ long) over the extension pole and down to the handle (Drawing VIII-1). This will rest at the base of the handle and put a constant weight on the roller, thus removing the need to press the roller to the floor. Arms and back will note a remarkable difference in fatigue. Many scenic artists dislike rollers, but others embrace their wide variety of surfaces and availability. Some embrace things we cannot discuss.

SPRAY GUNS

Spray guns, both hand-pump and compressor-driven, are useful painting tools. While hand sprayers have been around for many years, it was only in 1909 when the DeVilbiss Company applied the same principles as their medical atomizer to a paint gun and combined it with compressed air that the paint sprayer came into being. It revolutionized the infant automobile painting industry and had a profound impact on painted furniture, too. But, as with most things which save time at one end, more is required at the other. Clean-up and maintenance cannot be ignored with sprayers. Adequate time and care must be assured or the major investment will quickly bankrupt the theatre. Spray equipment requires a pressured air supply, available in many shops, but it must be regulated for the required pressure of the individual gun. Spray equipment usually requires a compressor with a large capacity air tank, unlike most shop tools which require high pressure, but little volume. Spray guns not compatible with shop tools can use a pressure regulator and one compressor and tank will make both viable.

PAINT TIP   One good source for spray guns and related items is an automotive parts and supply store. These establishments often clean and repair spray equipment. These health spas for sprayers can be most refreshing between shows.

Because much theatre painting is done with different paints of different viscosities and particulate sizes, the guns must be able to accept these differences. Not all spray guns or spray heads are created equal. Check with your supplier. The old reliable "Hudson" sprayer, a hand-pump garden sprayer, can easily be converted to air. The tank must be metal. Drill a hole at the top to receive a male fitting for the air hose. After the fitting has been brazed into place, the tank will give excellent results on about 40 lbs. of pressure. It is also possible to replace the short hose between the tank and the nozzle wand with a long piece of air hose which will alleviate carrying about the heavy tank while painting. However, the long hose must be properly and thoroughly cleaned which seems to take forever. If you are setting up spray equipment remember you will also need more hose than you plan for, and don't even think you can use the shop construction hoses. Buy enough fittings to make up several sets of extra hoses, and some "T" fittings which will allow more than one gun to feed from the source. Additional regulators for air pressure will also be needed. Live it up. There are also "airless" sprayers which do not require an air supply. The feed hose goes directly into the paint bucket. Again, the heads need to have the ability it emit a variety of paints.

There are many small, hand-held sprayers on the market. These are usually made of plastic and are common in garden stores. They can become invaluable for smaller paint jobs, touch-up or on-site projects with no air supply. Check out the ability to push paint through the nozzle before buying a case. Of course, clean-up is essential or these little sprayers become instantly disposable.

Oil and water do not mix and this is particularly true with spray equipment. Don't try to use both or you will curse that last person who used a different paint. Spray equipment, regardless of the type of paint being applied, must be used with the proper protective masks, goggles and clothing. Adequate air movement is also a must. Spray painting must not be done in any area where others are working unless everyone is adequately protected. If you can see or smell the spray, it is dangerous.

One further caution on spray equipment. Make certain only trained personnel use it. In addition to the added health hazards, the health of the equipment is seriously jeopardized when used improperly or even badly adjusted. Clean-up is critically important. Dried paint and rusted parts will rapidly decrease the efficiency of spray guns and any advantage gained in their use will cease. Nothing is more frustrating than a spray gun which sputters, splatters and constipates to a complete halt in the middle of a project.

SAFETY

Paints fall into two rather loose categories: water-based and solvent-based products (often erroneously called "oil base"). The latter can be quite toxic and should be used only by professionals who understand the paint's unique properties. The painters must be prepared with proper safety protection for themselves and others working within the area of the fumes, overspray or in physical contact with the paint or its solvents. The dangers of toxic buildup in the body are real and the federal warnings noted on the manufacturer's label must be followed by the user. Because the toxic properties can be ingested, absorbed through the skin upon contact or through inhaling the fumes, toxic paint—read all paint—is dangerous. Protect your skin and certainly any cuts or abrasions with the proper clothing and gloves. Wear a respirator properly designed to filter the fumes and overspray unique to the product and solvents required for clean-up. Remember that the fumes created when paint dries and cures are also dangerous. Truly, the life you save will be your own. Even if you do not experience any reaction—sore throat, watery eyes, nausea or headaches—know that the paint is dangerous and protect yourself. Of course, if you react in any negative way, stop using the product immediately. No one has the right to insist you continue working and endangering yourself. That is the law. Call your local health authorities or the OSHA hotline if you feel you are being coerced. Workers who are well, work well. Off the soap box.

Become good friends with the knowledgeable people who run the paint store or supply house where you will be buying. Don't be afraid to ask questions and feel free to ask for the Material Safety Data Sheets (MSDS) which, by law, must be provided for every hazardous product sold. These should be available on the job site. This information, considered by too many to be "governmental overkill," is often eye opening to the dangers, both immediate and potential, and can help decide a product's appropriateness for a certain job or shop. Always try to find the best product for the job, but it is not a bad compromise to find a healthier product. While theatre is more important than life, the show will go on, and so should the people working in the shops. Who put that soap box back under me? Each solvent based product requires its own solvent for cleanup of equipment and painter, and these solvents are usually not only incompatible with other products, but more dangerous if combined. A good rule-of-thumb is to ban all toxic solvents from a non-professional paint shop. If used, keep these dangerous paints and solvents in a *locked*, combustion-proof cabinet. If this diatribe has not convince you, carefully read the section on solvents. As consumers become more aware of dangerous products and refuse to use them, safer substitutes will become available. There is usually a safer product already on the market. Try to use it. Commercial paints are designed for years of wear, a situation luckily not common to most theatrical endeavors where the everlasting finish can be faked.

SOLVENTS

Paint, including what is generically called "latex paint" is potentially a health hazard. However the risk of toxic poisoning is drastically increased with solvent based products, especially those misnamed "oil paints." This includes various varnishes, shellacs, lacquers and other finishes sold both by the bucket and aerosol can. It must also include paint removers and paint strippers. The solvent required is often a clue to the health hazard.

A solvent is a liquid which will thin down or dissolve another material. Water is an excellent example and should be the solvent of choice. Unfortunately, water will not always work but with educated choices and careful selection of materials, especially paints, water can become the dominant solvent in any shop. The price is right, it is easily disposed of and except for the most serious whiskey drinker, non toxic. Most shop health hazards—and they are serious—can be alleviated, even eliminated by using only water solvent paints and finishes. That said, here is some information on common organic solvents used to clean, dissolve or thin non-water based products. In addition to prepping the surfaces for some highly toxic finishes, organic solvents are used to clean up tools, brushes, rollers and all too often the worker's hands, face and other exposed areas. Some solvents found in paint shops include acetone, turpentine, ethyl alcohol and pre-mixed solvents created with a variety of often changing components, including mineral spirits, petroleum distillates, lacquer thinner and naphthas. Many of these solvents disguise their toxicity under a trade name and sweet perfume. Read the labels and these Mata Haris will be exposed. Every hazardous product sold in the paint store must have a Material Safety Data Sheet (MSDS)—which will identify the contents and note any dangers. Federal law requires these sheets list hazardous ingredients. The sheets must be available where the products is sold and should be given to you upon request. MSDS are also available on the Internet.

Organic solvents are hazardous to your health. They can affect the nervous system, respiratory system, skin, eyes and internal organs. They will adversely affect the reproductive systems in both men and women. With the already evaporating gene pool, don't add fuel to the fire. Pregnant women must avoid toxic solvents at all times. Pregnant men should have used more protection.

Both the toxicity of and the exposure to a solvent can affect the worker. This, of course, varies with the material, conditions in the workplace and the worker. However the following guidelines are useful. Avoid breathing vapors. Adequate ventilation is a must. An open window doesn't cut it. Central air conditioning doesn't cut it because it recycles the air. However, once the foul fumes find their way into the front office, things will change. Large amounts of fresh air must move through the work area and be exhausted to the outside.

Avoid skin contact with toxic solvents. Wear appropriate protective gloves. Many household gloves simply melt away. When finished with the work, wash up with soap and water. Do not clean skin with solvents. There are many non-toxic skin cleaners available but baby oil or olive oil will remove most paints from the skin.

Wear proper body protection. This is important when painting and when pouring solvent. Do not expect protection from normal eye glasses. Never wear contact lenses unless protected by goggles. If using solvents, a plumbed eye-wash fountain should be in the area.

Always wear gloves when handling solvents. Make certain there is good ventilation but wear the proper vapor respirator if required. Smoking can also draw the toxic chemicals into the mouth, throat and lungs. Do not eat or drink around solvents. The food can hold toxic waste which will be ingested. Even though odor is often the least harmful part of a toxic solvent, remember, if you can smell—tell. This is particularly important on first notice of solvent odor. The nose will often "shut down" as a part of its protective reaction after extended presence of toxic fumes.

FIRE PRECAUTION

Almost all solvents will combust or explode. They must be stored in proper metal cabinets. Open flame (which includes smoking), electrical sparks (which includes welding), and carving Styrofoam with knives heated on a gas stove (which includes your certain death) must be avoided. While it is an excellent idea to have a class ABC multi-purpose, dry chemical fire extinguisher in any shop; it is mandatory if using solvents.

USEFUL AIDS FROM THE SHOP

The snapline may seem common enough but those used in the scene shop are usually a box filled with colored chalk. This chalk is excellent at depositing a bright red, yellow or blue line. For the painter, this line never disappears and tints the paint job accordingly. The chalk, beautifully designed for what it does, will not easily blow away, flog away or brush off. Blame the colorant in the powdered chalk. Painters prefer stick charcoal or even white chalk-board sticks which can be pulled over a line and then snapped onto the object which will eventually be painted. Buy a chalk box and fill it with powdered charcoal or whatever is ideal. The most long lasting chalk-line is a piece of 1 x 2 about 6″ long with the edges slighted rounded upon which you wind up a long piece of mason's line, a strong heavyweight cotton string. To use, unwind what you need, fix the end, whether with a loop over a nail or hand it to an assistant, and pull a piece of stick charcoal along the string. Its a bit messy as the string cuts through the charcoal but the charged line, when snapped, leaves a beautiful, straight impression. The charcoal line can be "erased" in quick order with a flogger. A bow-line can facilitate one person snapping and is especially useful for vertical work. To make one, think of flat frame construction and take a piece of one-by stock as long as the line you wish to snap. Attach a short "rail" (about 10 inches) to each end of this "stile" using corner blocks. Affix a piece of mason's line to the back of one end. Place the line around the front of one rail to the other. Stretch the line tightly and attach to the back of the second rail. You now have a taut line which can be charged with charcoal, placed against a surface and snapped.

FLOGGERS

Floggers are useful tools for urging on sluggish workers and also cleaning up charcoal lines and stray debris from objects being painted (Drawing VIII-3). To make one, and they must be made, take a piece of one-by, about two feet long. Smooth the edges to be comfortable in the hand. Next, tear muslin scraps into one-inch strips about 1'-6" long. Attach a dozen or so strips to the end of a stick. A quick "whip" across the surface and no longer needed charcoal lines will be removed. (When asked why he was so happy living with the sadist, the masochist answers, "Beats me." This explains nothing about scenic artists.) Avoid breathing charcoal dust. Remember what it does to coal miners.

LINING STICKS

Lining sticks can also be useful to the scenic artist. There are two basic styles: hand-held for vertical painting and floor based, with extended handle, for working horizontally. Both must be light, rigid and well balanced. They must also have an edge which is raised from the surface to be painted. This prevents capillary action which can pull the paint under the stick and deposit it onto the surface.

Lining sticks for vertical painting rarely exceed five feet in length, mostly because it is awkward to reach farther when painting. A piece of one-by stock with the edges beveled will work well. A wood block handle centered on the stick helps holding it. If the edges are rough and grab the bristles of the brush, a strip of ever-useful duct tape can be wrapped around the beveled edge to smooth it. Variations on lining sticks abound and they are often crafted for specific jobs and then discarded.

Floor sticks for lining (Drawings VIII-3, 4 and 5) are almost always double sided to alleviate the need to twirl the stick and clip a bucket of paint, or even the ankle of a neighbor painter. The board is often a bit wider than the hand-held horizontal stick so it will stand upright but lightness is still a major consideration. Many scenic artists mark off the blade to help measure on the floor. It does save the back, and even some time trying to find a tape measure.

Note how the handle mounts to the lining stick (Drawing VIII-4). To keep the handle centered and as thin as possible, thus avoiding getting in the way of the brush being pulled along the blade, the ¼" straps on both sides attach it to a base block. The dado for the base block is centered and runs the length of the blade. This locks in the handle. The dado also helps eliminate tension in the wood which builds as the wood ages. The kerfs running along the bottom of the blade also lessen the chance of tension warps. Scenic artists who travel often cut their favorite lining sticks in half. The base block snugly locked into the dado, bolts the two pieces together. The handle also

A NICELY CRAFTED LINING STICK WILL GREATLY AID IN QUALITY PAINTING. SUGGESTIONS ARE 6'0" LONG. HANDLE TAPERS INTO BLOCK WHICH CAN LOCK INTO DADO OR BOLT DIRECTLY TO THE BLADE.

NOTE HOW HANDLE BOLTS TO BLOCK WHICH BOLTS INTO DADO AND HOLDS BLADE TOGETHER. ONLY A HAND FULL OF NUTS AND THE SCENIC ARTIST IS OFF AND RUNNING.

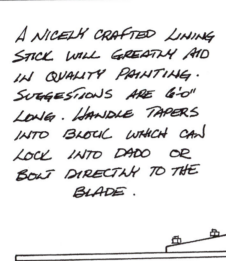

BLADE MARKED FOR EASY END MEASURE

BLADE MARKED FOR CENTER WORK

BLADE HAS OLD TAPE MEASURE ATTACHED

DETAIL VIEWS OF BLADES:

ROUTED, MITERED, KERFED AND DADOED

ROUTED AND KERFED

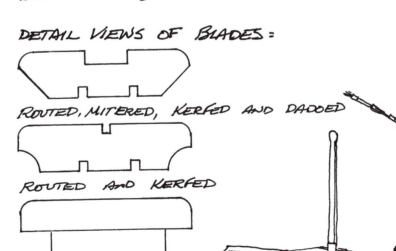

ROUTED LAMINATED STOCK

BUCKET CARRIER (MADE IN SHOP) WITH BROOM-HOLDERS FACILITATES MOVES AND AVOIDS SPILLS.

ADJUST BAMBOO TO FIT PAINTER

RUBBER NON-SKID BUTTONS ON BOTTOM

LAY-IN

CHARCOAL CARTOONING

LINING

bolts on. This easily lets the long and somewhat awkward stick break down and pack into an overhead compartment on airlines or become carefully checked baggage.

BAMBOO

Floor painting should be done with a minimum of back bending. This requires brushes with long handles. Some European manufacturers make brushes with handles which are threaded on one end and screw into the block. However, the utilization of bamboo sticks and poles (Drawing VIII-5) is a very practical and inexpensive way to temporarily extend any brush handle. By inserting the handle into the pole and not taping it to the side of a broom handle, the bristles are still in a straight line with the handle and the painter has good balance and control of the brush. A collection of bamboo poles is just the ticket. Bamboo has joints or knees along the stalk which are solid through the piece. To create an extension handle, cut the bamboo on an angle just past a joint. Sand down the sharp edge. Take a chisel and place it in the cut end. A slight tap will split the hollow shaft to the next joint. Rotate the chisel 90 and split the shaft again. There should be four "legs" into which you can insert the brush handle. A large rubber band can be wrapped near the cut end creating a sphincter like grip. Be careful rolling this rubber band up and down— the edges of the split bamboo are razor sharp and will easily cut into hands, fingers or anything else you may find useful. You may want to do a bit more sanding. Another thing which will make the bamboo more efficient on the insertion end is several wraps of duct tape just above the first joint. While the joint will stop the splits from continuing through the pole, continual use will eventually encourage the cracks ever upward until the pole disintegrates. Tape round the top end will also help hold the pole together and gives a smooth finish to protect your hand. A bamboo pole should last or years, especially if it is not dropped, stepped on or run over by trucks.

Because bamboo poles should not be longer than comfortable for the painter (usually not much past the wrist), they become "individualized" to each painter (Drawing VIII-5). The extended family of bamboos will eventually over-run even the most controlled shop. Variations include thin bamboo poles to hold charcoal sticks and felt markers for layout work and larger diameter poles for lay-in brushes.

Bamboo grows in many parts of the world but if not native to your theatre area, try a garden supply store, import market or craft store. They can even be ordered from catalogs.

Phew. Final curtain!

APPENDIX

DEALERS AND SUPPLIERS

A local lumber yard can supply the wood, glue and nails you need to build scenery. But where do you buy scenic paint, or muslin to cover flats, or special hardware, like trim chains or stage screws? Theatrical dealers and manufacturers, too numerous to list here, can be found in the membership directory of the Entertainment Services and Technology Association (ESTA), and in industry buyers guides like those published by *Entertainment Design* magazine (a.k.a. *Theatre Crafts International*) and *Lighting Dimensions* magazine. The *New York Theatrical Sourcebook* (available from Broadway Press), is an exhaustive collection of sources, primarily in the New York City area, for renting and buying everything to do with props, costumes and scenery. Other good resources include *Dramatics* magazine, *Theatre Design & Technology*, a quarterly journal published by the United States Institute for Theatre Technology, *Stage Directions* magazine, and, of course, the Internet. The last name on this short resource list is one of the best bookstores specializing in the performing arts, Drama Bookshop in New York City. Other local performing arts bookstores come and go, please support them too.

ESTA
875 Sixth Ave. #2302
New York, NY 10001
212-244-1505
www.esta.org

Entertainment Design, and
Lighting Dimensions
Primedia Intertec Publications
32 West 18th St.
New York, NY 10011
212-229-2965
www.etecny.net

Theatre Design & Technology
USITT
6443 Ridings Rd.
Syracuse, NY 13206-1111
315-463-6463
www.usitt.org

Dramatics
3368 Central Parkway
Cincinnati, OH 45225
513-559-1996
www.etassoc.org/pubs.htm

Stage Directions
3101 Poplarwood Ct. #310
Raleigh, NC 27604
919-872-7888
www.stage-directions.com

The Drama Book Shop (theatre/film books)
723 Seventh Ave., 2nd floor
New York, NY 10019
212-944-0595

INDEX

THE END